P9-APD-833

Peter Brydon

**COMPASS: COMPUTER APPLICATIONS
SOFTWARE SERIES**
Dennis P. Curtin, Series Editor

---

dBASE III PLUS ®: A Short Course
dBASE IV®: A Short Course
DOS 4: A Complete Course
DOS: A Short Course
LOTUS® 1-2-3® Release 2.2: A Short Course
LOTUS® 1-2-3®: A Complete Course
Telecommunications with ProCOMM® +:
  A Short Course
WordPerfect® 5.1: A Short Course
WordPerfect® 5.0: A Complete Course
WordPerfect® 5.0: A Short Course
Application Software WordPerfect® 5.1 Edition
Application Software Alternate, 2/E (WordPerfect®
  5.0, Lotus ®1-2-3®, and dBASE III PLUS®)
Application Software, 2/E (WordPerfect ® 5.0,
  Lotus® 1-2-3®, and dBASE IV®)
Application Software (WordStar Version)
Application Software (WordPerfect® 4.2 Version)

WordPerfect® 5.1
A Short Course

Dennis P. Curtin

Prentice Hall, Englewood Cliffs, New Jersey 07632

Library of Congress Cataloging-in-Publication Data

Curtin, Dennis P.
    WordPerfect 5.1 : a short course / Dennis P. Curtin.
        p.   cm. — (Computer applications software series)
    Includes index.
    ISBN 0-13-963083-X
        1. WordPerfect (Computer program)   2. Word processing.   I. Title.
    II. Series.
    Z52.5.W65C884   1991
    652.5′536 — dc20

                                                    90-19506
                                                    CIP

Editorial/production supervision: Lind Graphics Inc.
Interior design: Christine Gehring-Wolf
Cover design: Lundgren Graphics
Prepress buyer: Ilene Levy
Manufacturing buyer: Ed O'Dougherty

© 1991 by Prentice-Hall, Inc.
A Division of Simon & Schuster
Englewood Cliffs, New Jersey 07632

All rights reserved. No part of this book may be
reproduced, in any form or by any means,
without permission in writing from the publisher.

Printed in the United States of America
10 9 8 7 6 5 4 3 2

ISBN   0-13-963083-X

Prentice-Hall International (UK) Limited, *London*
Prentice-Hall of Australia Pty, Limited, *Sydney*
Prentice-Hall Canada Inc., *Toronto*
Prentice-Hall Hispanoamericana, S.A., *Mexico*
Prentice-Hall of India Private Limited, *New Delhi*
Prentice-Hall of Japan, Inc., *Tokyo*
Simon & Schuster Asia Pte. Ltd., *Singapore*
Editora Prentice-Hall do Brasil, Ltda, *Rio de Janeiro*

Contents

v

Preface

▼RATIONALE

This text has been designed to provide you with a introductory background in working with WordPerfect®. It does so by introducing you to the program on three levels: concepts, procedures, and activities.

CONCEPTS

Concepts are discussed because they provide the background for procedures. They explain principles, all of which apply to WordPerfect, but many of which also apply to other programs you will use on a microcomputer. When you understand concepts, procedures are easier to learn because they fit into a framework. Understanding concepts also makes it much easier to transfer your understanding to other programs and other computers.

PROCEDURES

Procedures are the specific skills one has to know to use WordPerfect. They include such fundamental steps as saving a file or making a printout. To work with a program, you have to understand more than one procedure because you almost always want to save your work and make printouts to share with others. In this sense procedures are like individual bricks, that when joined together make larger structures like arches, walls, and bridges. Some procedures are generally considered to be more advanced than others, and the organization of the procedures in this manual follows those conventions. This conventional classification of procedures into introductory and advanced can be misleading, however. Many procedures considered to be advanced are really quite simple and very useful. Although procedures in this text are presented in a sequence from simple to complex, don't hesitate to study the advanced procedures. You'll find many of them easy to use and quite exciting.

ACTIVITIES

Concepts and procedures tell you why to do something and how to do it, but they don't tell you what to do it with. To gain that knowledge concepts and procedures have to be put to work in real-world situations. To fulfill this goal, many tutorials, exercises, and projects have been included in this text. These activities serve more than one purpose.

- They build skills in the specific procedures they need to know.

- They demonstrate a variety of situations in which specific procedures are useful.

- They introduce important business, and other, principles that have been, or will be, introduced in other courses in the curriculum.

- They develop problem solving skills. Exercises provide less help than tutorials, and projects provide even less. Moving through this sequence of activities challenges you to think about what you should do and why you need to do it.

ORGANIZATION

This text is designed to be used in a lab-oriented course. It is organized into three parts.

Part I Procedures covers the procedures you use to work with WordPerfect and contains 27 topics that have the following elements:

- **Concepts** at the beginning of each topic introduce the basic principles discussed in the topic—the why, when, and where of word processing.

- **Procedures** describe step-by-step how you execute commands—the how of word processing with WordPerfect.

KEY/Strokes boxes (indicated with the accompanying icon) summarize all of the steps you follow for each procedure. These sections serve a dual function. You can refer to them when working on the activities in this text or when working on your own projects. Their format makes it easy to find the step-by-step procedures when you need them. A complete list of KEY/Strokes follows the table of contents.

- **Tips** in most topics suggest shortcuts, discuss advanced procedures, or cross-reference you to other topics where related procedures are discussed.

- **Summary** briefly explains the key terms and concepts introduced in the topic.

- **Tutorials** demonstrate step by step how to use the procedures discussed in the topic.

- **Exercises** provide additional opportunities to practice and gain experience with the concepts and procedures discussed in the topic. Unlike tutorials, you are not guided step by step. You have to determine the correct procedures to use. These exercises have been selected so they are relevant to business and should prove both interesting and challenging.

Optional disk-based exercises (indicated with the accompanying icon) use text already entered into files on the *WordPefect 5.1 Student Resource Disk* that accompanies this text. For ordering information, see the "Supplements" section of this preface. These exercises allow students to practice many procedures without taking up valuable lab time typing in the text that they need to format or perform other procedures with.

► A list of all KEY/Strokes boxes is in a file named KYSTROKE.WP5. Students can retrieve this file in Topic 20 to search for information they need.

They can then use the file as an on-line index to the information they need to find in this text.

► A list of all files that students create while completing tutorials, exercises, and projects is stored in a file named FILELIST.WP5. Students can retrieve this file and use it as a reference.

• **Questions** test understanding of the concepts and procedures discussed in the topic.

PART II Projects contains a number of projects that build skills and introduce problem solving. The projects are typical of those that people encounter in school and business. They include the preparation of a resume, cover letter, and follow-up letters used when seeking a job. Step-by-step instructions for the completion of these projects is not provided. To complete them, you must first have mastered the procedures listed for each project.

PART III DOS presents brief summaries and step-by-step tutorials for the most frequently used DOS commands.

▼ THE COMPASS SERIES

This text is part of an integrated series, *Computer Applications Software Series,* or *COMPASS.* The texts in this series, like this one, use a standardized approach to introducing operating systems and applications software. Many of the texts in the series are available in two versions, for complete courses or short courses.

• The complete course versions cover all features of the program and are suitable for a full-semester course or when you want extensive coverage of a program.

• The short-course versions are adapted from the complete-course versions. They are designed to be used in a course where more than one program is being covered or when time is limited and you want to cover only the most important features of the program. They are similar to the complete-course versions but contain fewer topics, tutorials, exercises, and projects.

TITLES

The COMPASS series contained the following texts at the time this one was published. Each text covers the latest version of their respective programs.

DOS 4: A Complete Course
WordPerfect 5: A Complete Course
Lotus 1-2-3 Release 2.2: A Complete Course
dBASE IV: A Complete Course

DOS 4: A Short Course
WordPerfect 5: A Short Course
WordPerfect 5.1: A Complete Course
Lotus 1-2-3, Release 2.2: A Short Course
dBASE IV: A Short Course
Communications with ProCom: A Short Course

These texts are updated as soon as a new version of the program is introduced, and previous versions of the text are kept in print as long as there is demand for them. Also, new titles are introduced when major new programs gain wide acceptance in college and university courses. To obtain an up-to-date listing of the titles in the series, contact your Prentice Hall representative.

SUPPLEMENTS

The publisher has developed many supplements for the COMPASS series that are free on adoption. These supplements include the following:

- **Instructor's Resource Manual** contains suggested course outlines and teaching suggestions and test questions.
- **WordPerfect 5.1 Resource Disk** is available and contains the files for all of the tutorials, exercises, and projects in this text. You can use these files for your own reference or copy-selected files for student use. You can obtain a free master copy by contacting your local Prentice Hall representative or calling Prentice Hall's Software Department toll-free at 1-800-842-2958. Be sure to specify whether the disk should be in the $5\frac{1}{4}$- or $3\frac{1}{2}$-inch format.
- **Videos** on the programs covered in this series are available to qualified adopters of this text. Contact your local Prentice Hall representative for details.

▼ ACKNOWLEDGMENTS

No book is the result of the efforts of a single person. Although the author accepts responsibility for the final results, he was assisted during the development of this text and would like to express his appreciation to the following people: Peggy Curtin handled all communications with computer companies and coordinated the art program for the series. Meredith Flynn tested all the tutorials, Bruce Emmer copyedited the manuscript, and Bob Tebbenhoff and Cheryl Smith oversaw the production process. And last, but by no means least, Michele Jay oversaw the last-minute marketing plans that brought this new edition to everyone's attention.

Dennis P. Curtin
Marblehead, Massachusetts

Word Processing Procedures
An Overview and Tutorial

When you want to use your computer to create documents, you use a *word processing* program. When you load one of these programs into the computer, you can quickly and easily create, edit, and format documents. There are many word processing programs on the market, but WordPerfect is the most popular. This program is popular because it is both easy to learn and very powerful. Let's look briefly at how you use WordPerfect, from loading the program to clearing the screen or quitting. Later in this text, we explain these procedures in detail.

▼ Fast-Start Tutorial

If you actually want to create this document while following this example, ask your instructor for help in loading WordPerfect, or refer to Topics 1 and 2, then follow the instructions in the boxes for each step. Don't worry about why you are doing some things; you'll learn about them in this text.

STEP 1: LOAD THE PROGRAM

A computer can perform a number of tasks. You tell it what task to perform by loading a program into the computer's memory. To use the computer for word processing, you load WordPerfect from the disks it is stored on (Figure 1). If you are using a computer with floppy disk drives, you insert a disk into drive B to save your work on. If you are working on a hard disk system, you insert a disk in drive A to save your work on if you are not saving it on the hard disk drive.

When you load WordPerfect, the blank document screen appears (Figure 2). This screen always displays a cursor, a one-character-wide underline. The cursor indicates where the next character you type will appear. When you type a character, it appears on the screen, and the cursor moves one space to the right.

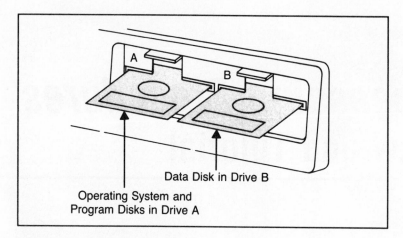

FIGURE 1   Loading WordPerfect.   To load WordPerfect from a floppy disk, you always insert the *WordPerfect 1* disk into drive A. If you want to save your work on a floppy disk, you insert a formatted data disk into drive B (on a floppy disk system) or drive A (on a hard disk system).

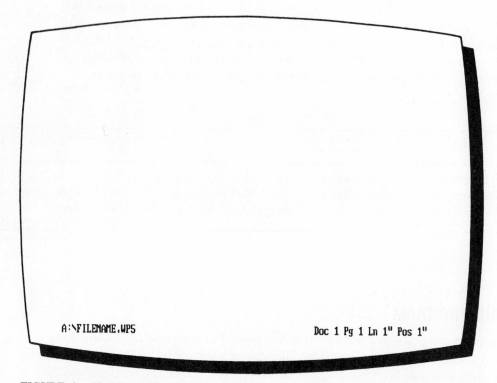

FIGURE 2   The Document Screen.   When you load WordPerfect, the document screen appears automatically. The cursor is initially in the upper left-hand corner of the screen. It indicates where the next character that you type will appear. The status line at the bottom of the screen gives the current position of the cursor.

STEP 2: ENTER THE DOCUMENT

Entering text is similar to entering it on a typewriter. The main difference is that you do not have to press **Enter** at the end of each line as you have to press the carriage return on a typewriter. WordPerfect automatically "wraps" the lines as you enter them, so they do not extend past the right margin. You have to press **Enter** only at the end of paragraphs and when you want a line to end before it reaches the right margin (Figure 3).

```
April 6, 1992 ↵

TO: Stuart Lewis ↵
FR: Mary Cranston ↵
RE: Word Processing Software ↵
↵
Dear Stuart, ↵
↵
We completed the evaluation of some leading software programs. We
will be making an oral presentation and demonstration of their
features on Wednesday morning. The presentation will cover the
program's ease-of-use, formatting capabilities, and advanced
features such as desktop publishing and merge-printing
capabilities. If you can attend, please let me know. ↵
↵
Sincerely yours, ↵
↵
↵
↵
Mary ↵



                                                    Doc 1 Pg 1 Ln 1" Pos 1"
```

FIGURE 3   Entering the Document.   You enter a document by typing it in, just as if you were typing on a typewriter. You press **Enter** only to end lines before they reach the right margin, to end paragraphs, or to insert blank lines.

▼Fast-Start Tutorial

To enter the document, type in the text shown in Figure 3. Press **Enter** only where indicated by the ↵ symbols. Do not worry about mistakes since you can correct them later.

STEP 3: EDIT AND REVISE THE DOCUMENT

After you enter the document, you proofread it and correct any mistakes. Generally, it is easier to proofread a printout of a document than to proofread the document on the screen (Figure 4). To edit the document on the screen, you use the arrows and other designated keys to move the cursor through the text. You then delete or insert characters, words, or phrases, or you highlight blocks—large sections of text—to copy, move, or delete in one step. You can also use advanced editing features like search and replace and spell checking to speed up the editing.

▼Fast-Start Tutorial

To edit the document, use the four directional arrow keys (↑ , ↓ , ←, and →) to move the cursor through the document and insert characters where needed. If you need to delete characters, the **Backspace** key deletes characters to the left of the cursor, and the **Del** key deletes the character above the cursor.

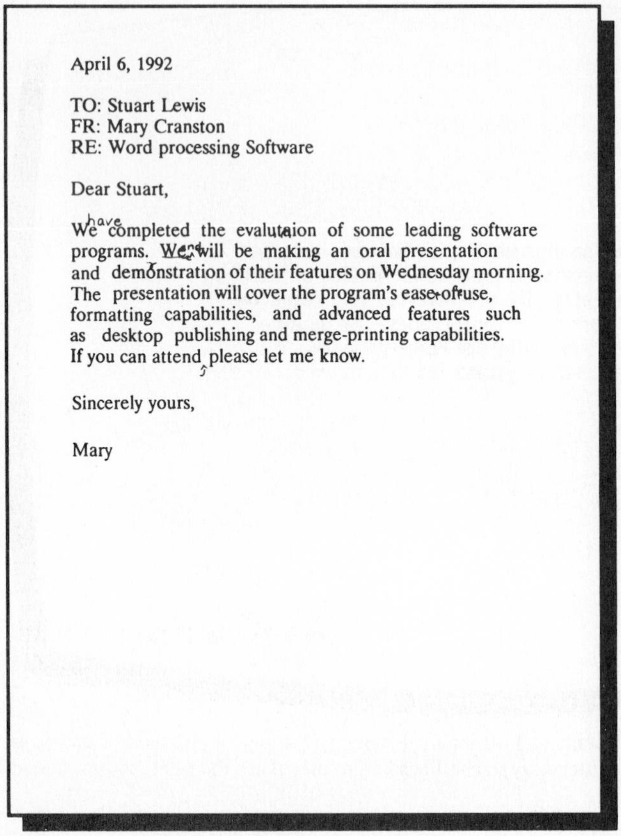

April 6, 1992

TO: Stuart Lewis
FR: Mary Cranston
RE: Word processing Software

Dear Stuart,

We have completed the evaluation of some leading software programs. We will be making an oral presentation and demonstration of their features on Wednesday morning. The presentation will cover the program's ease of use, formatting capabilities, and advanced features such as desktop publishing and merge-printing capabilities. If you can attend, please let me know.

Sincerely yours,

Mary

FIGURE 4 Editing the Document. To edit your document, print it out to make proofreading easier. If you find any errors, you edit the document on the screen by moving the cursor through it to insert or delete text.

STEP 4: FORMAT THE DOCUMENT

You format a document to control its layout and appearance (Figure 5). You do not need to know much about formatting when you begin since WordPerfect is already set to print a document single-spaced on an 8½-by-11-inch sheet of paper. These default settings anticipate the most frequent applications of the program—the preparation of memos, letters, and reports. However, you can format a document at any time—before you enter the document, while you enter it, or after you enter it. You can change margins, emphasize keywords by boldfacing them, or indent paragraphs. Unlike typing a document, formatting is separate from printing. If you decide to change formats, you don't have to retype the entire document; you just make a new printout.

▼ Fast-Start Tutorial

To format the document so that it looks similar to Figure 5:

1. Add a colon after the sentence *The presentation will cover the program's*.
2. Position the cursor under the first letter in each phrase that is to become a separate line, and then press **Enter**. When the cursor is under the *E* in *ease of use*, press **Enter** twice.
3. Capitalize the first letter in each phrase and insert an asterisk in front of each, followed by a space.
4. Delete extra commas, the word *and* at the ends of lines, and the one extra period, using the **Del** or **Backspace** key.
5. Position the cursor under the first letter of *If*, and press **Enter** twice.

```
April 6, 1992

TO: Stuart Lewis
FR: Mary Cranston
RE: Word Processing Software

Dear Stuart,

We have completed the evaluation of some leading software programs
and will be making an oral presentation and demonstration of their
features on Wednesday morning. The presentation will cover the
program's:

■ Ease of use
■ Formatting capabilities
■ Advanced features such as desktop publishing and merge-printing
  capabilities

If you can attend, please let me know.

Sincerely yours,


Mary
                                            Doc 1 Pg 1 Ln 1" Pos 1"
```

FIGURE 5 Formatting the Document. You format a document to change its layout or appearance. Here, a paragraph was broken up into a bulleted list.

STEP 5: SAVE THE DOCUMENT

When you have completed the document, you assign it a filename and save it in a file on the disk. The Save command copies the document on the screen and in the computer's memory to a file on the disk (Figure 6). If the document is long, you normally save it several times while entering it so that it would not be lost if the power failed or something else went wrong.

Fast-Start Tutorial

To save the file:

1. Press **F10** and the prompt reads *Document to be saved:*. (If a screen with the heading *Document Summary* is displayed, press **Enter** to display the prompt.)

2. Type **B:TUTORIAL.WP5** (on a floppy disk system) or **A:TUTORIAL.WP5** (on a hard disk system), and then press **Enter**.

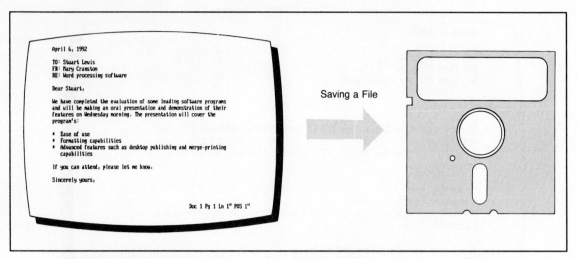

FIGURE 6 Saving a File. When you save a file, the computer copies the version currently on the screen and stored in the computer's memory to a file on the disk so that you can retrieve it later when you need it.

STEP 6: PRINT THE DOCUMENT

You make a printout using the Print command. This command sends the document to the printer, where it is printed using the formats you specified in Step 4 (Figure 7). To print a document, your computer must be connected to a printer and the printer must be on.

 Fast-Start Tutorial

To print the document, press **Shift-F7** to display the Print menu and then press **1** for *Full Document*.

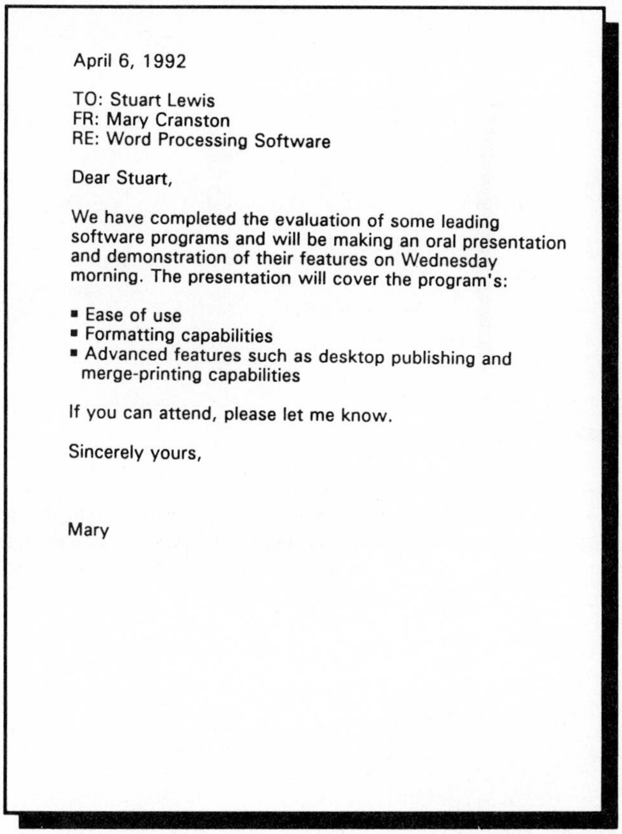

April 6, 1992

TO: Stuart Lewis
FR: Mary Cranston
RE: Word Processing Software

Dear Stuart,

We have completed the evaluation of some leading
software programs and will be making an oral presentation
and demonstration of their features on Wednesday
morning. The presentation will cover the program's:

- Ease of use
- Formatting capabilities
- Advanced features such as desktop publishing and
  merge-printing capabilities

If you can attend, please let me know.

Sincerely yours,

Mary

FIGURE 7   Printing the Document.   WordPerfect is set so that documents
are automatically printed on 8½-by-11-inch paper with 1-inch margins. (Yours
will look different from this because some of your lines will end at different
places.)

STEP 7: CONTINUE OR QUIT

When you have finished a document, you have three choices: enter a new document, edit an existing document, or exit the program.

- If you want to create a new document, you clear the current document from
  the screen.
- To edit an existing document, you retrieve it onto the screen from its file on a
  disk (Figure 8).
- If you are done for the day or want to run another program, you use the Exit
  command. This removes WordPerfect and any document you are working on
  from the computer's memory and from the screen. You can then quit for the
  day or load another program.

▼ Fast-Start Tutorial

To continue or exit, press **F7** and the prompt
reads *Save document? (Y/N) Yes*. (If a screen with
the heading *Document Summary* is displayed,
press **Enter** to display the prompt.) Press **N** and

the prompt reads *Exit WP? (Y/N) No*. Press **Y** to exit
the program, or press **N** to clear the screen and
work on your own document.

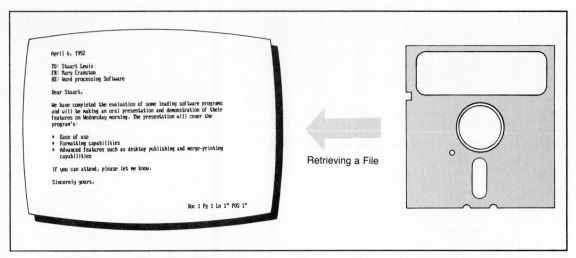

FIGURE 8   Retrieving a File.   When you retrieve a document from the disk on which it is stored, the computer copies it into its memory and displays it on the screen. The document in the file on the disk remains unchanged.

▼ QUESTIONS

1. What are word processing programs used for?
2. List the seven steps in creating a document with WordPerfect, and briefly describe each of them.
3. What happens when you save a file?
4. What happens when you retrieve a file?

TOPIC 1
Loading and Quitting the Operating System

Although you do your computer work with applications programs like WordPerfect, the heart of the computer's software is another type of software, called the operating system. The operating system coordinates activity between you and the computer and between parts of the computer like the keyboard and display screen. Through the operating system, WordPerfect tells the computer to display on the screen the characters you type, save your work into a file on the disk, print a file, and so forth.

LOADING THE OPERATING SYSTEM

Because the operating system coordinates activity between any applications program you run and the computer's hardware, you must load the operating system into the computer's memory before you load WordPerfect. This is called booting the system. The term comes from the expression "pulling oneself up by the bootstraps." Once the operating system is loaded, you can load WordPerfect or use the operating system's commands to manage your files.

If your system is off, you load the operating system by turning it on. When you do so, it automatically looks to the disk in the startup drive for the operating system files it needs.

- On a floppy disk system, the startup drive is drive A, so you insert the DOS disk labeled IBM DOS, MS-DOS, or Startup disk into that drive (see the box "Inserting Floppy Disks").
- On a hard disk system, the startup drive is drive C, but the computer still looks to drive A first. Therefore, before you turn on a hard disk system, be sure to open the door to drive A or eject the disk so that the program does not try to load the operating system from that drive (see the box "Error Messages").

With the drives set, you turn on the computer. The position of the on/off switch varies from computer to computer. Frequently, it is on the right side toward the back. Also, on some systems, you have to turn on the display screen using its own switch.

When you turn on the computer, it pauses for a few moments, and then the startup drive spins. All computers have built-in clocks, and many computers set them automatically. If your system's clock is not set automatically, you are prompted to enter the date and time each time you turn it on. If you are prompted to do so, see the box "Entering Dates and Times."

▼ Inserting Floppy Disks

The way you insert floppy disks depends on the type of system you are using. Most floppy disk systems have two drives, A and B. When loading a program from a floppy disk, you insert it into drive A, the startup drive. To save your work onto a floppy disk, you insert it into drive B on a floppy disk computer and into drive A on a computer with a hard disk (after booting the system). The arrangements of floppy disk drives vary.

- **To insert a 5¼-inch disk,** open the door to the disk drive. Hold the disk with the label facing up to insert it into a horizontal drive. Hold it with the label facing to the left and with the write-protect notch up to insert it into a vertical drive.

Point the oblong read/write slot toward the slot in the drive, and insert the disk into the slot. (On some systems, it "clicks" into place.) Never push

hard because a 5¼-inch disk will buckle if it gets caught on an obstruction. Carefully jiggle the disk to make sure it is inserted all the way into the disk drive. Gently close the disk drive's door, or press the button that locks the disk into the drive. If you encounter any resistance, jiggle the disk and then close the door or press the button again. To remove the disk, open the door and pull the disk out. On some drives, gently pushing the disk in and then quickly releasing the pressure pops it out of the drive; on others, you have to press a button.

- **To insert a 3½-inch disk,** hold it so that the arrow embossed on the case is gently into the drive, and press until it clicks into place. To remove the disk, press the disk eject button just above or below the drive's slot.

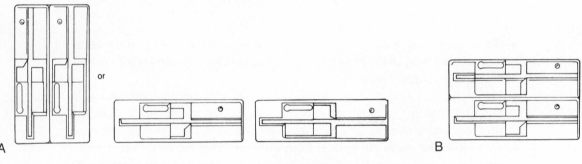

A. If your floppy disk drives are side by side, drive A is the one on the left.
B. If one drive is above the other, drive A is the one on the top.

▼ Error Messages

When you boot an IBM computer system, you may see the message *Non-bootable disk* or *Non-System disk or disk error* (or a similar message on compatible computers). One of these error messages appears when you turn on the computer with a disk in drive A that does not contain the operating system files that the computer needs.

- On a floppy disk system, insert the DOS disk into drive A, and then press any key to continue.
- On a hard disk system, open drive A's door or eject the disk in that drive, and then press any key to continue.

▼ Entering Dates and Times

When you first turn on some computers, you are prompted to enter the date and time. Entering the correct date and time is important because the computer's clock date and time marks files that you save. The clock is also used by WordPerfect to enter dates and times into files and to display them on the screen.

You enter the date and time as described below, and then press **Enter** (◄┘ on IBM and compatible keyboards). If you enter either incorrectly, an error message is displayed, and you are prompted to reenter them.

ENTERING DATES
Enter dates in the format MM-DD-YY.

- MM (month) is a number from 1 to 12.
- DD (day) is a number from 1 to 31.
- YY (year) is a number from 80 to 99 or from 1980 to 1999.

  You can use hyphens (-), slashes (/), or periods (.) to separate the day, month, and year. For example, to enter the date January 10, 1992, enter it as 1-10-92, 1/10/92, or 1.10.92.

  If you fail to enter a date, the system's clock remains set to 1-01-80, and all files that you save are marked with that date. You cannot enter a date earlier than 1/1/1980. To enter a date later than 12/31/1999, you must enter all four digits for the year. For example, to enter January 1, 2001, type **1/1/2001**.

ENTERING TIMES
Enter times in the format HH:MM.

- HH (hours) is a number between 0 and 23.
- MM (minutes) is a number between 0 and 59.

  Separate the hours and minutes with colons (:) or periods (.).
  You can use military time or, if you are using DOS 4, standard time.

- Military time is based on a 24-hour day. For example, to set the clock to 1:30 p.m., enter **13:30**.
- Standard time is based on a 12-hour period. To specify the time when using DOS 4, you enter a **p** or an **a** after the last time unit. For example, to set the clock to 1:30 p.m., enter **1:30p**. To set it to 10:30 a.m., enter **10:30a**. Do not enter spaces between the time and the letters.

THE COMMAND PROMPT AND THE DOS 4 SHELL

When you load DOS, either the command prompt (Figure 9) or the DOS 4 Shell (Figure 10) is displayed. Which appears depends on the version of DOS that you are using and how your system has been set up. The command prompt is available on all versions of DOS, but the Shell was added only to DOS 4.0 and later versions. (If you are loading DOS from a floppy disk, the program may appear instead of the operating system. See the box ''System Disks.'')

The Command Prompt

On many systems, the command prompt appears on the screen when you boot the system (Figure 9). It will normally be *A>* or *A:\>* if you loaded from a floppy disk or *C:\>* if you loaded from a hard disk drive. However, the command prompt can be customized, so it may be different on your system.

The command prompt tells you that you are in DOS and that the default, or active, disk drive is drive A or C. From this command prompt, you can execute all DOS commands (see Part Three) or start applications programs like WordPerfect® (see Topic 2).

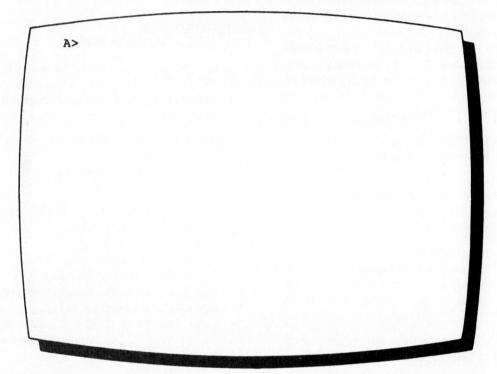

FIGURE 9   The Command Prompt.   All versions of DOS can display the command prompt. From this prompt, you load applications programs and execute DOS commands.

The DOS 4 Shell

If you are using DOS 4 and your system has been set up to do so, the DOS 4 Shell appears on the screen when you boot the system. The first screen displayed is the Start Programs screen (Figure 10). The menu-operated Shell makes it easy to execute commands without remembering cryptic commands. All you have to know is how to use the Shell's menus.

Although you might want to use the Shell for most of your work, some advanced procedures can be completed only from the command prompt. Also, when the command prompt is displayed, the system works just like earlier versions of DOS. You can quickly switch back and forth between the Shell and the command prompt whenever you want to.

- To display the Shell from the command prompt, type **DOSSHELL** and then press **Enter** (◄┘ on IBM and compatible keyboards). However, before doing so
  - If you are working on a hard disk system, first type **C:** and then press **Enter** to change the default drive to drive C.
  - If you are working on a floppy disk system, first insert the Shell disk into drive A, type **A:** and then press **Enter** to change the default drive to drive A.

- To display the command prompt when the Shell is on the screen, press **F3** from Start Programs to remove the Shell from memory. (You first have to press **F3** if you are in the File System, or **Esc** if you are in the DOS Utilities' subgroup, to return to Start Programs.) You can also select *Exit Shell* from the Start Programs' Exit menu on the Action Bar. After using either command, type **DOSSHELL** and then press **Enter** to return to the Shell.

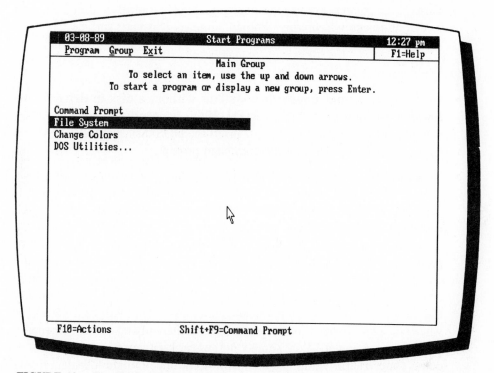

FIGURE 10   The DOS 4 Shell.   When you load DOS 4 and later versions, the Shell is displayed if your Startup disk is set up to do so. (Your screen may look slightly different if you do not have a graphics display or a mouse.)

▼ System Disks

If the operating system files have been copied to your *WordPerfect 1* disk, the disk is called a system disk. It is called a system disk because you can load both the operating system and WordPerfect from the same disk. If you have a disk of this kind, you insert the *WordPerfect 1* disk into drive A instead of the DOS disk. (Your teacher can tell you if your disk is a system disk.)

If the disk also has a file called an AUTOEXEC.BAT file, both DOS and the WordPerfect program may be loaded automatically when you turn on the computer with the *WordPerfect 1* disk in drive A.

QUITTING DOS

When you are done for the day, you should always turn off the computer. If you are using the DOS 4 Shell, you should always press **F3** to exit the Shell and return to the command prompt before turning off your system. If you turn the computer off without first exiting the Shell, temporary files may be left on your disk. If you do this repeatedly, you will eventually run out of room on the disk.

If you are quitting for the day, you should do three things:

- Open all floppy disk drive doors or eject the disks in the drives so that the disk drives' read/write heads don't leave indentations in the disks' surfaces.
- Remove any floppy disks from the disk drives to prevent their loss, increase security, and ensure that no one mistakenly erases them.
- Turn off the computer or use the display monitor's controls to dim the screen so that an image will not be "burned" into its phosphor surface.

▼ TIPS

➤ **If you turn on some floppy disk systems without a disk in drive A, the Basic program is loaded from ROM**. If this happens (the screen indicates that you are in the Basic program), insert the DOS disk, type **SYSTEM** and then press **Enter** to display the command prompt.

➤ **You can boot a computer that is already on**. When you first turn on a computer it is called a cold boot because the system has not been running. If you want to reboot a system that is already on, perhaps to start over if you encounter a serious problem with a program, you warm-boot the system. To warm boot the system, you hold down **Ctrl** and **Alt** while pressing **Del** or press the computer's Reset button. This command clears all data from the computer's memory and has almost the same effect as turning the computer off and then back on again. Use this command with restraint. You normally use this procedure only when you encounter a problem with your system or when you have changed some system settings that only take effect when you reboot the computer. You should not warm-boot on a regular basis. It doesn't cause harm, but it is a bad habit because you might lose data if you do it at the wrong time.

➤ **If you are already running an applications program, you do not have to boot the system to return to DOS** since it is already in memory. You just use the applications program's Quit or Exit command, and that returns you to the operating system.

➤ **When you turn your computer off**, you should wait 20 to 30 seconds before turning it back on. Some systems will not reboot without this pause. If you turn one of these systems back on too quickly, nothing happens.

▼ TUTORIALS

The way you load the operating system depends on whether you are loading DOS 3 or 4. For this reason, there are two tutorials in this topic, but you complete only the one for the version of the operating system that you are using.

- Tutorial 1A describes loading and quitting DOS 3.
- Tutorial 1B describes loading and quitting DOS 4.

Also, if the computer that you are working on is connected to a network, you may have special procedures to follow to access the operating system. If so, your instructor will provide you with information on how to begin (see Exercise 1A).

TUTORIAL 1A   Loading and Quitting DOS 3

In this tutorial, you load DOS 3 and then quit it. To begin this tutorial, your computer should be off.

Step 1   **Get Ready.** Before proceeding:
- On a floppy disk system, insert the DOS disk into drive A (see the box ''Inserting Floppy Disks'').
- On a hard disk system, open the door to drive A or eject the disk in that drive.

Step 2   **Load the Operating System.** To load the operating system, turn the computer on. The on/off switch is usually located on the side of the computer toward the rear. When you turn the computer on, a bright underline flashes in the upper left corner of the screen as the computer runs its internal diagnostic program. In a few moments, the computer may beep, and then drive A spins and its light comes on while the operating system is loaded. If there is no disk in drive A, the computer looks to drive C for the program if the system contains a hard disk drive. If nothing appears on your screen, your display may not be on. On some systems, the display has a separate on/off switch.

Step 3   **Enter the Date and Time.** If your computer's clock is not set automatically, in a moment the prompt reads *Enter new date:* (If you make a typo when entering any commands, press **Backspace** to delete the incorrect characters, and then type them in correctly before pressing **Enter**—the key labeled ◄⌐ on IBM and compatible keyboards.)

1. Enter the date as month-day-year (for example, type **1-30-92** for January 30, 1992), and then press **Enter**. The prompt then reads *Enter new time:*
2. Enter the time as hour:minute (for example, type **10:30**), and then press **Enter**.

Result: The command prompt appears on the screen.

Step 4   **Check the Version Number.** After loading DOS, you can check the version number whenever the command prompt is displayed.

Note: In all the instructions in this text, the characters you type are shown in uppercase letters, but whether you use uppercase or lowercase letters usually does not matter. For example, in the following command, you can type **VER**, **ver**, **Ver**, **vEr**, or **veR**; the computer accepts them all.

To check the version number
  Type   **VER** and then press **Enter**

Result: The screen displays the version number of DOS in memory.

Step 5   **Continue or Quit.** You have now completed this tutorial. Either continue to the next tutorial or quit for the day. If you want to quit, remove your disks from the drives and turn off the computer.

TUTORIAL 1B   Loading and Quitting DOS 4

In this tutorial, you load DOS 4 and then quit it. To begin this tutorial, your computer should be off.

Step 1   **Get Ready.** Before proceeding:

- On a floppy disk system, insert the Startup disk into drive A (see the box ''Inserting Floppy Disks'').
- On a hard disk system, open the door to drive A or eject the disk in that drive.

Step 2   **Load the Operating System.** To load the operating system, turn the computer on. The on/off switch is usually located on the side of the computer toward the rear. When you turn the computer on, a bright underline flashes in the upper left corner of the screen as the computer runs its internal diagnostic program. In a few moments, the computer may beep, and then drive A spins and its light comes on while the operating system is loaded. If there is no disk in drive A, the computer looks to drive C for the program if the system contains a hard disk drive. If nothing appears on your screen, your display may not be on. On some systems, the display has a separate on/off switch.

Step 3   **Enter the Date and Time.** If your computer's clock is not set automatically, in a moment the prompt reads *Enter new date:* (If you make a typo when entering any commands, press **Backspace** to delete the incorrect characters, and then type them in correctly before pressing **Enter**.)

1. Enter the date as month-day-year (for example, type **1-30-92** for January 30, 1992), and then press **Enter**. The prompt then reads *Enter new time:*
2. Enter the time as hour:minute (for example, type **10:30** and add an **a** or a **p** to specify a.m. or p.m.), and then press **Enter**.

Result: The command prompt *A:\>* or *C:\>* appears on the screen, or the DOS 4 Shell is displayed. If the command prompt is displayed and you are working on a floppy disk system, insert the Shell disk into drive A. (On a hard disk system, this isn't necessary.) On either kind of system, type **DOSSHELL** and then press **Enter**.

Step 4   **Return to the Command Prompt.** Whenever the Shell is displayed, you can remove it from memory and return to the command prompt.

To return to the command prompt
    Press   **F3**

Result: The command prompt appears on the screen.

Step 5   **Check the Version Number.** After loading DOS, you can check the version number whenever the command prompt is displayed.

Note: In all the instructions in this text, the characters you type are shown in uppercase letters, but whether you use uppercase or lowercase letters usually does not matter. For example, in the following command, you can type **VER**, **ver**, **Ver**, **vEr**, or **veR**; the computer accepts them all.

To check the version number
    Type   **VER** and then press **Enter**

Result: The screen displays the version number of DOS in memory.

Step 6 **Return to the Shell.** Now return to the Shell.

To reload the Shell

Type   **DOSSHELL** and then press **Enter**

Result: The Shell reappears on the screen.

Step 7 **Continue or Quit.** You have now completed this tutorial. Either continue to the next tutorial or quit for the day.

To return to the command prompt

Press   **F3**

Result: If you want to quit, remove your disks from the drives and turn off the computer.

EXERCISES

EXERCISE 1A Boot Your System

The way you boot a system varies, depending on how your system has been set up. If your system is on a network, or if for some other reason your startup does not follow the same rules described in this topic, enter your startup procedures here.

1. _____

_____

_____

2. _____

_____

_____

3. _____

_____

_____

4. _____

_____

_____

EXERCISE 1B View a Video

Many videocassettes have been developed to introduce users to specific operating systems. Visit your library, learning center, and computer lab to see if any on DOS are available for you to view. If so, view one of them, and then summarize its key points.

▼ QUESTIONS

1. What does booting a computer mean?

2. What is the startup drive? Which drive is it on a floppy disk system? On a hard disk system?

3. When you turn on the computer and are prompted to enter the date, what two formats can you enter it in? What two formats can you enter the time in?

4. If the command prompt is *A*>, what does that mean? If *C:*>?

5. What is the difference between a warm boot and a cold boot? How do you do each?

6. What is the purpose of a shell, like the one that comes with DOS 4?

7. Why should you remove the DOS 4 Shell from memory before you turn off your computer?

Microcomputers are versatile tools, and you can use them to perform many tasks. To do so, you load the program you want to use into the computer's memory. The type of program that you load, called an applications program, determines the kinds of tasks you can perform. For example, to use your computer for word processing, you can load the WordPerfect program.

LOADING WORDPERFECT FROM A FLOPPY DISK

Once the operating system is loaded, you can load WordPerfect. The way you do so depends on the type of computer you are using and the operating system you loaded. You only have to follow one of the procedures described below.

KEY/Strokes

LOADING WORDPERFECT FROM A FLOPPY DISK AND THE COMMAND PROMPT

1. Insert the disk labeled *WordPerfect 1* or *WordPerfect 1/WordPerfect 2* into drive A. (If the command prompt is not *A>*, type **A:** and then press **Enter**.)
2. Type **WP** and then press **Enter** to load the program. On some systems, the prompt reads *Insert diskette labeled "WordPerfect 2" and press any key*. Insert the requested disk, and then press any key to continue. The message reads **Please wait** and in a moment the document screen appears (see Figure 12)

KEY/Strokes

LOADING WORDPERFECT FROM A FLOPPY
DISK AND THE DOS 4 SHELL

1. Insert the disk labeled *WordPerfect 1* or *WordPerfect 1/WordPerfect 2* into drive A

2. To display the File System (Figure 11), highlight *File System* on the Start Programs' Main Group, and then press **Enter**. All the files on the disk in the default drive are automatically listed

3. To update the File List, press **Tab** to move the highlight to the Drive Identifier area, highlight the drive that contains the program files, and then press **Enter**

4. To load the program, press **Tab** to move the highlight to the File List, highlight the program file named WP.EXE, and then press **Spacebar** to select the file. Press **F10** to activate the Action Bar, press **F** (for *File*) to pull down the File menu, and then press **O** (for *Open (start)*) to display a pop-up box with the cursor in the Options entry field. Press **Enter** without specifying any options. The drive spins, and the program is loaded

Note. On some systems, the prompt reads *Insert diskette labeled "WordPerfect 2" and press any key to continue*. Do so, and the document screen appears (Figure 12)

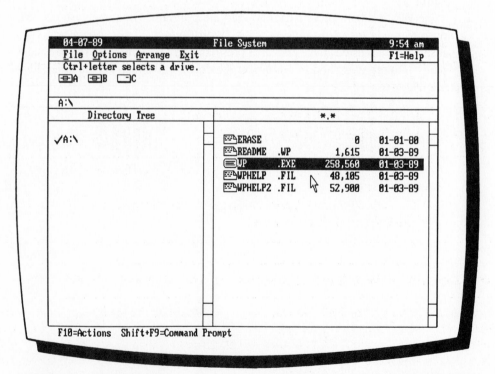

FIGURE 11   The File System.   When you display the File System, all the files on the disk in drive A are automatically displayed in the File List. (Your screen may look slightly different if you do not have a graphics display or a mouse.) To load a program:

1. You highlight its name on the File List and press **Spacebar** to select it.

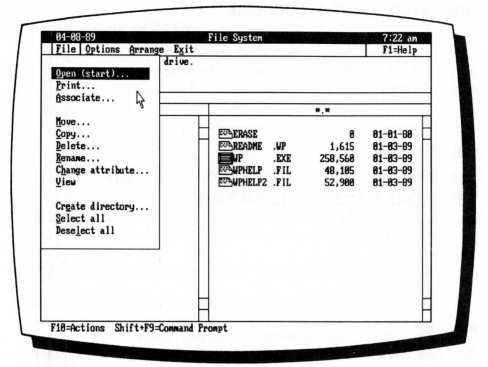

```
04-08-89                    File System                    7:22 am
 File  Options  Arrange  Exit                            F1=Help
                          drive.
  Open (start)...
  Print...
  Associate...        �k

  Move...                                    *.*
  Copy...
  Delete...             ERASE            0      01-01-80
  Rename...             README  .WP    1,615    01-03-89
  Change attribute...   WP      .EXE  258,560   01-03-89
  View                  WPHELP  .FIL   48,105   01-03-89
                        WPHELP2 .FIL   52,900   01-03-89
  Create directory...
  Select all
  Deselect all




  F10=Actions  Shift+F9=Command Prompt
```

2. You pull down the File menu, and then select *Open (start)*.

When you save files, they are saved to the disk in the default drive. Default drives are discussed in detail in Topic 4, but you should know that WordPerfect usually saves files to the disk that was the default drive when you loaded the program. By making drive B the default drive when you load the program from drive A, you can set the default drive to drive B automatically.

KEY/Strokes
LOADING WORDPERFECT FROM A FLOPPY DISK SO DRIVE B IS THE DEFAULT DRIVE

1. Insert the *WordPerfect 1* disk into drive A and a data disk on which to save your files into drive B
2. Type **B:** and then press **Enter** to change the command prompt to *B>*
3. Type **A:WP** and then press **Enter**

 Are other copies of WordPerfect currently running? (Y/N)

If you did not quit the program correctly the last time you used it, the prompt reads *Are other copies of WordPerfect currently running? (Y/N)* when you load the program. If you are not running the program on a network or under the WordPerfect Library's Shell with another copy of the program running, press **N**.

If you press **Y**, the prompt reads *Directory is in use. New WP Directory:*. Type the name of a new drive or directory in which to store temporary files, and then press **Enter**. If you do not specify a new drive or directory, these files are automatically overwritten.

TABLE 1   Key Lock Indicators

Key	When Engaged	When Not Engaged
Caps Lock	*POS* in uppercase	*Pos* in lowercase
Num Lock	*Pos* flashes	*Pos* does not flash

EXITING WORDPERFECT

At the end of a session, you press **F7** to exit WordPerfect when you want to load another program or turn the computer off. It is important to exit the program using the commands designed for this purpose. Although you can exit by simply turning off the computer, this is a bad habit to get into because WordPerfect creates temporary files on the disk while you are working and these are deleted only if you exit correctly.

When you press **F7** to exit WordPerfect, you are given the option of saving the document on the screen. Saving documents is discussed in Topic 4. KEY/Strokes ''Exiting WordPerfect'' describes how to exit the program without saving the document. You may want to do this because you have no further use for the document or because you saved it earlier and have not made any changes that you want to save. If you have not made any changes since you retrieved the document or last saved it, when you press **F7** to exit, a message on the status line reads *(Text was not modified)*. If this message appears, you have no reason to save the file.

After pressing **F7** to begin the exit sequence, you can always press **F1** at any point to cancel the command and leave the current document on the screen.

When you exit WordPerfect, the operating system's command prompt or Shell is displayed. From this prompt or Shell, you can load another program, format disks or copy files, or turn off the computer to quit for the day.

KEY/Strokes
EXITING WORDPERFECT

1. Either press **F7**

    Or   pull down the File menu and select *Exit*

    The prompt reads *Save document? Yes (No)*
    - If a screen with the heading *Document Summary* is displayed, it means that a previous user has changed a default setting (see the box ''The Document Summary Screen'' in Topic 5). Just press **Enter** to display the prompt.
    - If you have a document on the screen that has not been changed since you last saved it, the status line displays the message *(Text was not modified)*. This means that you can exit the program without saving the file without losing any text. If this message does not appear, you should save the document if you want to save your changes.

2. Press **N** to abandon the file, and the prompt reads *Exit WP? No (Yes)*
3. Press **Y** to return to the operating command prompt or the Shell

Note: If the message *Insert disk with COMMAND.COM* appears on the screen, insert the *WordPerfect 1* disk, and then press any key to continue.

If the message *Insert disk with batch file Press any key to continue* appears, insert the DOS 4 Shell disk into drive A, and then press any key. In a few moments, the prompt reads *Press Enter (◄┘) to return to the File System*. Press **Enter**, and the File System reappears.

▼ TIPS

➤ **If you load WordPerfect from a floppy disk in drive A on a hard disk system**, be sure to turn on the computer and load the operating system before inserting the *WordPerfect 1* disk into drive A. If you turn on the computer with the *WordPerfect 1* disk in drive A, the computer will not read two key files on the hard disk: the AUTOEXEC.BAT file and the CONFIG.SYS file, which customize your system.

➤ **Do not turn off the computer or remove the WordPerfect disk from drive A** (unless copying files) until you exit the program.

➤ **If you have a document on both windows** (see Topic 15), when you exit from the first one, you are asked if you want to exit that document. If you answer Yes, the other document appears on the screen. You then have to exit that document to quit the program.

▼ TUTORIALS

The way you load WordPerfect depends on the operating system and hardware you are using. For this reason, there are three tutorials on loading the program, but you should complete only the one for the version of the operating system that you are using.

- Tutorial 2A describes loading from a floppy disk and the command prompt.
- Tutorial 2B describes loading from a hard disk and the command prompt.
- Tutorial 2C describes loading from a floppy or hard disk using the DOS 4 Shell.

Also, if the computer that you are working on is connected to a network, you may have special procedures to follow to load WordPerfect. If so, your instructor will provide you with information on how to begin (see Exercise 2C).

TUTORIAL 2A   Loading WordPerfect from Floppy Disks and the Command Prompt

In this tutorial, you load and then exit WordPerfect from the operating system's prompt. To begin this tutorial, the operating system must be loaded. To complete this tutorial, you need the disks labeled *WordPerfect 1* and *WordPerfect 2* (for some 5¼-inch floppy disk systems) or the disk labeled *WordPerfect 1/WordPerfect 2* (for a 3½-inch system). (Both disks are referred to in this text as the *WordPerfect 1* disk.)

Note: Some computers are connected to networks that have their own menu systems to load programs. If you are working on such a system, your instructor will explain how to load WordPerfect. Once the program is loaded, continue at Step 2.

Step 1   **Load WordPerfect.** Before you can use the WordPerfect program, you must load it into your computer's memory.

- If you are working on a floppy disk system, insert the *WordPerfect 1* disk into drive A. If the command prompt is not *A>* or *A:\>*, type **A:** and then press **Enter**.
- To load the program, type **WP** and then press **Enter**. (On some 5¼-inch floppy disk systems, the prompt reads *Insert diskette labeled "WordPerfect 2" and press any key*. Insert the requested disk, and then press any key to continue.)

Result: The blank WordPerfect document screen appears. The screen displays a cursor, a flashing one-character-wide underline that you use to enter and edit text. A status line is displayed at the bottom of the screen.

Step 2   **Have Some Fun.** If this is your first time using WordPerfect, type in some text. Don't worry about what you type because you won't save or print it. The only commands you have to know are these:

- Press **Enter** twice to end a paragraph and insert a blank line.
- Press the directional arrow keys to move the cursor through text you have already entered.
- Press **Backspace** to delete the character to the left of the cursor.

Step 3 **Continue or Exit.** You have now completed this tutorial. Either continue on your own document or another tutorial or exit WordPerfect and return to the operating system.

To continue or exit

Press **F7** and the prompt reads *Save document? Yes (No)*. (If a screen with the heading *Document Summary* is displayed, press **Enter** to display the prompt.)

Press **N** and the prompt reads *Exit WP? No (Yes)*

Press **Y** to exit the program, or press **N** to clear the screen and work on your own document

Result: If you did not exit the program, the document screen is now blank so that you can enter your own document. If you did exit the program, the command prompt is displayed on the screen. Remove your program and data disks, and then turn off the computer or load another program.

TUTORIAL 2B Loading WordPerfect from a Hard Disk and the Command Prompt

In this tutorial, you load and then exit WordPerfect from the operating system's prompt. To begin this tutorial, the operating system must be loaded.

Note: Some computers are connected to networks that have their own menu systems to load programs. If you are working on such a system, your instructor will explain how to load WordPerfect. Once the program is loaded, continue at Step 2.

Step 1 **Load WordPerfect.** Before you can use the WordPerfect program, you must load it into your computer's memory.

To change the default drive

Type **C:** and then press **Enter** to make drive C the default drive

To change the default directory

Type the name of the directory, and then press **Enter**. For example, if the WordPerfect files are stored in a directory named WP51, type **CD\WP51** and then press **Enter** to make that the default drive

To load the program

Type **WP** and then press **Enter**

Result: The blank WordPerfect document screen appears. The screen displays a cursor, a flashing one-character-wide underline that you use to enter and edit text. A status line is displayed at the bottom line of the screen.

Step 2 **Have Some Fun.** If this is your first time using WordPerfect, type in some text. Don't worry about what you type because you won't save or print it. The only commands you have to know are these:

- Press **Enter** twice to end a paragraph and insert a blank line.
- Press the arrow keys to move the cursor through text you have already entered.
- Press **Backspace** to delete the character to the left of the cursor.

Step 3 **Continue or Exit.** You have now completed this tutorial Either continue on your own document or another tutorial or exit WordPerfect and return to the operating system.

To continue or exit

Press   **F7** and the prompt reads *Save document? Yes (No)*. (If a screen with the heading *Document Summary* is displayed, press **Enter** to display the prompt.)

Press   **N** and the prompt reads *Exit WP? No (Yes)*

Press   **Y** to exit the program, or press **N** to clear the screen and work on your own document

Result: If you did not exit the program, the document screen is now blank so that you can enter your own document. If you did exit the program, the command prompt is displayed on the screen. Remove your program and data disks, and then turn off the computer or load another program.

TUTORIAL 2C   Loading WordPerfect from the DOS 4 Shell

In this tutorial, you load and then exit the WordPerfect program from the DOS 4 Shell. You can complete this tutorial only if you are using DOS 4 or later versions. To begin this tutorial, the operating system must be loaded and the Shell displayed.

Note: Some computers are connected to networks that have their own menu systems to load programs. If you are working on such a system, your instructor will explain how to load WordPerfect. Once the program is loaded, continue at Step 3.

Step 1 **˙Display the File System.** The command you use to load programs is contained in the File System. Before proceeding, if you are using a floppy disk system, insert the disk labeled *WordPerfect 1* into drive A.

To display the File System

Highlight   *File System*, and then press **Enter**

To change the default drive

Press   **Tab** to move the highlight to the Drive Identifier area

Highlight   *A* (on a floppy disk system) or *C* (on a hard disk system) and then press **Enter**. On a hard disk system, press **Tab** to move the highlight to the Directory Tree, highlight the directory that contains the WordPerfect program files, and then press **Enter**

Result: The File List for the WordPerfect disk or the WordPerfect directory is displayed.

Step 2 **Load WordPerfect.** To load WordPerfect, you select the program's name on the File List and then select Open (start) from the File menu.

To load WordPerfect

Press   **Tab** to move the highlight to the File List

Highlight   the file named *WP.EXE*

Press   **Spacebar** to select the file

Press   **F10** to activate the Action Bar

Press   **F** (for *File*) to pull down the File menu

Press   **O** (for *Open (start)*) to display a pop-up with the cursor in the *Options* entry field

Press   **Enter** without specifying any options

Result: The drive spins, and in a moment the prompt reads *Insert diskette labeled "WordPerfect 2" and press any key to continue*. Do so, and the blank WordPerfect document screen appears. The screen displays a cursor, a flashing one-character-wide underline that you use to enter and edit text. A status line is displayed at the bottom of the screen.

Step 3 **Have Some Fun.** If this is your first time using WordPerfect, type in some text. Don't worry about what you type because you won't save or print it. The only commands you have to know are these:

- Press **Enter** twice to end a paragraph and insert a blank line.
- Press the directional arrow keys to move the cursor through text you have already entered.
- Press **Backspace** to delete the character to the left of the cursor.

Step 4 **Continue or Exit.** You have now completed this tutorial. Either continue on your own document or another tutorial or exit WordPerfect and return to the operating system.

To continue or exit

Press   **F7** and the prompt reads *Save document? Yes (No)*. (If a screen with the heading *Document Summary* is displayed, press **Enter** to display the prompt.)

Press   **N** and the prompt reads *Exit WP? No (Yes)*

Press   **Y** to exit the program, or press **N** to clear the screen and work on your own document

Result: If you did not exit the program, the document screen is now blank so that you can enter your own document. If you did exit the program, a prompt may read *Insert disk with batch file Press any key to continue*. If this prompt appears, insert the Shell disk into drive A, and then press any key. In a few moments, the prompt reads *Press Enter (◄┘) to return to the File System*. Press **Enter**, and the File System reappears.

Step 5 **Quit for the Day.** When you are finished working with the computer, you quit for the day.

To quit for the day

Press   **F3** to return to the Start Programs screen

Press   **F3** to return to the command prompt

Result: The command prompt is displayed. Remove your disks from the drives, put them in their envelopes, and then turn off the computer.

TUTORIAL 2D   Exploring the Screen Display

In this tutorial, you explore the WordPerfect document screen display. To begin this tutorial, you must first load the program.

Step 1 **Explore the Key Lock Indicators.** The *Pos* indicator on the status line indicates the status of the **Num Lock** and **Caps Lock** keys.

To lock Num Lock and Caps Lock

Press   **Caps Lock**

Press   **Num Lock**

Result: When you press these keys, you engage them and they remain engaged until you press them again. Notice that the *Pos* indicator is both flashing and uppercased (*POS*). The flashing indicates that the **Num Lock** key is engaged, and the caps indicates that the **Caps Lock** key is also engaged. Press each key to turn it off, then press each again twice to turn it on and off. Notice the *Pos* indicator as you do so.

Step 2 **Explore the Cursor Position Indicators.** The other indicators on the status line indicate the cursors position in the document. The initial settings should indicate that the cursor is in document 1 (*Doc 1*), on page 1 (*Pg 1*), line 1 (*Ln 1*) and 1 inch from the left edge of the paper when the document is printed (*Pos 1"*). To see these change, you have to enter some text.

To enter text

Type	**As I type text, the status line always indicates the current position of the cursor.**
Press	**Enter** twice
Type	your name
Press	**Enter**

Result: The status line now indicates the current position of the cursor. Neither the document nor the page has changed, but the line has. Press the arrow keys to move the cursor through the text while watching the status line *Ln* and *Pos* indicators.

Step 3 **Explore the Filename Indicator.** To see the file's name displayed on the status line, you must first save the document. If you have not done so already, insert a data disk into drive B on a floppy disk system or drive A on a hard disk system. When you save the document here, you specify the drive on which you want to save it.

To save the file

| Press | **F10** and the prompt reads *Document to be saved:*. (If a screen with the heading *Document Summary* is displayed, press **Enter** to display the prompt.) |
| Type | **B:DOCSCRN.WP5** (on a floppy disk system) or **A:DOCSCRN.WP5** (on a hard disk system), and then press **Enter** |

Result: The drive spins, and the document is saved onto the disk in the specified drive. The document remains displayed on the screen so that you can continue editing it. If your program is set up to do so, the file's name is now displayed on the status line at the bottom of the screen (unless a previous user changed one of WordPerfect's default settings on the Setup menu).

Step 4 **Continue or Exit.** You have now completed this tutorial. You may either continue with your own work or exit WordPerfect and return to the operating system. If you are quitting for the day, remove your program and data disks, and then turn off the computer.

▼ EXERCISES

EXERCISE 2A   Load WordPerfect from a Network

The way you load WordPerfect varies, depending on how your system has been set up. If your system is on a network, or if for some other reason your procedures do not follow the same rules described in this topic, enter your loading procedures here.

1. _____
   _____
   _____

2. _____
   _____
   _____

3. _____
   _____
   _____

4. _____
   _____
   _____

EXERCISE 2B   Load WordPerfect So the Default Drive Is B

When you load WordPerfect on a floppy disk system, the default drive is automatically set to drive A. This means that when you save a file, it is automatically saved to the disk in that drive. Normally, however, you want to save your work on the disk in drive B. To do so, you make drive B the default drive, then load WordPerfect from drive A.

1. Insert the *WordPerfect 1* disk into drive A.
2. Insert a data disk into drive B.
3. Type **B:** and then press **Enter** to change the command prompt to *B>*.
4. Type **A:WP** and then press **Enter**.
5. Press **F5** and the current default drive is listed. The message should read *Dir B:*. Press **F1** to remove the message.

EXERCISE 2C   Loading WordPerfect from a Hard Disk

The way you load WordPerfect varies, depending on how your system has been set up. If your system has its own menu, or if for some other reason your procedures do not follow the same rules described in this topic, enter your loading procedures here.

1. _____
   _____
   _____

2. _____
   _____
   _____

3. _____
   _____
   _____

4. _____
   _____
   _____

EXERCISE 2D Identify the Items on the Screen

After loading WordPerfect, turn your printer on. Press **Shift-PrtSc** (or just **Print Screen** on an enhanced keyboard) to make a printout of the screen display, and then advance the paper out of the printer. Using Figure 12 as a guide, identify the items that appear on the status line by circling them and writing a brief description of what they indicate. Graphics characters may not print or may print as other characters. If this happens, draw them on your printout.

EXERCISE 2E View a Video

Many videocassettes about WordPerfect are available. Obtain one of these from your school or public library or from a video rental store, and watch it. These videos give you an overview of the procedures offered by the program.

▼QUESTIONS

1. If you are loading WordPerfect from a floppy disk, which disk should you insert first if your program disk is not a system disk? Why?

2. What steps would you follow to load WordPerfect from the command prompt and a floppy disk drive? From the command prompt and a hard disk drive? From the DOS 4 Shell?

3. What steps would you follow to load WordPerfect from the command prompt on a hard disk system? From the DOS 4 Shell?

4. What two ways are there to exit WordPerfect? Which one should you use? Why?

5. If you are quitting for the day, what steps should you take?

TOPIC 3
Executing Commands

To operate WordPerfect, you use either its traditional function key approach or the new pull-down menus.

GETTING HELP

Since WordPerfect has so many commands and function key combinations, you should use the keyboard template as a guide (Figure 13). These templates are color-coded to identify key combinations (see Table 2).

TABLE 2   Color Codes on Keyboard Template and Quick Reference Card

Color	Meaning
Black	Press the indicated function key by itself. If more than one key is listed in black (as they are on the Quick Reference card), press the keys in sequence.
Blue	Hold down **Alt** while you press the indicated function key.
Green	Hold down **Shift** while you press the indicated function key.
Red	Hold down **Ctrl** while you press the indicated function key.

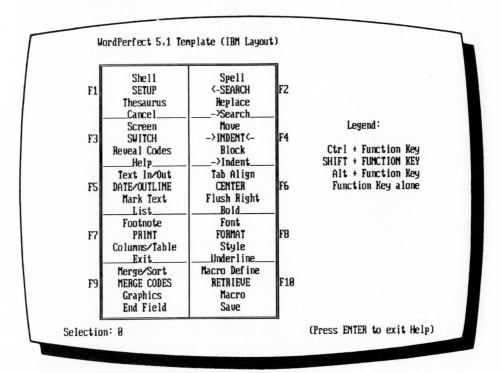

FIGURE 13   Keyboard Template.   The keyboard template provides a quick guide to Word-Perfect's commands.

One type of keyboard template fits over the function keys at the left end of the keyboard.

```
WordPerfect 5.1 Template (Enhanced Layout)

 ┌─F1──────┬─F2──────┬─F3──────┬─F4──────┐   Legend:
 │ Shell   │ Spell   │ Screen  │ Move    │ Ctrl + Function Key
 │Thesaurus│ Replace │Reveal Codes│ Block │ Alt + Function Key
 │ SETUP   │ <-SEARCH│ SWITCH  │->Indent<-│ SHIFT + FUNCTION KEY
 │ Cancel  │ ->Search│ Help    │ ->Indent │ Function Key alone
 └─────────┴─────────┴─────────┴─────────┘

     ┌─F5──────┬─F6──────┬─F7──────┬─F8──────┐
     │Text In/Out│Tab Align│Footnote │ Font   │
     │Mark Text│Flush Right│Columns/Table│ Style │
     │DATE/OUTLINE│ CENTER │ PRINT  │ FORMAT │
     │ List    │ Bold    │ Exit   │Underline│
     └─────────┴─────────┴─────────┴─────────┘

         ┌─F9──────┬─F10─────┬─F11─────┬─F12─────┐
         │Merge/Sort│Macro Define│     │         │
         │Graphics │ Macro   │        │         │
         │MERGE CODES│RETRIEVE│        │         │
         │End Field│ Save    │Reveal Codes│ Block │
         └─────────┴─────────┴─────────┴─────────┘

 Press 1 to view the PC/XT keyboard template
 Selection: 0                     (Press ENTER to exit Help)
```

Another type of template fits above the function keys on enhanced keyboards.

WordPerfect also has a color-coded Quick Reference card listing all of the program's commands. A copy of this card is printed in one color on the inside front cover. This card does not describe each command in detail, but it gives you the keystrokes that get you started.

WordPerfect contains extensive on-line help that you can display at any time by pressing **F3**. If you press **F3** before you begin an operation, a screen describing the help system is displayed. This screen also lists your program's registration number. You may need to know this number if you call WordPerfect's customer service for assistance.

WordPerfect's on-line help is context-sensitive, so the help displayed may be directly related to what you are trying to do at the moment. For example, if you pressed **F10** to begin to save a file and cannot remember how to complete the sequence, pressing **F3** displays help on saving files.

Sometimes you don't even know how to start a command. In these cases, you can use the index to speed up your search. For example, let's say you want to know how to save a file. After pressing **F3**, press **S** since that is the most likely index listing for the Save command. This displays a screen listing various save keystrokes. For example, it shows that to display help on saving text, you press **F10**. If you want additional help, press another letter to return to the index.

When you have finished with help, you press **Spacebar**, **Enter**, or **0** to return to where you were in your procedure before you asked for help. If you are using a mouse, click the right button.

KEY/Strokes
USING ON-LINE HELP

1. Either   press **F3**

   Or   pulldown the Help menu and select *Help*, *Index*, or *Template*
2. To display other screens
   - Press any letter key (**A** through **Z**) to see an alphabetized list of commands. Each key displays a list of topics that begins with the letter you press. For example, for help on deleting text, press **D**; for help on the GoTo command, press **G**
   - Press any function key labeled **F1** through **F10** (or **F1** through **F12** on enhanced keyboards) for information on the command the key is used for. You can also press **F3** again to display an illustration of the keyboard template
   - Hold down **Alt**, **Shift**, or **Ctrl** while you press any of the function keys **F1** through **F10** for information on the commands that these key combinations execute
   - If any of the menu choices on the screen have a highlighted number or letter, you can press the number or letter to display help on that option
3. Repeat any of the procedures described in Step 2 until you find the help you are looking for. Some help screens also display lists of features you can display help on by pressing the number of the feature
4. When finished viewing help, press **Spacebar**, **Enter**, or **0** to return to the document screen, or click the right mouse button

▼ Using Help on a Floppy Disk System

On a floppy disk system, when you press **F3** for help, the program looks for the help files. If the program cannot find them, a prompt reads *WPHELP.FIL not found. Insert the diskette and press drive letter:*. If this prompt appears, insert the disk labeled *WordPerfect 1* into one of the drives (usually A or B), and then press the letter of the drive. When you are finished with help, remove the disk and replace it with the disk that was originally in the drive.

USING FUNCTION KEYS

You execute most WordPerfect commands from the keyboard by pressing one of the ten function keys, **F1** through **F10**, on the keyboard. (Some newer computers and enhanced keyboards have 12 or more function keys.) The function keys are assigned more than one task; for example, the **F2** key can perform four tasks. To change its function, you hold down another key while you press it. Using combinations of keys in this way makes it possible to assign many more tasks to the keyboard than there are keys. The other keys that you hold down are called control or modifier keys: **Ctrl**, **Alt**, and **Shift**. These keys do not send characters or commands to the computer; rather, they change what is sent when you press other keys. For example, when using **F2**:

- Press **F2** by itself to search down through a document.
- Hold down **Shift** and then press **F2** to search toward the top of the document.
- Hold down **Ctrl** and then press **F2** to spell-check the document.
- Hold down **Alt** and then press **F2** to search and replace in the document.

When you use these modifier keys, you hold them down first, and then press the other key. The sequence in which you press the keys is important—so follow these procedures:

1. Hold down the **Alt**, **Shift**, or **Ctrl** key. These keys do not repeat or send commands to the computer, so you can hold them down as long as you want.

2. Press the function key just as if you were typing a character. If you hold it down, the command will repeat until you release it, and you will soon find the computer beeping. This can create problems.

PULL-DOWN MENUS

WordPerfect 5.1 added a new feature, ***pull-down menus***. These menus make it easier to execute many commands since you choose them from a list. To display the pull-down ***menu bar*** at the top of the screen (Figure 14), press **Alt-=**. The menu bar lists the names of menus. Figure 15 shows all of the commands listed on all of the pull-down menus. To operate the menus, you use the following procedures.

- To move the highlight between menu titles:
  - Press ← or →.
  - Press **Home**, ← or **Home**, → to move the highlight to the first or last choices on the menu bar.
- To pull down a menu:
  - Highlight its name and then press ↓ or **Enter**.
  - Press the highlighted letter in the command. The highlighted letter is called a mnemonic because it is easy to remember: *F* for *File*, *E* for *Edit*, and so on.
- To make a choice from a pulled-down menu:
  - Use the arrow keys to move the highlight over one of the command names on the menu, and then press **Enter**. (Press **Home**, ↑ or **Home**, ↓ to move the highlight to the first or last choice on the menu.)
  - Press the highlighted letter in the command.

When choosing commands from menus, keep the following points in mind:

- Choices in brackets, like *[Paste   ]*, cannot be selected at the point where you are in the operation. You cannot highlight a bracketed command.
- Choices followed by an arrow head (▶), like *Appearance*, have submenus.
- To exit the menus without making a choice, press **F1** or **Esc**.

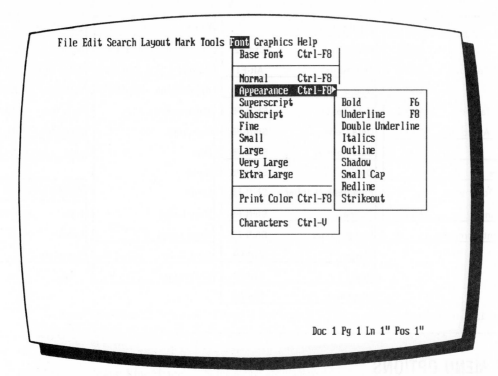

File Edit Search Layout Mark Tools **Font** Graphics Help

```
                              Base Font   Ctrl-F8

                              Normal      Ctrl-F8
                              Appearance  Ctrl-F8
                              Superscript          Bold            F6
                              Subscript            Underline       F8
                              Fine                 Double Underline
                              Small                Italics
                              Large                Outline
                              Very Large           Shadow
                              Extra Large          Small Cap
                                                   Redline
                              Print Color Ctrl-F8  Strikeout

                              Characters  Ctrl-V
```

Doc 1 Pg 1 Ln 1" Pos 1"

FIGURE 14   Pull-down Menus.   Pull-down menus make WordPerfect easier to learn and use.

File		Edit		Search		Layout	
Retrieve	Shift-F10	Move (cut)	Ctrl-Del	Forward	F2	Line	Shift-F8
Save	F10	Copy	Ctrl-Ins	Backward	Shift-F2	Page	Shift-F8
Text In	Ctrl-F5	Paste		Next		Document	Shift-F8
Text Out	Ctrl-F5	Append		Previous		Other	Shift-F8
Password	Ctrl-F5	Delete	Backspace	Replace	Alt-F2	Columns	Alt-F7
List Files	F5	Undelete	F1	Extended		Tables	Alt-F7
Summary		Block	Alt-F4	Go to	Ctrl-Home	Math	Alt-F7
Print	Shift-F7	Select				Footnote	Ctrl-F7
Setup	Shift-F1	Comment	Ctrl-F5			Endnote	Ctrl-F7
Go to DOS	Ctrl-F1	Convert Case	Shift-F3			Justify	
Exit	F7	Protect Block	Shift-F8			Align	
		Switch Document	Shift-F3			Styles	Alt-F8
		Window	Ctrl-F3				
		Reveal Codes	Alt-F3				

(Continued)

FIGURE 15   Pull-down Menu Commands.   This figure shows all of the commands listed on the pull-down menus.

Many menus have more than one level, so choosing a command listed on a menu may display another menu, called a submenu. Getting to the actual command you want to execute occasionally means that you must select a series of commands from the displayed submenus. When you reach the menu you want and make your choice, any one of several things might happen:

- The document screen may automatically reappear.
- You may have to press **Enter** and make another selection from the same menu.
- The cursor may automatically move to another part of the same menu choice if it has more than one part.
- A prompt may be displayed; for example, when printing a file from the disk, the prompt *Document name:* asks you to enter the name of the document.

If the menu does not automatically disappear after you finish making choices, or if you want to cancel a command in progress, you use one of the following keys:

- Press **F7** to have the computer accept any changes you have made in menu choices and return directly to the document screen. Sometimes you may have to press it more than once to return to the document screen.
- Press **0** or **Spacebar** to have the computer accept any changes you have made in menu choices and back up through any submenus. Each time you press one of these keys, you retrace your steps one menu until you return to the document screen. This is helpful when you want to back up a menu or two so that you can take a new branch.
- Press **F1** to cancel a command that displays a menu or a message on the status line. This command cancels any changes you have already made in the menus. You may have to press it more than once to back entirely out of the command.

  If a prompt or menu is not displayed, pressing **F1** executes the Undelete command, and previously deleted text may be inserted into your document (see Topic 7). If this happens to you by mistake, press **F1** again to remove the Undelete menu and any highlighted text inserted into your document.

PROMPTS

When you press a function key or make a choice from a menu, a prompt may appear. Prompts are questions that WordPerfect wants you to answer. For example, you may be asked to enter a page number to print, the name of a file to save or retrieve, or a word you want to find.

- To answer prompts, you type a response. For example, when saving a file, the prompt reads *Document to be saved:*. To save a file named LETTER, you would type **LETTER**. You can type responses to prompts in any combination of uppercase or lowercase letters. For example, when prompted to enter a filename, you can type it as **LETTER**, **letter**, or **Letter**. If you make any typos while typing an answer, press **Backspace** to delete them, and then type the answer correctly. When the response is complete and correct, press **Enter** to enter it.
- When some prompts are displayed the second and subsequent times in a session, like those displayed when saving files or using search and replace, your previous response is displayed following the prompt. You can press **Enter** to accept the suggested response or enter a new response (the first character you type automatically deletes the previous response). You can

also edit the previous response. To do so, press **Ins** or → to enter edit mode. Then

- Use the arrow keys to move the cursor through the text to edit it.
- Press **Backspace** to delete the character to the cursor's left or **Del** to delete the character the cursor is under. You can also press **Ctrl-End** to delete all characters from the cursor to the end of the response.
- Press **Ins** to switch between insert and typeover modes to insert new characters or type over existing characters (see Topic 7).
- When you are finished editing the response, press **Enter**.

• Some prompts have a suggested answer, for example, *Replace B:\FILENAME.EXT? No (Yes)*. The *Yes* in parentheses is the suggested response. To accept the suggested response (in this example, *Yes*), press **Y** or just press **Enter**. To reject the suggested response, press **N** or any key other than Y.

USING A MOUSE

WordPerfect 5.1 added support for a mouse (Figure 18). A mouse can be used for a number of procedures, including the following:

- Making menu choices from pull-down menus.
- Moving the cursor through the document (see Topic 7).
- Selecting (blocking) text so that it can be copied, moved, deleted, or formatted (see Topic 14).

Specific procedures for using a mouse are described in the relevant topics. However, here are some principles of using a mouse that will make its use easier.

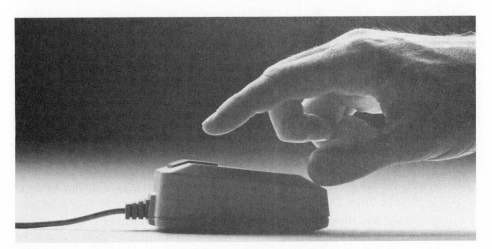

FIGURE 18　A Mouse.　A mouse can have either two or three buttons. *Courtesy of Apple Computer, Inc.*

Holding and Dragging the Mouse

When you use a mouse, you roll it across the surface of the desk. This motion tells the mouse which way to move the mouse pointer on the screen. To make the mouse pointer move in a predictable direction, it is important that you hold the mouse so that it is oriented parallel to the middle line of the screen (Figure 19). This way, when you move the mouse up, down, or sideways, the mouse pointer moves in the expected direction. If you hold the mouse at an angle, your hand motion and the motion of the mouse pointer will not be coordinated.

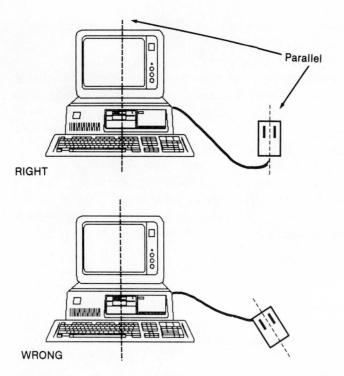

FIGURE 19   Holding and Dragging a Mouse.   Hold the
mouse parallel to the center line of the screen.

Basic Mouse Commands

When using a mouse, here are some of the basic commands to remember.

- The *mouse pointer* (■) appears when you move the mouse and disappears when you press a key.
- *Point* means to position the mouse pointer over or on some items on the screen.
- *Clicking* refers to pressing one of the buttons on the mouse.
- *Drag* means to hold down one of the mouse buttons while you move the mouse.
- Cancel (same as **F1**) by pressing the middle button on a three-button mouse or holding down either button and clicking the other on a two-button mouse.
- *Double clicking* refers to pressing one of the buttons on the mouse twice in rapid succession. Double clicking the left button is the same as clicking the left button and then pressing **Enter**. The first click highlights an item, and the second click selects it. For example, if a prompt like *Document to be saved: FILENAME* is displayed, double-clicking on the file name following the prompt with the left button displays the prompt *Replace FILENAME? No (Yes)*.
- Clicking the right button performs one of three procedures:
  - If a menu is displayed, it is the same as pressing **F7**. The menu is exited.
  - If no menu is displayed, it displays the pull-down menu bar. Pressing it again removes the menu bar.
  - Holding down the button and dragging the mouse scrolls the document on the screen.

- Clicking the left button performs several procedures:
  - It moves the cursor to the same position as the mouse pointer.
  - It highlights a menu item pointed to with the mouse pointer.
  - It cancels a menu if the mouse pointer is not positioned on a menu choice.

Using the Mouse with Pull-down Menus

You can use a mouse to execute commands listed on the pull-down menus (Table 3). To display the pull-down menu bar, click the right mouse button (click it again to remove the menu).

To pull down a menu from the menu bar, point to the menu name, then click the left button. You can also point to any menu name, hold down the left button, and drag the mouse pointer along the menu bar to pull down other menus.

To select a command from a pulled-down menu (or any other menu), point to the command with the mouse pointer and click the left button. You can also point to any command, hold down the left button, and then drag the mouse pointer to highlight any other command. Once the desired command is highlighted, release the left button.

To exit the menus without making a choice, point anywhere but to a command and click the left button. If you are holding the left button down to drag between choices, release it when not pointing to a command.

TABLE 3   Mouse Commands and the Menu

Action	Button to Click
Activate the menu	Right
Remove the menu	Right
Pull down a menu	Left
Make a menu choice	Left

 TIP

> ➤ **When help screens are displayed, many of them are identical to the screens that appear during the execution of commands.** To let you know when you are in the help system, the help screens always display the message *(Press ENTER to exit help)*.

▼ TUTORIAL

TUTORIAL 3A   Executing Commands

In this tutorial, you explore commands and on-line help. To begin this tutorial, you must first load the program (see Topics 1 and 2).

Step 1   **Explore Help.** Take a few minutes to experiment with the help commands. You will find this on-line help very useful.

Note: When you execute the Help command on a floppy disk system, the prompt reads *WPHELP.FIL not found. Insert the diskette and press drive letter:*. When this prompt appears, insert the disk labeled *WordPerfect 1* into drive A or B, and then press **A** or **B**.

To display help

Press   **F3** to display a screen that introduces you to help

Press   **F3** again to display an illustration of the keyboard template (if you are using a keyboard with the function keys on the left, press **1**)

Press   each of the other function keys labeled **F1** through **F10** (or **F1** through **F12** on enhanced keyboards) to display a brief description of their function

Hold   **Alt**, **Shift**, or **Ctrl** down when you press each of the function keys **F1** through **F10** to display help on the commands these key combinations execute

Press   any letter key (**A** through **Z**) to see an alphabetized list of features. Each key displays a list of topics that begins with the letter you press. To get help on a topic of interest, press the appropriate key. For example, for help on deleting text, press **D** and for help on the *GoTo* command, press **G**

Press   **Spacebar** to return to the document screen

Result: The document screen reappears. (If you swapped disks, remove the *WordPerfect 1* disk from drive B.)

Step 2   **Display Menus.** Let's display one of WordPerfect's multilevel menus, the one you use to change formats.

To display a menu

Press   **Shift-F8** to display the Format menu

Press   **1** (for *Line*) to display the Line Format menu (Figure 20)

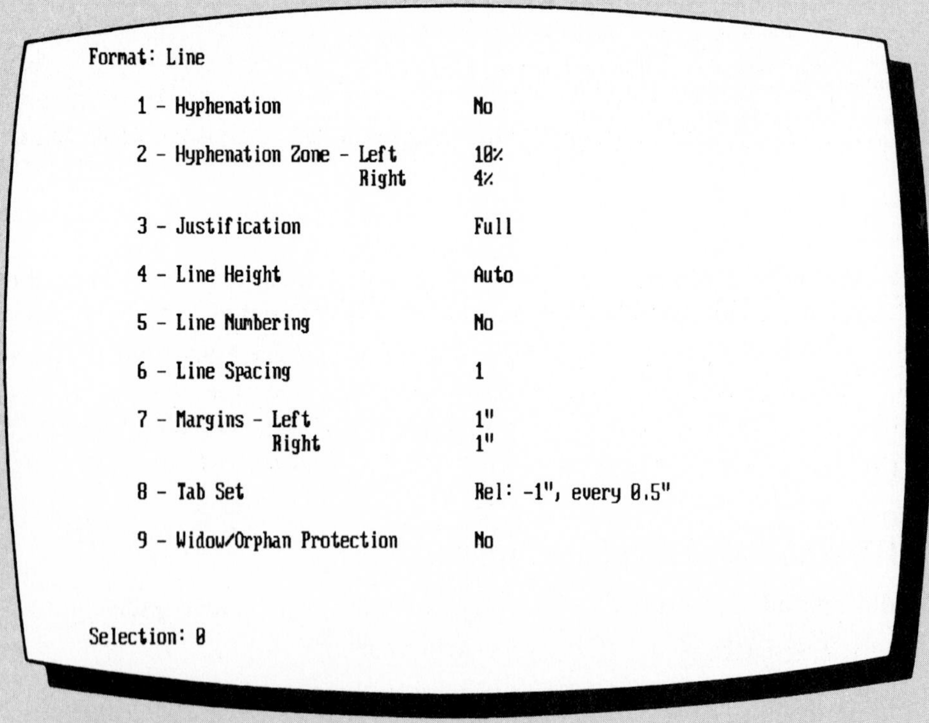

```
Format: Line

    1 - Hyphenation                    No

    2 - Hyphenation Zone - Left        10%
                          Right         4%

    3 - Justification                  Full

    4 - Line Height                    Auto

    5 - Line Numbering                 No

    6 - Line Spacing                   1

    7 - Margins - Left                 1"
                 Right                 1"

    8 - Tab Set                        Rel: -1", every 0.5"

    9 - Widow/Orphan Protection        No


  Selection: 0
```

FIGURE 20   **The Line Format Menu.**   When the Format menu is displayed, pressing **1** for *Line* displays the Line Format menu. This menu lists commands you use to format lines of text in a document.

Result: The Line Format menu lists commands you use to format lines of text in a document. Press **0** (the number) to back up to the Format menu. Press **0** again to back out of the menus completely. Repeat the command above to display the Line Format menu, but this time press **F7** to exit the menu. Notice how you return directly to the document screen without backing up through the menus?

Step 3 **Display a Prompt.** Now let's display a prompt and then cancel the command.

To display a prompt

Press   **F10** and the prompt reads *Document to be saved:*. (If a screen with the heading *Document Summary* is displayed, it means that a previous user has changed a default setting. Just press **Enter** to display the prompt.)

Result: If you wanted to save the document on the screen, you would type a filename and then press **Enter**. Since there is no document, press **F1** to cancel the command and remove the prompt.

Step 4 **Explore Some Other Menus and Prompts.** WordPerfect's Quick Reference card lists the keys you press to use all WordPerfect commands. A copy of the Quick Reference card is printed at the back of this text.

Use the Quick Reference card or your printout to experiment with commands to display menus and prompts. Remember that you cancel commands and return to the document screen by pressing **F7**. You can back up through menus by pressing **0** (the number zero). Continue experimenting until you feel comfortable with the procedures. Don't worry while experimenting. The worst thing that can happen is that you inadvertently exit the program. If this happens, just reload the program and continue.

Step 5 **Continue or Exit.** You have now completed this tutorial. You may either continue with your own work or exit WordPerfect and return to the operating system. (If you need help on quitting, refer to Topic 2.) If you are quitting for the day, remove your program and data disks, and then turn off the computer.

EXERCISES

EXERCISE 3A   Explore WordPerfect's Help

Load WordPerfect; then press the key you use to display help. With the help screen displayed, and using your keyboard template as a guide, press the keys you would normally press to execute the commands listed below. When you are finished, press one of the keys you use to exit help and return to your document.

Cancel (**F1**)	Help (**F3**)	Indent (**F4**)
Bold (**F6**)	Exit (**F7**)	Underline (**F8**)
Save (**F10**)	Block (**Alt-F4**)	Reveal Codes (**Alt-F3**)
Search (**F2**)	Replace (**Alt-F2**)	Spell (**Ctrl-F2**)
Format (**Shift-F8**)	Retrieve (**Shift-F10**)	List Files (**F5**)

EXERCISE 3B   Print a Copy of the Keyboard Template

If you do not have a keyboard template, you can print one from the help screen. Be sure the printer is on and has paper in it.

1. Display help, and then press the help key again to display on the screen the template for an enhanced keyboard. (If you are using a keyboard with the ten

function keys on the left, press **1** to display a template for those function keys.)

2. Print the screen display
   - On standard keyboards, hold down **Shift**, and then press the key labeled **PrtSc**.
   - On enhanced keyboards, press **Print Screen** without holding down **Shift**.
3. Advance the paper out of the printer. Note that graphics characters may not print or may print as other characters.
4. Exit help and return to the document screen.

▼QUESTIONS

1. What are help screens? How do you display them?
2. What is the keyboard template? What do the colors indicate?
3. What is a Quick Reference card?
4. What are function keys? What is their purpose?
5. What are the **Ctrl**, **Alt**, and **Shift** keys used for? How do you use them?
6. What is a pull-down menu? How do you display one?
7. What is a menu? What keys do you press to make menu choices?
8. What is a submenu?
9. What key do you press to have the computer accept any menu choices you have made and return directly to the document screen?
10. What key do you press to back up through menus? To cancel a command?
11. What is a prompt? How do you answer prompts?

Before you can create a new document with WordPerfect, you must display a blank document screen. This happens automatically when you load the program. However, if you are already working on a document and want to create a new one, you first clear the current document from the screen. When you do so, you are given the option of saving or abandoning the document. When you do either, the screen is cleared, and you can then enter a new document. If you want to work on an existing document, you retrieve it onto the screen from the disk on which it is stored in a file. When saving and retrieving files, you have to understand how to specify the drives and directories that you save files to and retrieve them from.

SAVING FILES

You should frequently save the file you are working on. If you turn off the computer, experience a power failure, encounter hardware problems, or make a mistake, you may lose files that are in the computer's memory. Your files are not safe from these disasters until you save them onto a disk—a more permanent form of storage. When preparing a document, you should always save it:

- Before experimenting with unfamiliar commands.
- Before making major revisions.
- Before printing (in case something goes wrong during the process).
- Before exiting the program.

When you work with applications programs like WordPerfect, you save the files that you create onto a disk. On many systems, you save them to a hard disk. On others, especially those you use in school, you save them onto a floppy disk so you can take your files with you. These floppy disks are called data disks because they are used to save data files instead of program files. (To prepare data disks for use on your computer, you use the DOS Format command—see the DOS Appendix.) If you want to save your work onto a floppy disk, you usually insert it into drive B on a floppy disk system or drive A on a hard disk system. You then use one of WordPerfect's commands to save the file on the screen onto the disk in the drive.

- Press **F10** to save the document and leave it in memory and on the screen so that you can continue working on it.
- Press **F7** to save the document in a file on the disk, remove it from memory, and clear the screen or return you to the operating system.

When you save a file the first time, you must assign it a filename that follows DOS conventions. Filenames can have up to eight characters and be followed by an optional period and extension of up to three characters. WordPerfect does not automatically add extensions to files, but you can add your own. If you add the extension .WP5 to your files, you will always be able to identify the program used to create them. Table 4 lists the characters that you can use in filenames and extensions. (Extensions that you should avoid using are listed in the ''Tips'' section of this topic.)

TABLE 4 Characters Acceptable in Filenames

Letters	**A** through **Z**
Numbers	**0** through **9**
Characters	! @ # $ % & ( ) - ^ { } _ ` ' ~

KEY/Strokes

SAVING A FILE AND LEAVING IT ON THE SCREEN

1. Either press **F10**

   Or pull down the File menu and select *Save*
   The prompt reads *Document to be saved:* (If a screen with the heading *Document Summary* is displayed, press **Enter** to display the prompt)

2. Either type a filename, and then press **Enter** to save a new file

   Or press **Enter** if the file's name is displayed following the prompt. The prompt reads *Replace* followed by the path and filename. Press **Y** to save the file under the current name, or press **N** to edit the filename

---

KEY/Strokes

SAVING A FILE AND CLEARING IT FROM THE SCREEN

1. Either press **F7**

   Or pull down the File menu and select *Exit*
   The prompt reads *Save document? Yes (No)*

   - If the document has not been revised since it was last saved, a message on the status line reads *(Text was not modified)*
   - If a screen with the heading *Document Summary* is displayed, press **Enter** to display the prompt

2. Press **Y** and the prompt reads *Document to be saved:*

3. Either type a name for the file, and then press **Enter** if no name is suggested or you want to save it under a different name

   Or press **Enter** to save the file under the suggested name if you had saved the file previously, and the prompt reads *Replace FILENAME? No (Yes)*. Press **Y** to continue
   The prompt reads *Exit WP? No (Yes)*

4. Press **N** to stay in the WordPerfect program and clear the screen

▼ The Document Summary Screen

WordPerfect's default settings can be changed so that a document summary form is displayed whenever you save a file or exit the program. To change the setting, press **Shift-F1** to display the Setup menu. Press **3** for *Environment* and then press **4** for *Document Management/Summary*. Press **1** for *Create Summary on Save/Exit*, then press **Y** for *Yes* or **N** for *No*. Press **F7** to return to the document screen.

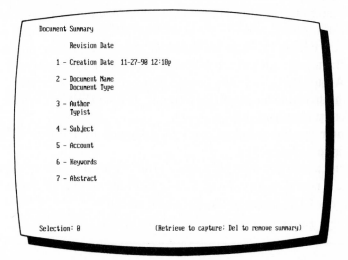

When the document summary screen is displayed, you press **1** though **7** to select each entry that you want to make. Enter the information, and then press **Enter**. (Press **F7** when you are finished entering the abstract.) Press **F7** to save your entries and return to the document screen

SPECIFYING DRIVES AND DIRECTORIES

WordPerfect saves files to the default drive and the default directory unless you specify otherwise (see Part III). The default drive and directory is initially set to the one you loaded the program from. You can specify another drive and directory in one of three ways:

- You can specify a path in the Save command. When the prompt asks you to enter a filename, you can specify a drive and directory in front of the filename. For example, to save a file named JOHN.WP5 to a subdirectory named LETTERS on drive C, you would type **C:\LETTERS\JOHN.WP5** and then press **Enter**.
- You can change the default drive and directory for the session. This is the easiest approach because you need not specify the path when saving files. (To see what the default drive is, you can press **F5**. The current drive is listed at the left end of the status line. Press **F1** to remove the message.)
- You can specify a permanent drive or directory for all files, regardless of the default drive setting. The only way to send them to another drive or directory is to change this setting or specify a path in front of the filename when saving a file.

➤ **The error message** *Disk Full – Press any Key to Continue* **appears when you try to save a file and there is no room for it on the disk**. If this happens, delete some files from the disk and try again (see Topic 27), put a new disk into the drive and save the file, or if working from a hard disk, insert a disk into drive A and then save the file on that drive.

▼ TUTORIAL

TUTORIAL 4A   Saving and Abandoning Files

In this tutorial, you explore saving and abandoning files. to begin this tutorial, you must first load the program (see Topics 1 and 2). You should insert your data disk into one of the disk drives. If necessary, clear any existing document from the screen.

Step 1   **Create a Document.** Type the paragraph of text shown in Figure 21. Don't worry about making mistakes or typos. You are not concerned at this point with the accuracy or content of the document.

> I won't be like everyone else. I will save my work frequently so that it won't be lost if the power fails, my computer dies, or I make a mistake. While others are crying about their loss, I'll smile and try not to look too superior.

FIGURE 21   The MYFILE Document.   Type this document to use as a sample file to save.

Step 2   **Save the Document.** If you have not done so already, insert a data disk into drive B on a floppy disk system or drive A on a hard disk system. When you save the document here, you specify the drive on which you want to save it.

To save the file

Press   **F10** and the prompt reads *Document to be saved:*. (If a screen with the heading *Document Summary* is displayed, press **Enter** to display the prompt.)

Type   **B:MYFILE.WP5** (on a floppy disk system) or **A:MYFILE.WP5** (on a hard disk system), and then press **Enter**

Result: The drive spins, and the document is saved onto the disk in the specified drive. The document remains displayed on the screen so that you can continue editing it. If your program is set up to do so, the file's name is now displayed on the status line at the bottom of the screen (unless a previous user changed one of WordPerfect's default settings).

Step 3   **Save the Document Again.** When you execute the Save command this time, the program remembers the name you assigned to the document the last time you saved it. You can press **Enter** to accept that name, or you can type in a new name and then press **Enter** to save the document under the new name. Here you want to save it under the same name.

To save the document

Press   **F10** and the prompt reads *Document to be saved: B:\MYFILE.WP5* or *Document to be saved: A:\MYFILE.WP5*. (If a screen with the heading *Document Summary* is displayed, press **Enter** to display the prompt.)

Press   **Enter** to accept the default filename, and the prompt reads *Replace B:\MYFILE.WP5? No (Yes)* or *Replace A:\MYFILE.WP5? No (Yes)*

Press   **Y**

Result: The drive spins as the document is saved onto the same disk that you specified in Step 2.

Step 4   **Change the Default Drive.** Now let's change the default drive so it is not the same as the one you are saving your files on.

To change the default drive

Press   **F5** and the message reads *Dir* followed by the current directory

Press   **=** (the equal sign), and the prompt reads *New directory* = followed by the current directory

Press   **Ins** to enter edit mode

Type   **A** (on a floppy disk system so that the prompt reads *New directory = A:*) or **C** (on a hard disk system so that the prompt reads *New directory = C:*) and then press **Enter**. The message reads *Dir* followed by the current directory

Press   **F1** to return to the document screen

Result: The default drive is now drive.A (on a floppy disk system) or C (on a hard disk system).

Step 5   **Save the Document and Change Its Name.** Whenever you save a file, you can change its name. Here you do so by editing the suggested filename.

To save and rename a file

Press   **F10** and the prompt reads *Document to be saved: B:\MYFILE.WP5* or *Document to be saved: A:\MYFILE.WP5*

Press   **→** to move the cursor under the period that separates the filename and the extension

Type   **2** so that the prompt reads *Document to be saved: B:\MYFILE2.WP5* or *Document to be saved: A:\MYFILE2.WP5*

Press   **Enter** to save the file

Result: You now have two copies of the file on the disk, one under the original name and one under the new name.

Step 6   **Save the Document while Exiting.** When you exit WordPerfect to return to the operating system, you are given an opportunity to save the file.

To save and exit

Press   **F7** and the prompt reads *Save document? Yes (No)*

Press   **Y** and the prompt *Document to be saved B:\MYFILE2.WP5* or *Document to be saved A:\MYFILE2.WP5*

Press   **Enter** and the prompt reads *Replace B:\MYFILE2.WP5? No (Yes)* or *Replace A:\MYFILE2.WP5? No (Yes)*

Press   **Y** and the prompt reads *Exit WP? No (Yes)*

Press   **Y** to exit the program, or press **N** to clear the screen and work on your own document

Result: If you did not exit the program, the document screen is now blank so that you can enter your own document. If you did exit the program, the command prompt is displayed on the screen. Remove your program and data disks, and then turn off the computer or load another program.

▼ EXERCISE

EXERCISE 4A   Load WordPerfect and Name a File

When you load WordPerfect, you can specify a filename for a new or existing file by typing the command **WP FILENAME.EXT**. Do this now, and name the document TEST.WP5. If the file existed, it would have been retrieved. Since it does not exist, the file on the screen is assigned the name. When you are finished, press **F7** to exit. Then press **N** twice to clear the screen but remain in the program.

▼ QUESTIONS

1. What happens to a file you are working on if you turn off the computer without first saving the file onto a disk?

2. List four stages at which it is prudent to save your files.

3. What two commands can you use to save a file? How do they differ?

4. Which of the following filenames are acceptable to DOS? If not acceptable, why not?

[FILE].DOC	ABC.ABC	A.A	STANFORDS.WP5
1.1	1.1234	LETTER	MEMO.*

5. Assume that you are writing three term papers for each of your classes on a computer. List the filename you would assign to each paper so that you could later identify the course and the papers from them.

6. Why would you want to abandon a file instead of saving it?

7. You are working on a document named MEMO.DOC and want to save it on a disk or in a directory other than the default. For each of the following, what path and filename would you specify when the prompt reads *Document to be saved:*?

To save the file on Drive	Directory	I would specify this path
B:	None	_____
A:	None	_____
C:	None	_____
C:	LETTERS	_____
C:	LETTERS\1987	_____

If you want to work on an existing document, you retrieve it onto the screen from the disk on which it is stored in a file. When retrieving files, you have to understand how to specify the drives and directories that you save files to and retrieve them from (see Topic 4).

RETRIEVING FILES

After you create and save a file on a disk, you can retrieve it later for further editing. Before retrieving a file:

1. Save the file currently displayed on the screen if you want to retrieve it later.
2. Clear the screen so that the file you retrieve is not merged into the one on the screen.
3. If the file was saved onto a floppy disk, insert that disk into drive B (on a floppy disk system) or drive A (on a hard disk system with a single floppy disk drive).

To retrieve a file, press **Shift-F10** or pull down the File menu and select *Retrieve*, and then enter the name of the file. WordPerfect retrieves files from the default drive and directory unless you specify otherwise. The default drive and directory is initially set to the one you loaded the program from. You can specify another drive and directory in one of three ways:

- You can change the default drive and directory. This is the easiest approach because you need not specify the path when retrieving files. (To see what the default drive is, you can press **F5**. The current drive is listed at the left end of the status line. Press **F1** to remove the message.)
- You can specify a path in the Retrieve command. When the prompt asks you to enter a filename, you can specify a drive and directory in front of the filename. For example, to retrieve a file named JOHN.WP5 from a subdirectory named LETTERS on drive C, you would type **C:\LETTERS\JOHN.WP5** and then press **Enter**.
- You can specify a document's drive by changing the Location of Files setting on the Setup menu as described in Topic 4. If you specify a document's drive or directory, files are automatically retrieved from there, regardless of the default drive setting.

When the file is retrieved, the disk drive operates as the computer copies the file from the disk into the computer's memory. The file is then displayed on the screen for you to edit. The copy of the file on the disk remains unchanged until you change the document on the screen and save it back onto the disk. At that time it overwrites the old file.

KEY/Strokes

RETRIEVING A FILE BY ENTERING ITS NAME

1. Either press **Shift-F10**

   Or   pull down the File menu and select *Retrieve*

   The prompt reads *Document to be retrieved:*

2. Type the path if the desired file is not in the current directory, followed by the filename and extension, and then press **Enter**

USING LIST FILES TO RETRIEVE FILES

WordPerfect's List Files screen and menu simplifies retrieving files and lists many other commands you can use to simplify your work. To display the List Files screen (Figure 22), press **F5** and then press **Enter** or pull down the File menu and select *List Files*. The instructions that follow describe the functions you can perform from this screen and menu. When finished, press **F7** to return to the document screen.

```
05-08-90  02:59a            Directory A:\*.*
Document size:       0  Free:    500,736 Used:    927,657   Files:      108

   .  Current   <Dir>              ..   Parent    <Dir>
   1-UP     .WP5   1,503  02-18-89 11:17a  3-UP    .WP5   7,061  02-18-89 11:32a
   3-UPA    .WP5   7,061  02-18-89 11:32a  A1      .WP5  21,492  04-24-90 02:53p
   A2       .WP5   7,691  04-24-90 03:02p  A3      .WP5  21,318  04-24-90 02:54p
   ABUSE    .WP5   9,151  03-06-90 07:27p  ABUSE2  .WP5   8,747  01-23-89 01:44p
   ACCOUNTS .WP5  11,947  01-23-89 02:04p  ADDGRPH .WP5  23,165  04-07-89 09:31a
   ADVANCE  .WP5   7,773  01-23-89 02:05p  ALIGN   .WP5   7,256  02-18-89 11:11a
   ALIGNDOC .WP5  14,188  04-20-90 10:23a  APPEND  .WP5   8,088  03-06-90 07:27p
   BLOCKON  .WP5   1,581  06-24-89 06:56a  BLOCKS  .WP5   7,321  02-18-89 11:09a
   BOLD1    .WP5     519  03-06-90 06:16p  BOLD2   .WP5   1,061  03-06-90 06:19p
   CELLS    .WP5     838  04-20-90 08:56a  CHART   .WP5   8,860  01-23-89 02:06p
   CLOSE    .MAC      33  08-04-87 01:55p  CODE1   .WP5  14,008  01-01-80 03:12p
   CODE2    .WP5  10,243  06-23-89 06:09p  CODES   .WP5   7,628  04-19-90 06:32p
   COLUMN   .WP5   8,130  03-06-90 07:27p  COLUMNS .WP5  25,521  04-07-89 09:25a
   CURLTR   .WP5   9,945  02-18-89 10:23a  CURLTR1 .WP5   9,945  02-18-89 10:23a
   CURLTR2  .WP5   1,968  03-06-90 06:21p  DOCSUM  .WP5     516  05-01-90 02:16p
   DOS      .WP5   2,672  03-06-90 06:24p  DOSTEXT .WP5     766  05-05-90 04:47p
   DRAW     .WP5   2,167  02-18-89 11:19a  EMPHASIS.WP5   7,219  02-18-89 11:12a
   ENTER    .WP5   7,030  02-18-89 11:07a ▼ENTER1  .WP5   6,652  01-03-90 11:03a

 1 Retrieve; 2 Delete; 3 Move/Rename; 4 Print; 5 Short/Long Display;
 6 Look; 7 Other Directory; 8 Copy; 9 Find; N Name Search: 6
```

FIGURE 22   The List Files Screen and Menu.   The List Files screen displays the names of the files, their extensions, their size (in bytes), and the date and time they were last saved. Any subdirectory is listed followed by *<Dir>* in the size column. A header indicates the current date and time, the name of the directory, the size of the document currently on the screen, the number of bytes on the disk that are still free and already used, and the number of files on the disk or in the directory. The List Files menu at the bottom of the screen lists choices used in file management.

Moving Around the List Files Screen

When the List Files screen is displayed, if an arrow appears at the top or bottom of the vertical center line, additional files are listed. To see them, press ↑ or ↓, **PgUp** or **PgDn**, or the **+** and **-** keys on the numeric keypad. To move to the top or bottom of the list, press **Home** twice, and then press ↑ or ↓.

To move the highlight to a specific file, press **N** for *Name Search* and the prompt reads *(Name Search; Enter or arrows to Exit)*. Begin typing the file's name. As you type each character, the highlight moves closer to the file. (You can press **Backspace** to delete characters as you type.) When you have typed enough characters to uniquely identify the file, it is highlighted. Press **Enter** to display the menu again.

To move quickly through directories, highlight the directory (including *<Parent> <Dir>*, which is the directory one level up), and then press **Enter** twice to display the files it contains. When you locate the directory containing the file you want, highlight the file's name, and then press **1** for *Retrieve*. You can also press **7** for *Other Directory* and then press **Enter** twice to make the highlighted directory the current directory.

To change the default directory or create a new one, press **7** for *Other Directory*. Type the new directory (for example, **C:\LETTERS**), and then press **Enter**. If the directory you specify does not exist, the prompt reads *Create:* followed by the name of the directory and the prompt *No (Yes)*. Press **Y** to create a new directory.

Retrieving Files

When the List Files screen is displayed, to retrieve a file, you highlight its name on the list of filenames and then press **1** for *Retrieve*. If a document is already on the screen, the prompt reads *Retrieve into current document? No (Yes)*. Press **N** to return to the List Files menu.

If a disk or directory has a lot of files, you can look at just selected ones using wildcards. For example, when you press **F5** the prompt reads *Dir* followed by the current path and then **.**. The **.** is called a ***filename specification***, and it tells WordPerfect to display files with any filename or any extension. To display just selected files, use the question mark or asterisk wildcards.

- The question mark can be used to substitute for any single character.
- The asterisk is more powerful; it represents any character in a given position and all following characters.

For example, if you change the **.** to CHPT?.* all files that begin with CHPT and have one other character are listed when you then press **Enter**. For example, it would list the files CHPT1.DOC, CHPT2.BAK, CHPT3.DOC, and so on.

If you have already displayed the List Files screen, you can change the filename specification by highlighting *Current <Dir>* and pressing **Enter**. When the message reads *Dir PATH*.**, revise the filename specification. For example, type **B:*.WP5** and then press **Enter** to list all the files on drive B that end with the extension .WP5.

Previewing Files or Directories

To preview the contents of a file that does not contain a document summary, highlight it, and then press **6** for *Look* or press **Enter**. (If a document does have a document summary with more than just the name and type, the document summary is displayed instead of the document. If this happens, see the box "The

Document Summary Screen'' in Topic 4.) The Look command does not actually load the entire file, so you cannot edit it. It does, however, provide a way for you to scan the contents of several files quickly until you find the one you want. The top of the screen tells you the file's name and size in bytes (Figure 23). If the document is longer than the screen:

- Press ↑ or ↓ , or the + or - keys on the numeric keypad, to scroll through it.
- Press **S** to start and stop continuous scrolling. (You can also press just **S** to stop scrolling.)
- Press **Home** twice and then press one of the directional arrow keys to move to one of the four edges of the document.
- Press **End** to display the right side of a document that is too wide for the screen.
- Use the Search commands (see Topic 20) to move the cursor to a specific line in the document.

To view additional documents, you can press **PgUp** or **PgDn** or press **1** for *Next Doc* or **2** for *Prev Doc* on the Look menu.

You can also highlight a directory (indicated by *<Dir>*) and then press **Enter** or **6** for *Look*. The prompt reads *Dir* followed by the name of the directory. Press **Enter** to look at the files in the directory. You can then retrieve a file or press **F7** or **Spacebar** to return to the document screen.

```
File: A:\POEM.WP5                    WP5.1       Revised: 04-19-90 04:05p


     Not like the brazen giant of Greek fame,
     With conquering limbs astride from land to land,
     Here at our sea-washed, sunset gates shall stand
     A mighty woman with a torch, whose flame
     Is the imprisoned lightening, and her name
     Mother of Exiles. From her beacon-hand
     Glows world-wide welcome; her mild eyes command
     The air-bridged harbor that twin cities frame.
     "Keep, ancient lands, your storied pomp!" cries she
     With silent lips. "Give me your tired, your poor,
     Your huddled masses yearning to breathe free,
     The wretched refuse of your teaming shore.
     Send these, the homeless, tempest-tost to me,
     I lift my lamp beside the golden door!"

     Emma Lazarus




Look: 1 Next Doc: 2 Prev Doc: 0
```

FIGURE 23   The Look Command.   You can use the Look command on the List Files menu to preview the contents of a file on the disk before you retrieve it.

▼TIPS

➤ **If you enter a filename that WordPerfect cannot find**, the message reads *ERROR: File Not Found*. If you wait a second, the prompt *Document to be retrieved:* reappears. You can either edit the filename or path or press **F1** to cancel the command.

➤ **When the List Files screen is displayed**, you can press **Shift-F7** to print out a list of the files.

➤ **You can retrieve and then work on two separate documents** at the same time using windows (see Topic 15).

▼TUTORIAL

TUTORIAL 5A   Retrieving Files

In this tutorial, you explore retrieving files. To begin this tutorial, you must first load the program (see Topic 2). You should insert the data disk on which you saved the files you created in Tutorial 4A into one of the disk drives. If necessary, clear any existing document from the screen.

Step 1   **Getting Ready.** Begin by inserting the data disk on which you saved the MYFILE.WP5 file into drive A (on a hard disk system) or drive B (on a floppy disk system).

Step 2   **Retrieve a Document.** Now let's retrieve the document that you saved by entering its name, preceded by the drive on which you save it.

To retrieve the file

Press   **Shift-F10** and the prompt reads *Document to be retrieved*:
Type   **B:MYFILE.WP5** (on a floppy disk system) or **A:MYFILE.WP5** (on a hard disk system) and then press **Enter**

Result: The document appears on the screen just as it was when you saved it.

Step 3   **Clear the Screen.** If you want to continue working, on either a new document or an old document stored on the disk, first clear the current document from the screen. When doing so, you have the option of saving the current document or abandoning it. Here, you abandon the document.

To clear the screen

Press   **F7** and the prompt reads *Save document? Yes (No)*
Press   **N** and the prompt reads *Exit WP? No (Yes)*
Press   **N** to clear the screen but not exit

Result: The document you were working on is cleared from the screen. However, you remain in the program so that you can enter your own document or retrieve an existing one.

Step 4   **Change the Default Drive and Display the List Files Screen and Menu.** Now change the default drive to B on a floppy disk system or A on a hard disk system.

To change the default drive

Press   **F5** and the message reads *Dir* followed by the current directory

Press   **=** (the equal sign), and the prompt reads *New directory =* followed by the current directory

Type   **B:** on a floppy disk system or **A:** on a hard disk system, and then press **Enter**. The message reads *Dir* followed by the path of the new default drive and directory

Press   **Enter** again to display the list of files on the new default drive and directory

Result: The default drive is now drive B on a floppy disk system or A on a hard disk system, and a list of the files in that drive is displayed.

Step 5 **Preview and Then Retrieve a File.** The List Files' Look command lets you preview the contents of a file before you retrieve it. The Look command displays the file, but you cannot edit it until you retrieve it. You see how the Look command works in this step.

To preview and then retrieve a file

Press   the arrow keys to move the highlight over the desired file, in this case, *MYFILE.WP5*

Press   **6** for *Look* to display the contents of the file

Press   **F7** to return to the List Files screen and menu

Press   **1** for *Retrieve* to retrieve the same file so that you can edit it

Result: The file appears on the screen.

Step 6 **Clear the Screen.** Clear the current document from the screen but remain in the program. When prompted *Save document? Yes (No)*, press **N** (for *No*), since you have previously saved this document.

Step 7 **Continue or Exit.** You have now completed this tutorial. You may either continue with your own work or exit WordPerfect and return to the operating system. If you are quitting for the day, remove your program and data disks, and then turn off the computer.

▼**EXERCISE**

EXERCISE 5A Load WordPerfect and Retrieve a File

When you load WordPerfect, you can automatically retrieve a file by typing the command **WP FILENAME**. For example, to retrieve a file named EXAMPLE.WP5 from a disk in drive A, type **WP A:EXAMPLE.WP5**. Do this now, and retrieve the document named MYFILE.WP5. Since the file exists, it is retrieved onto the screen after WordPerfect is loaded. When you are finished, press **F7** to exit. Then press **N** twice to clear the screen but remain in the program.

▼**QUESTIONS**

1. What command do you use to retrieve a file from the disk?
2. What command do you use to display the List Files screen and menu?

Entering text with WordPerfect is no more difficult than typing it on a typewriter; in many ways, it is easier. With both, you use the keyboard to enter letters, numbers, and symbols. With WordPerfect, the cursor, a blinking one-character-wide underscore (_), indicates where the next character you type will appear. When you open a new document, the cursor rests in the upper left-hand corner of the screen. As you type a character, the character appears where the cursor is, and the cursor then moves one space to the right.

- To enter uppercase letters, either hold down **Shift** while typing a letter or press **Caps Lock** to enter all uppercase letters. (The *Pos* indicator on the status line changes to an all-uppercase *POS* when **Caps Lock** is engaged.) Press **Caps Lock** again to return to lowercase. (The *POS* indicator on the status line changes to *Pos* when **Caps Lock** is not engaged.) If you press **Shift** to enter text when **Caps Lock** is engaged, you enter lowercase letters.
- To enter shifted characters like !, @, and # that appear on the top half of some keys, hold down **Shift** while you press the key.
- To enter numbers, either use the number keys on the top row of the keyboard or use the numeric keypad. On some computers, the keys on the numeric keypad also move the cursor. When **Num Lock** is engaged, the *Pos* indicator flashes, and pressing the keys enters numbers. When **Num Lock** is not engaged, the *Pos* indicator does not flash, and pressing the keys moves the cursor. Some keyboards also have lights that indicate when **Num Lock** is engaged.

If you are an experienced typist and are used to typing a lowercase letter ell (**l**) for **1** (one), or an uppercase letter oh (**O**) for zero (**0**), do not do this on your computer. The computer treats numbers and letters differently, and although you usually won't have problems, you could run into difficulties by disregarding this distinction.

KEY/Strokes
ENTERING DOCUMENTS

- To end lines, press **Enter**
- To enter a soft space, press **Spacebar**
- To enter a hard space, press **Home**, **Spacebar**
- To delete characters, press **Backspace** or **Del**
- To scroll the screen, press arrow keys, **PgUp** and **PgDn**, or the plus and minus keys on the numeric keypad
- To boldface a word or phrase, press **F6**, type the text, and then press **F6** again
- To underline a word or phrase, press **F8**, type the text, and then press **F8** again

WORD WRAP

When you are typing paragraphs, you do not have to press **Enter** at the end of each line. WordPerfect has a feature, called word wrap, that automatically does this for you (Figure 24). When the end of a line is reached, the word processing program calculates whether the word being entered fits on the line. If it will not fit, the program automatically begins a new line of text by moving the entire word to the next line.

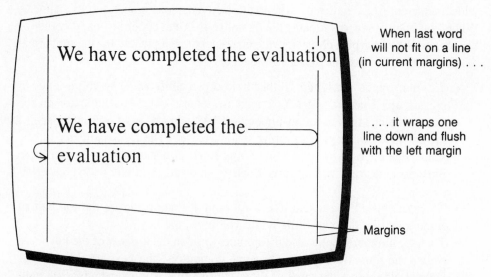

FIGURE 24   Word Wrap.   When you reach the end of a line, the program calculates whether the word you are entering will fit on the line. If it will not fit, the program moves, or wraps, the entire word to the beginning of the next line.

CARRIAGE RETURNS

Carriage returns are codes in the document that indicate where the lines end. When you print the document, these codes tell the printer to move down one line and back to the left margin. WordPerfect has two kinds of carriage returns: soft and hard.

Soft Carriage Returns

WordPerfect automatically enters soft carriage returns at the end of a line as you enter text whenever it reaches the right margin and wraps a word to the next line. Soft carriage returns automatically adjust their position if you revise the text. For example, when you insert or delete text or when you change the margins, existing soft carriage returns are automatically deleted, and new ones are inserted at the end of each line.

Hard Carriage Returns

You press **Enter** to enter a hard carriage return when you want to end a line before you reach the right margin. For example, you can press **Enter**

- To end a paragraph.
- To enter an inside address, a salutation, or a heading.
- To insert a blank line, as you would following an inside address, the date, and the closing of a letter. Each time you press **Enter**, you insert another blank line.

- To start a new paragraph. Here, you press **Enter** twice—once to end the current paragraph and again to insert a blank line before starting the first line of the next paragraph.

If you then add or delete text, hard carriage returns are not automatically rearranged, as soft carriage returns are. Hard returns remain where you entered them.

You can enter hard carriage returns as you type a document, or you can enter them into existing text.

- When entering hard carriage returns as you enter text, you press **Enter** to end a line before it reaches the right margin or to end one paragraph and start a new one. The cursor moves down a line and back to the left margin. You press **Enter** again to insert a blank line before starting the first line of the next paragraph. Each time you press **Enter**, the cursor moves down another line.
- You enter hard carriage returns in existing text whenever you want to break an existing paragraph or line into two paragraphs or lines. To do so:
  - You move the cursor under the character that you want to be the first character in the new paragraph or line.
  - You then press **Enter** to insert a hard carriage return. This moves the cursor, the character it was under, and all following text, down one line and back to the left margin. If you press **Enter** a second time, a blank line is inserted above the new paragraph or line.

WordPerfect treats hard carriage returns just like any other character, so you can delete them just like other characters with the **Backspace** or **Del** key. WordPerfect also has a command that allows you to see where they have been entered so that it is easier to delete them (see Topic 7).

SPACES

When entering text, you normally press **Spacebar** to insert spaces, just as you do on a typewriter. Like carriage returns, there are both soft and hard spaces.

- When you press **Spacebar** in a document, it enters a *soft space*. If the word following the space does not fit on the line, the word wraps at the space to the next line.
- Certain expressions, although they contain spaces, should not be split to print on different lines, for example,
  - a name like *Henry VIII* or *Mrs. Wilson*
  - a time like *8 p.m.*
  - an address like *32 Elm Street*
  - a formula like *1 + 1 = 2*

    To keep the two or more parts of the phrase together, you enter *hard spaces*. This way, if the phrase does not fit on one line, it all wraps to the next line. To enter a hard space, press **Home**, and then press **Spacebar**.

CORRECTING MISTAKES

There are several ways to correct mistakes (see Topic 7), but when entering text you usually use the **Backspace** or **Del** keys to do so. If you make any mistakes—and notice them immediately:

- Press **Backspace** to delete characters to the cursor's left; then retype the characters correctly.
- You can also use the directional arrow keys (→, ←, ↑, and ↓) to move the cursor through the text and press **Del** to delete any character the cursor is positioned under.

If you hold these keys down, they delete one character after another until you release them.

SCROLLING

As you enter text, the screen gradually fills up. When the last line on the screen is filled, the text begins to *scroll*, or move, up a line at a time so that the line you are entering is always displayed on the screen. To make room for the new lines, text at the top of the document scrolls off the top of the screen (Figure 25). But it is not gone for good; you can scroll back to it whenever you want using the cursor movement keys and commands (see Topic 7). For example, you can press the plus and minus keys on the numeric keypad to scroll up and down through the document a screen at a time. You can also press **PgUp** and **PgDn** to scroll through it a page at a time.

When you fill a page with text, a dashed line across the screen (-----) indicates where the previous page ends and the new one begins. This is called a soft page break. If you insert or delete text above this page break, it adjusts its position automatically. When you print the document, the page will be advanced out of the printer at the point where this page break is indicated.

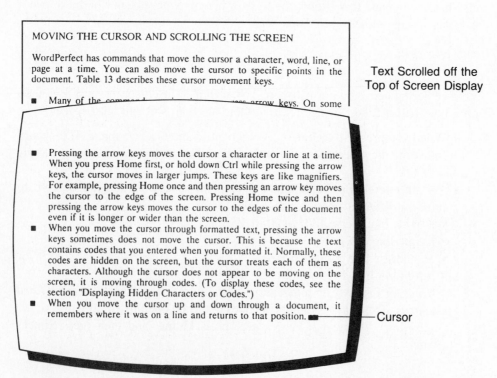

MOVING THE CURSOR AND SCROLLING THE SCREEN

WordPerfect has commands that move the cursor a character, word, line, or page at a time. You can also move the cursor to specific points in the document. Table 13 describes these cursor movement keys.

Text Scrolled off the Top of Screen Display

■ Many of the commands ... arrow keys. On some

■ Pressing the arrow keys moves the cursor a character or line at a time. When you press Home first, or hold down Ctrl while pressing the arrow keys, the cursor moves in larger jumps. These keys are like magnifiers. For example, pressing Home once and then pressing an arrow key moves the cursor to the edge of the screen. Pressing Home twice and then pressing the arrow keys moves the cursor to the edges of the document even if it is longer or wider than the screen.

■ When you move the cursor through formatted text, pressing the arrow keys sometimes does not move the cursor. This is because the text contains codes that you entered when you formatted it. Normally, these codes are hidden on the screen, but the cursor treats each of them as characters. Although the cursor does not appear to be moving on the screen, it is moving through codes. (To display these codes, see the section "Displaying Hidden Characters or Codes.")

■ When you move the cursor up and down through a document, it remembers where it was on a line and returns to that position. ■■———— Cursor

FIGURE 25   Scrolling.   When the screen is full, the document scrolls up as you enter new text. The line on which you are entering text always remains displayed on the screen.

BOLDFACING AND UNDERLINING

Two style formats, boldface and underline, are assigned to function keys. To boldface text, you press **F6**; to underline text, you press **F8**. When you are entering text, you can employ either of two approaches to use these formats:

- Press the function key for the desired format, type the text, and then press the same function key to end the format.
- Press the function key for the desired format, type the text, and then press → to move the cursor to the right of the hidden code that ends the format. (It was inserted automatically when you pressed the function key the first time.)

Any text you enter between the codes that begin and end boldfacing and underlining is formatted as bold or underlined. In the status line at the bottom of the screen, the *Pos* indicator indicates when the cursor is inside or outside of the codes. The way the number is displayed varies. For example, on some computers, the number changes color or intensity.

TIPS

➤ **The maximum size of a document is limited only by your computer's memory and the amount of disk storage space** available for the document and a backup copy if you are saving backup copies. However, WordPerfect suggests that you limit your largest documents to no more than 70 single-spaced pages (140 double-spaced pages) so that you do not experience delays when editing and scrolling.

➤ **When using underlining, you can choose to underline spaces and tabs or not**. To change the setting, move the cursor to above where you want to change the type of underlining. Press **Shift-F8** then press **4** for *Other* or pull down the Layout menu and select *Other* to display the Other Format menu. Then press **7** for *Underline*, and the prompt reads *Spaces*. Either press **Y** to underline spaces or press **N** to not underline spaces. The prompt then reads *Tabs*. Either press **Y** to underline tabs or press **N** to not underline tabs. Press **F7** to return to the document screen.

TUTORIALS

TUTORIAL 6A   Entering Text

In this tutorial, you enter and edit text. To begin this tutorial, you must first load the program. You should insert your data disk into one of the disk drives and make that drive the default. If necessary, clear any existing document from the screen.

Step 1   **Enter the Document.** Type in the text for the document shown in Figure 26, including the deliberate spelling mistakes in the underlined words. (Do not try to underline the words on your own screen.) As you enter the document:

To boldface and underline new text

Type	**These words were** and then press **Spacebar**
Press	**F6** to begin boldfacing
Press	**F8** to begin underlining
Type	**boldfaced and underlined**
Press	**F6** to end boldfacing
Press	**F8** to end underlining
Press	**Spacebar**
Type	**as they were being entered.**
Press	**Enter**

Result: The words you boldfaced and underlined may stand out from the rest of the text.

Step 4 **Change the Type of Underlining.** You can specify whether the spaces between words are underlined or not when you use the underline format. You can do the same with spaces entered by pressing **Tab**. The default setting is for spaces to be underlined but not tabs. Let's change the setting so that spaces are not underlined.

To change the kind of underline

Move	the cursor under the *T* in *These* in the last line
Press	**Shift-F8** to display the Format menu
Press	**4** for *Other* to display the Other Format menu
Press	**7** for *Underline*, and the prompt reads *Spaces*
Press	**N** for *No*, and the prompt reads *Tabs*
Press	**N** for *No*
Press	**F7** to return to the document screen

Result: If your screen displays underlining, spaces are no longer underlined. If not, you will see that they are not when you print out the document.

Step 5 **Save the Document.** Now that you have finished the document, save it under the filename BOLD1.WP5 so that you can retrieve it later but leave it on the screen.

Step 6 **Print the Document.** Now make a printout to see how it looks. Be sure that the printer is on and has paper in it and that the paper is aligned.

To print the document

Press	**Shift-F7** to display the Print menu
Press	**1** for *Full Document*

Result: The printer immediately begins printing. The words you boldfaced should be darker than the rest of the text, and the words you underlined should have a line under them as shown in Figure 27. The spaces between the words in the last sentence should not be underlined if your printer supports this option.

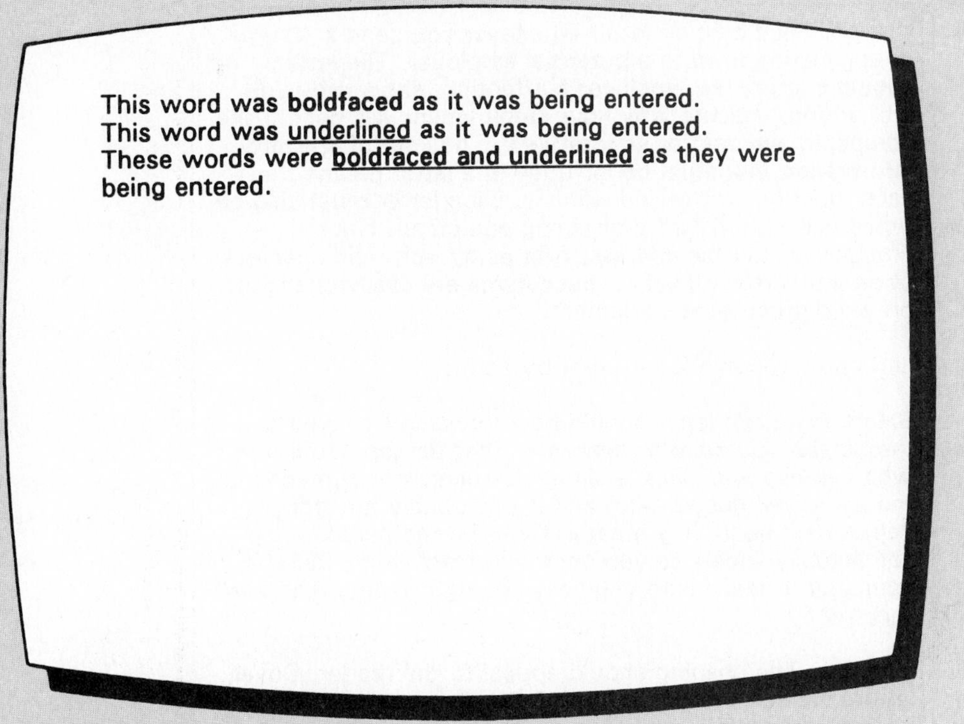

This word was **boldfaced** as it was being entered.
This word was <u>underlined</u> as it was being entered.
These words were <u>**boldfaced and underlined**</u> as they were
being entered.

FIGURE 27   The BOLD1 Document.   After completing this tutorial, your document should
look like this.

Step 7   Continue or Exit. You have now completed this tutorial. You may either continue with your own work or exit WordPerfect and return to the operating system. If you are quitting for the day, remove your program and data disks, and then turn off the computer.

▼EXERCISES

EXERCISE 6A   Enter a Document on Cover Letters

Enter the document that describes cover letters shown in Figure 28. (Do not correct any mistakes that you make. You edit them in the Topic 7.)

1. Save the document as CVRLTR1.WP5 but leave it on the screen.
2. Print the document.

You will need a cover letter whenever you send a resume or application form to a potential employer. The letter should capture the employer's attention, show why you are writing, indicate why your employment will benefit the company, and ask for an interview. The kind of specific information that must be included in a letter means that each must be written individually. Each letter must also be typed perfectly. Word processing equipment helps. Frequently only the address, first paragraph, and specifics of an interview will vary. These items are easily changed on word processing equipment.

Let's go through a letter point by point.

Salutation. Each letter should be addressed by name to the person you want to talk with. That person is the one who can hire you. This is almost certainly not someone in the personnel department, and it is probably not the department head. It is most likely to be the person who will actually supervise you once you start work. Call the company to make sure you have the right name. And spell it correctly.

Opening. The opening should appeal to the reader. Cover letters are sales letters. Sales are made after you capture a person's attention. You capture the reader's attention most easily by talking about the company rather than yourself. Mention projects under development, recent awards, or favorable comments recently published about the company. You can find such information in the business press, including the business section of local newspapers and many magazines that are devoted to particular industries. If you are answering an ad, you may mention it. If someone suggested that you write, use his or her name (with permission, of course).

Body. The body of the letter gives a brief description of your qualifications and refers to the resume, where your sales campaign can continue.

Closing. At the end of the letter, request an interview. Suggest a time, and state that you will confirm the appointment. Use a standard complimentary close, such as "Sincerely yours," leave three or four lines for your signature, and type your name. Either type your phone number under your name or include it in the body of the letter, but it will be more difficult to find there should the reader wish to call you.

FIGURE 28   The CVRLTR1 Document.

EXERCISE 6B   Enter the RIGHTS Document

Enter the document shown in Figure 29 in the order in which the paragraphs are shown. As you enter each paragraph, save the file as RIGHTS.WP5. When finished, make a printout.

Clause 10
Reserved Powers of the States
The powers not delegated to the United States by the
Constitution, nor prohibited by it to the States, are
reserved to the States respectively, or to the people.

Clause 2
Militia and the Right to Bear Arms
A well regulated Militia, being necessary to the security of
a free State, the right of the people to keep and bear
Arms, shall not be abridged.

Clause 4
Searches and Seizures
The right of the people to be secure in their persons,
houses, papers, and effects, against unreasonable
searches and seizures, shall not be violated, and no
Warrants shall issue, but upon probable cause, supported
by Oath or affirmation, and particularly describing the
place to be searched, and the persons or things to be
seized.

Clause 5
Grand Juries, Self-Incrimination, Double Jeopardy, Due
Process, and Eminent Domain
No person shall be held to answer for a capital, or
otherwise infamous crime, unless on a presentment or
indictment of a Grand jury, except in cases arising in the
land or naval forces, or in the Militia, when in actual
service in time of War or public danger; nor shall any
person be subject for the same offense to be twice put in
jeopardy of life or limb; nor shall be compelled in any
criminal case to be witness against himself, nor be
deprived of life, liberty, or property, without due process
of law; nor shall private property be taken for any public
use, without just compensation.

Clause 1
Religion, Speech, Assembly, and Politics
Congress shall make no law respecting an establishment
of religion, or prohibiting the free exercise thereof; or
abridging the freedom of speech, or the press; or the right
of the people peaceably to assemble, and to petition the
Government for a redress of grievances.

FIGURE 29   The RIGHTS Document.

> **Clause 6**
> **Criminal Court Procedures**
> In all criminal prosecutions, the accused shall enjoy the right to a speedy and public trial, by an impartial jury of the State and district wherein the crime shall have been committed, which district shall have been previously ascertained by law, and to be informed of the nature and cause of the accusation; to be confronted with the witnesses against him; to have compulsory process for obtaining Witnesses in his favor, and to have the Assistance of Counsel for his defence.

> **Clause 7**
> **Trial by Jury in Common Law Cases**
> In Suits at common law, where the value in controversy shall exceed twenty dollars, the right of trial by jury shall be preserved, and no fact tried by a jury shall be otherwise re-examined in any Court of the United States, than according to the rules of the common law.

> **Clause 8**
> **Bail, Cruel and Unusual Punishment**
> Excessive bail shall not be required, nor excessive fines imposed, nor cruel and unusual punishments inflicted.

> **Clause 3**
> **Quartering of Soldiers**
> No Soldier shall, in time of peace be quartered in any house, without the consent of the Owner, nor in time of war, but in a manner prescribed by law.

> **Clause 9**
> **Rights Retained by the People**
> The enumeration in the Constitution, of certain rights, shall not be construed to deny or disparage others retained by the people.

FIGURE 29   *(Continued)*

▼ **QUESTIONS**

1. Describe word wrap. When does it happen?
2. What are carriage returns? What is the difference between a hard and a soft carriage return?
3. How do you break a paragraph into two paragraphs?
4. What is the difference between hard and soft spaces? When would you want to use a hard space?
5. What is the most common way to correct mistakes when entering text?
6. What happens to the document on the screen once the screen is full?

TOPIC 7
Editing Documents

After you type a document, you proofread and then edit it. To edit a document on the screen, you use the cursor movement keys or commands to move the cursor through the document to delete or insert characters, words, or phrases.

KEY/Strokes

EDITING DOCUMENTS

- To scroll the screen, press arrow keys, **PgUp** and **PgDn**, or the plus and minus keys on the numeric keypad
- To switch between insert and typeover modes, press **Ins**
- To undelete text, press **F1**

MOVING AROUND THE DOCUMENT WITH THE KEYBOARD

WordPerfect provides you with several ways to move the cursor through a document. The four directional arrow keys (Figure 30) move the cursor one character or line at a time and repeat if you hold them down. On some computers, these keys are on the numeric keypad, which is also used to enter numbers. When pressing these keys to move the cursor, be sure the *Pos* indicator is not flashing on the status line. If it is, pressing the arrow keys on the numeric keypad enters numbers. To turn off the flashing *Pos* indicator, press **Num Lock** to disengage the key.

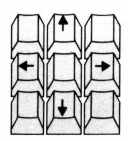

FIGURE 30 Directional Arrow Keys. The four directional arrow keys (sometimes called cursor movement keys) move the cursor one character or line at a time in the direction of the arrow.

All computers have directional arrow keys on the numeric keypad that work only when **Num Lock** is not engaged.

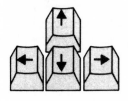

Newer computers also have a separate set of directional arrow keys that work at any time.

- You cannot move the cursor off the screen, and you cannot move it past the last line of text in the document.
- Pressing the arrow keys moves the cursor one character or line at a time. When you press **Home** first or hold down **Ctrl** while pressing the arrow keys, the cursor moves in larger jumps. These keys are like magnifiers. For example, pressing **Home** once and then pressing an arrow key moves the cursor to the edge of the screen. Pressing **Home** twice and then pressing an arrow key moves the cursor to the edges of the document even if it is longer or wider than the screen.

MOVING AROUND THE DOCUMENT WITH A MOUSE

You can move the cursor to any point in the document by pointing to it with the mouse pointer and then clicking the left button. If the position you point to contains no text or codes, the cursor jumps to the nearest position that does.

To scroll the document, hold down the right mouse button, then drag the mouse pointer toward the edge of the screen in the direction you want to scroll. For example, to scroll down through a document, hold down the right button and drag the mouse pointer toward the bottom of the screen. The screen will continue scrolling as long as you hold the button down and position the mouse pointer on the border of the document screen.

The GoTo Command

WordPerfect's GoTo command makes it easy to move the cursor quickly to specific points in a document. To use this command, press **Ctrl-Home** or pull down the Search menu and select *Go to* to display the prompt *Go to*. Press any of the cursor movement keys or commands described in Table 6.

You can also press **Ctrl-Home** twice to return to where the cursor was originally after using the GoTo command, or after pressing **Home** and any arrow keys, **PgUp** or **PgDn**, Search (**F2**), Replace (**Alt-F2**), or the **+** or **-** keys on the numeric keypad.

TABLE 6   GoTo Commands

To Move the Cursor to	Press
Top of current page	**Ctrl-Home**, ↑
Bottom of current page	**Ctrl-Home**, ↓
Next occurrence of a specific character	**Ctrl-Home**, Character
Next hard carriage return	**Ctrl-Home**, **Enter**
Next space	**Ctrl-Home**, **Spacebar**
Top of specific page	**Ctrl-Home**, Number of page, **Enter**
Original position after search or move	**Ctrl-Home** twice

INSERTING AND REPLACING TEXT

To edit text, you move the cursor through the document and insert and delete characters as needed. WordPerfect's default setting is the insert mode, so if you enter characters into existing text, the text moves over to make room for them. To switch back and forth between insert and typeover mode, press **Ins**. The message *Typeover* appears at the left end of the status line when you are in typeover mode. In typeover mode, characters you enter type over and replace any existing characters already there. Pressing **Ins** toggles between insert and typeover mode. When using typeover mode, you do not type over the codes you entered when formatting text (see Topic 9); instead, they are automatically pushed to the right to make room for the new text.

Backspace, **Spacebar**, **Tab**, and **Shift-Tab** act differently, depending on the mode you are in.

- With insert on, **Backspace** deletes the character to the cursor's left and closes up the space. With typeover on, **Backspace** deletes the character to the cursor's left and inserts a space.
- With insert on, pressing **Spacebar** inserts a space, and text to the right of the cursor moves over to make room for it. With typeover on, pressing **Spacebar** deletes the character the cursor is positioned under and moves the cursor one space to the right; text to the right of the cursor does not move over.
- With insert on, **Tab** pushes text ahead of the cursor to the next tab stop. With typeover on, **Tab** moves the cursor through the text to the next tab stop without entering tab codes.
- With insert on, **Shift-Tab** inserts a margin release code (see Topic 13) at the cursor's position. With typeover on, pressing **Shift-Tab** moves the cursor to the left margin. Pressing it with the cursor at the left margin inserts a margin release code.

DELETING TEXT

Deleting text removes it from the screen and the computer's memory. Table 7 lists the keys you can delete text with.

As you format a document, you enter codes that control the printer. These codes are discussed in detail in Topic 9, but you may encounter them, even though you don't see them, when you use the **Del** or **Backspace** keys to delete text in existing documents. If you use one of these keys to delete a code whose deletion will not have a noticeable affect of the way the document looks on the screen, a prompt may ask you if you want to delete the code. If this prompt appears, press **Y** to do so or **N** to leave the code undeleted.

TABLE 7   Keys That Delete Text

To Delete	Press
The character to the left of the cursor	**Backspace**
The character above the cursor	**Del**
The word containing the cursor or, if the cursor is on a space, the word to the left	**Ctrl-Backspace**
From the cursor to the beginning of the word	**Home, Backspace**
From the cursor to the end of the word	**Home, Del**
From the cursor to the end of the line	**Ctrl-End**
From the cursor to the end of the page	**Ctrl-PgDn**

UNDELETING TEXT

WordPerfect stores the previous three deletions, including typed-over text, in a buffer—a small portion of the computer's memory allocated to saving material that you delete. It also has an Undelete command (**F1**) that allows you to recover a deletion if you notice the mistake soon enough. Deletions are defined as any sequence of characters that you delete before you move the cursor with one of the cursor movement commands. The buffer stores only the three most recent deletions; thus you must undo mistakes before you make enough additional deletions to move the one out of the buffer that you want to recover.

KEY/Strokes
UNDELETING TEXT

1. Move the cursor to where the mistake was originally made. (Text and codes are restored at the cursor's position.)
2. Either press **F1**

    Or   pull down the Edit menu and select *Undelete*

    The Undelete menu appears along with the most recent deletion in reverse video
3. Either press **1** for *Restore*

    Or   press **2** for *Previous Deletion* repeatedly to cycle through up to three previous deletions (you can also press ↑ or ↓ to display them), and then press **1** for *Restore* to restore the desired one

    Or   press **F1** to remove the Undelete menu and return to the document screen without restoring a deletion

▼ **TUTORIAL**

TUTORIAL 7A   Editing a Document

In this tutorial, you edit the document named ENTER1.WP5 that you created in Tutorial 6A. To begin this tutorial, you must have completed that tutorial and must load the program. You should insert your data disk into one of the disk drives and make that drive the default. If necessary, clear any existing document from the screen.

Step 1 **Retrieve the Document.** Insert the disk on which you saved the ENTER1.WP5 document into one of the disk drives, and then retrieve the document.

Step 2 **Move the Cursor.** Now that you have retrieved the document, you can move the cursor through it. Practice moving the cursor with the commands described in Table 5, and notice how the cursor moves through the text. (Not all of them will work since the document isn't long enough.) Remember that keys connected with hyphens (for example, **Ctrl-←**) are pressed simultaneously, whereas those separated by commas (for example, **Home**, ↑) are pressed one after the other. Hold down some of the keys to see how they repeat until you release them.

Step 3 **Correct Mistakes.** Now that you know how to move the cursor, let's correct some mistakes. First correct the intentional errors in the document. Figure 32 shows the document after editing.

To delete characters
    Move   the cursor to under either *c* in *proccessing* on the first line
    Press   **Del** to delete the extra letter *c*

To insert characters
    Move   the cursor to under the *t* in *leters* on the third line
    Type   **t** to insert the missing letter *t*

To type over characters
    Move   the cursor to under the first *s* in *resorts* on the third line
    Press   **Ins** to turn on typeover mode, and the status line reads *Typeover*
    Type   **p** over the letter *s*
    Press   **Ins** to return to insert mode, and *Typeover* disappears from the status line

To delete a word
    Move   the cursor to the beginning of *numerous* on the third line
    Press   **Ctrl-Backspace**

To break a paragraph into two paragraphs
    Move   the cursor to under the *Y* in *You can enter* at the beginning of the third sentence
    Press   **Enter** twice to insert a blank line between the two paragraphs

To join lines separated by carriage returns
    Move   the cursor to the right of the period at the end of the first paragraph
    Press   **Del** until the two paragraphs are joined
    Press   **Spacebar** (if necessary) to insert a space between the joined sentences

Word processing is probably the most common application of microcomputers. The ease with which you can draft and revise memos, letters, reports, and other documents with a word processing program increases both the speed and the quality of your writing. You can enter, edit, change, reorganize, format, and print text without having to retype all of it each time you make a change. This ease of use encourages you to revise and reorganize your material more frequently so that you can express your ideas more clearly.

There are many word processing programs on the market. They differ from one another in the ease with which you can edit text and in the capacities of the the program, especially with respect to formatting documents for printing.

your initials

FIGURE 32   The Edited ENTER1 Document.   When you are finished editing the document, it should look like this.

Result: Now, using what you have learned, correct any additional mistakes. Table 7 summarizes the editing commands you have just learned as well as some others. When you have finished, your document should look like Figure 32.

Step 4   Save the Document under a New Name. Now that you have finished editing the document, save the latest version. When doing so, you change the name of the document to ENTER2.WP5.

Note: The path in front of the filename when you execute the Save command in this and the following steps may be *A:* if you retrieve the file from that drive.

To save the document

Press   **F10** and the prompt reads *Document to be saved: B:\ENTER1.WP5*

Press   → to move the cursor under the number *1*

Press   **Del** to delete the number *1*

Type   **2** to change the filename to *B:\ENTER2.WP5*, and then press **Enter**

Result: The drive spins as the document is saved onto the disk under the new filename.

Step 5   Print the Document. Now that you have edited the document, make a printout to see how it looks. Be sure that the printer is on and has paper in it and that the paper is aligned.

To print the document

Press   **Shift-F7** to display the Print menu

Press   **1** for *Full Document*

Result: The printer immediately begins printing.

Step 6   Continue or Exit. You have now completed this tutorial. You may either continue with your own work or exit WordPerfect and return to the operating system. If you are quitting for the day, remove your program and data disks, and then turn off the computer.

EXERCISES

EXERCISE 7A   Edit the CVRLTR1 Document

Retrieve the CVRLTR1.WP5 file you created in Exercise 6A.

1. Edit the document to correct any mistakes you may have made.
2. Save the document under the same name.
3. Print the edited document.

EXERCISE 7B   Edit the RIGHTS Document

Retrieve the RIGHTS.WP5 file you created in Exercise 6B.

1. Edit the document to correct any mistakes you may have made.
2. Save the document under the same name.
3. Print the edited document.

EXERCISE 7C   Edit a Document from Proofreaders' Marks

Occasionally, you may have to edit documents that have been professionally edited with proofreaders' marks.

1. Enter and correct the document shown in Figure 33 using the proofreaders' marks that indicate editing changes as your guide. Proofreaders' marks are described inside the back cover.
2. Save the document as PROOF.WP5.

It does not appear that the earliest printers had any method of correcting errors before the form was on the press. The learned. The learned correctors of the first two centuries of printing were not proof-readers in our sense, they were rather what we should term office editors. Their labors were chiefly to see that the proof corresponded to the copy, but that the printed page was correct in its latinity, that the words were there, and that the sense was right. They cared but little about orthography, bad letters, or purely printers' errors, and when the text seemed to them wrong they consulted fresh authorities or altered it on their own responsibility. Good proofs, in the modern sense, were impossible until professional readers were employed, men who had first a printer's education, and then spent many years in the correction of proof. The orthography of English, which for the past century has undergone little change, was very fluctuating until after the publication of Johnson's Dictionary, and capitals, which have been used with considerable regularity for the past 80 years, were previously used on the miss or hit plan. The approach to regularity, so far as we have, may be attributed to the growth of a class of professional proof readers, and it is to them that we owe the correctness of modern printing. More errors have been found in the Bible than in any other one work. For many generations it was frequently the case that Bibles were brought out stealthily, from fear of government interference. They were frequently printed from imperfect texts, and were often modified to meet the views of those who published them. The story is related that a certain woman in Germany, who was the wife of a printer, and had become disgusted with the continual assertions of the superiority of man over woman which she had heard, hurried into the composing room while her husband was at supper and altered a sentence in the Bible, which he was printing, so that it read Narr instead of Herr, thus making the verse read "And he shall be thy fool" instead of "and he shall be thy lord."

FIGURE 33   The PROOF Document.

QUESTIONS

1. What is the cursor used for when editing, and how do you move it?
2. What does scrolling the screen mean? When does it scroll? In which directions can you scroll it?
3. How do you execute the GoTo command?
4. What is the basic difference between insert mode and typeover mode?
5. If you press **Spacebar** to move the cursor, what happens when the program is in insert mode? In typeover mode?
6. Describe three ways of deleting text.
7. What is the Undelete command? Describe how it works.

To share your documents with others or to make proofreading easier, you make printouts. To begin, you first load the printer with paper, align the paper, and turn the printer on. The way you load paper varies, depending on the type of printer and paper you are using. If you are using single sheets, you usually stack them in a paper tray or bin. If you are using continuous-form paper, you feed it into the printer as shown in Figure 34. The settings you can make on the printer vary, but many have some or all of the switches described in the box "Printer Controls."

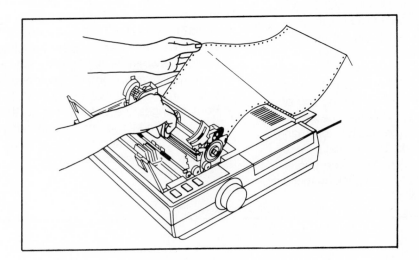

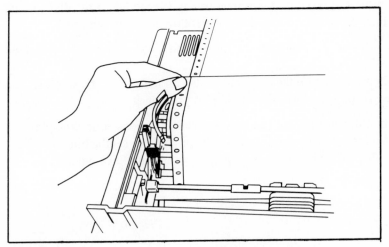

FIGURE 34   Loading Continuous-Form Paper.   To load continuous-form paper into a printer:

Feed it through a slot, around the platen, and back out of the printer.

In the process, you engage the holes in the perforated tear-off margins with the tractor or pin feed mechanism. *Courtesy of Epson*

Printer controls

The controls on printers vary from model to model, but most have some or all of the following (though their names may differ).

- **On/off** turns the power to the printer on and off. Knowing when to use this switch is important.
    - If you turn the printer off while it is operating, all data in the printer's buffer (text storage area) will be lost. If you immediately turn the printer back on, your document may resume printing, but a large block will have been missed. If you have canceled a print job and want to start over, turning the computer off and back on is a good way to ensure that text from the previous job does not remain in the buffer.
    - If after you turn the printer off, you turn it back on, it resets the top of the form so that the printer considers the line that the print element is resting on the top line of the sheet of paper. It uses this line as the starting point when calculating top margins and page length. This is useful since you can adjust your paper in the printer and just turn it off and then back on to set the top of the form.

- **Off-Line/On-Line** connects the printer to and disconnects it from the computer. The printer must be on line to print documents, but it must be off line to use some of the other switches on the printer like Form Feed and Line Feed.
- **Form Feed**, sometimes labeled FF, advances a sheet of paper out of the printer. If the printer has an automatic sheet feeder or a tractor feed, it inserts a new sheet. For this switch to work, the printer must be off line.
- **Line Feed**, sometimes labeled LF, advances paper in the printer by one line. This is useful when making fine adjustments to the paper's position in the printer. For this switch to work, the printer must be off line.
- **Letter Quality/Draft Quality** switches the printer between its high-quality but slower letter-quality mode and its lower-quality but faster draft-quality mode.
- **Font** changes the default font so that the entire document is printed in that font unless you specified otherwise by entering font change codes within the document.

PRINTING OPTIONS

You can print a file displayed on the screen or any file stored on the disk. When you choose which procedure to use, keep the following points in mind.

- When you print a document on the screen, you can print a selected block.
- When you print a file on the disk that is also on the screen, be sure they are the same. To be sure, save the file before printing it.

When you print a document, you can specify several options. For example, you can specify the printer that the document is to be printed on, set the binding offset, change the number of copies, and specify the text and graphics quality.

DOCUMENT PREVIEW

If you use several formatting commands, you may have a hard time visualizing what the document will look like when it is printed. Many formatting commands do not show their effects on the screen. For example, you do not normally see page numbers, headers, footers, footnotes, top and bottom margins, and font changes on the screen. To see these, you use the View Document command on the Print menu (Figure 35). Though you cannot edit the document when it is displayed with this command, you can see where improvements might be made before you print it out.

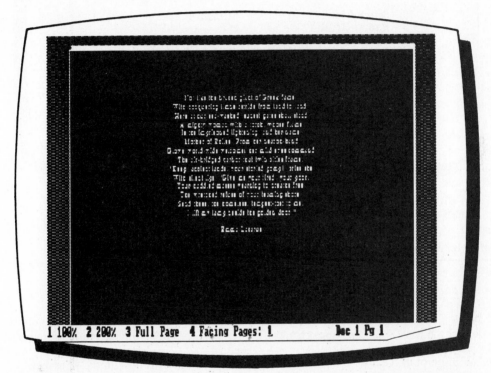

FIGURE 35   The View Document Command.   When you select *View Document* from the Print menu, the document is displayed on the screen exactly as it will print out. The menu choices at the bottom of the screen allow you to specify the enlargement. Here, a page is shown at 100%.

KEY/Strokes

PRINTING THE DOCUMENT ON THE SCREEN

1. Either leave the cursor anywhere in the document if you are printing the entire document

    Or   move the cursor to a single page to be printed

2. Either press **Shift-F7**

    Or   pull down the File menu and select *Print*

    The Print menu is displayed (Figure 36)

3. Select any of the options described in Table 8

4. Either press **1** for *Full Document*

    Or   press **2** for *Page*

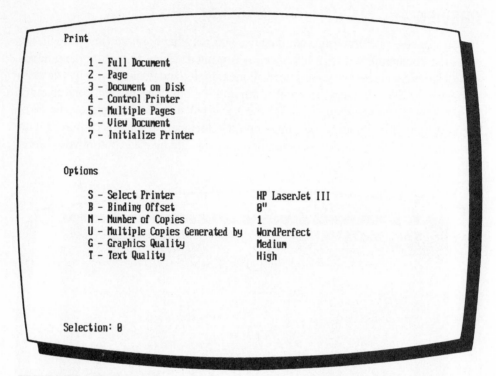

```
Print

        1 - Full Document
        2 - Page
        3 - Document on Disk
        4 - Control Printer
        5 - Multiple Pages
        6 - View Document
        7 - Initialize Printer


    Options

        S - Select Printer              HP LaserJet III
        B - Binding Offset              0"
        N - Number of Copies            1
        U - Multiple Copies Generated by WordPerfect
        G - Graphics Quality            Medium
        T - Text Quality                High




    Selection: 0
```

FIGURE 36   The Print Menu.   The Print menu lists the commands you use to print documents, change options, and control print queues.

TABLE 8   Print Menu Choices

Print

1   *Full Document* prints the entire document.

2   *Page* prints the page in which the cursor is positioned.

3   *Document on Disk* displays the prompt *Document name:* Type the name of a document on the disk (you can specify a path in front of the name), and then press **Enter**. This option also allows you to print a document that is formatted for another printer.

4   *Control Printer* displays the Control Printer menu, which is used to manage jobs in the print queue. This command is described in the section "Managing a Print Queue."

5   *Multiple Pages* specifies which pages of the document on the screen should be printed.

6   *View Document* displays the document on the screen the way it will look when printed so that you can preview it. If you use several formatting commands, you may have a hard time visualizing what the document will look like when it is printed. Many formatting commands do not show their effects on the screen. For example, you do not normally see page numbers, headers, footers, footnotes, top and bottom margins, and font changes on the screen. To see these, you use the View Document command on the Print menu (Figure 35). Though you cannot edit the document when it is displayed with this command, you can see where improvements might be made before you print it out. If you use this command, press + and - on the numeric keypad to scroll within a page. Press **PgUp** and **PgDn** to scroll between pages. Press **Shift-F3** to change colors. If your system has a graphics display, you also have the following menus choices
   - *1 100%* displays the page on the screen the same size it will be when printed.
   - *2 200%* displays the page on the screen twice the size it will be when printed.
   - *3 Full Page* displays a full 8½-by-11-inch page on the screen. The text may not be readable at this small size.
   - *4 Facing Pages* displays two facing pages. The first page is displayed as a single page, and all subsequent pages are displayed side by side, as they would appear if you were paging through a book.

7   *Initialize Printer* downloads soft fonts to the printer. You use this command only when you have marked soft fonts with asterisks to indicate that they must be available in the printer when the print job begins.

Options

S   *Select Printer* displays a list of printers that have been defined. Highlight the printer you want to use, and then press **1** for *Select*. Any document can be printed on any printer. When you select a new printer, WordPerfect reformats the document to match the capabilities of the selected printer as closely as possible.

B *Binding Offset* is used if your document is to be reproduced double-sided or printed on a duplex printer and bound. This command sets a gutter margin to shift text to the right on odd-numbered pages and to the left on even-numbered pages. This is useful when you want to leave room for punched holes for three-ring binders or for staples or other kinds of binders. The Binding command shifts the text to the right on pages with odd numbers and to the left on pages with even numbers. The binding offset that you enter is the distance from the edge of the page and is added to the margin settings specified for the document. For example, if the left margin setting is 1″ and you set the binding offset to .5″, the margin is 1.5″ on alternate pages.

N *Number of Copies* specifies the number of copies to be printed.

U *Multiple Copies Generated by* speeds up printing if your laser printer recognizes the command that prints multiple copies.
   • If WordPerfect controls multiple copies, they are printed more slowly, especially if they contain graphics or require downloadable fonts. However, copies are collated.
   • If the printer controls multiple copies, they are printed faster but are not collated.

G *Graphics Quality* controls the resolution used to print graphics. You can choose draft, medium, or high resolution. Higher resolutions take longer to print but give better results. You can also press **1** for *Do Not Print* if you want to print just text in the document without the included graphics. You can do this when just editing hard-copy text or when your printer will not print both text and graphics in the same pass.

T *Text Quality* controls the resolution used to print text. The choices and results are similar to those of the Graphics Quality command.

KEY/Strokes

PRINTING A DOCUMENT ON THE DISK

1. Either press **Shift-F7**

    Or   pull down the File menu and select *Print*

    The Print menu is displayed (Figure 36)

2. Press **3** for *Document on Disk* and the prompt reads *Document name:*

3. Type the document's name. (If it is not in the default directory, enter a path.)

4. Press **Enter** and the prompt reads *Page(s): (All)*

5. Either press **Enter** to print the entire document

    Or   type a range of pages (see the box ''Specifying Pages to Be Printed''), and then press **Enter**

6. Press **F7** to return to the document screen

▼ Specifying Pages to Be Printed

When printing a file, you can print selected pages. After you enter the name of the file or select it from the List Files screen and menu, the prompt reads *Page(s): (All)*. You can either press **Enter** to print the entire document or specify selected page numbers and then press **Enter** to begin printing. When specifying only certain pages, use the following procedures. (Do not enter spaces in the page specifications, for they may create problems.)

   • To print from the beginning of the document

to a specific page, type a hyphen and then the ending page number. For example, to print from the beginning of the document to page 10, type **-10**.

   • To print from a specific page to the end of the document, type the beginning page number followed by a hyphen. For example, to print from page 10 to the end of the document, type **10-**.

   • To print a single page, enter the page number. For example, to print page 7, type **7**.

(Continued)

- To print several consecutive pages, enter the starting and ending pages separated by a hyphen. For example, to print pages 2 through 5, type **2-5**.
- To print several nonconsecutive pages, separate them with commas. For example, to print pages 1, 5, and 10, type **1,5,10** and to print page 1 and then pages 6 through 8, type **1,6-8**.
- To print sections where you have specified Roman numbering (see Topic 11), enter Roman numerals to print the selected pages. For example, to print page 2, type **ii**; to print pages 2 through 5, type **ii-v**; and to print pages 1, 5, and 10, type **i,v,x**.
- If you have specified new page numbers anywhere in the document (see Topic 11), those changes divide the document into sections. To print selected pages, follow all the preceding rules, but add section numbers followed by a colon. For example, to print pages 2 through 5 in an introduction, and pages 2 through 5 in the second and third sections of the document, type **1:2-5,2:2-5,3:2-5**.
- Sections are numbered sequentially beginning at 1 unless you have used both Roman (i, ii, iii) and Arabic (1, 2, 3) numbers in the document. In these cases, each numbering style is numbered separately. For example, to print pages 2 through 5 in an introduction numbered with Roman numerals and pages 2 through 5 in the second and third sections of the document numbered with Arabic numerals, type **1:ii-v,1:2-5,2:2-5**.

USING LIST FILES TO PRINT

WordPerfect's List Files screen and menu simplifies printing files. To display the List Files screen, press **F5** and then press **Enter** or pull down the File menu and select *List Files*. To print out a file on the list, highlight it and then press **4** for *Print*. When you do so, the prompt reads *Page(s): (All)*. You can either press **Enter** to print the entire document or specify selected page numbers and then press **Enter** to begin printing. To specify only selected pages, see the box "Specifying Pages to Be Printed."

If you want to print a group of files, you can mark them.

- To mark or unmark individual files, move the highlight over the desired files, and then press **Shift**-* (or just the asterisk on the numeric keypad).
- To mark or unmark all files, press **Alt-F5**.

When you then press **4** for *Print*, a prompt reads *Print marked files?* Press **Y** to print them or **N** to cancel the command.

SETTING UP AND SELECTING PRINTERS

Before you can print documents, you must tell your program what printer you are using and what port it is connected to. This is usually done when the program is first installed for use on your system, but you can add printers or change settings at any time. Adding a printer copies the necessary driver from the *Printer* disk to your WordPerfect program disk. This driver lets your program "talk" to your printer. For example, if you boldface a word on the screen, the driver translates the command into one the printer needs to boldface the word on the printout. You must specify the correct printer driver to get the best results from your printer.

If you add more than one printer to WordPerfect's list of printers, and want to then change the printer used to print a document, you must first select the printer so that the correct driver is used. If you do not use the correct driver, you may get strange results when you print a document (Figure 37).

FIGURE 37 Wrong Printer Driver. Reprinted from *INFOSYSTEMS*, May 1985, © Hitchcock Publishing Company.

The best way to find out if your printer supports certain features is to make a trial printout using all the program's commands you are interested in. When you print the document, you see how they appear. WordPerfect provides a special PRINTER.TST file on the *WordPerfect 1* disk that you can use for this purpose.

MANAGING A PRINT QUEUE

Because the computer is generally tied up while the printer is printing, you lose time when you print out files, especially if the files are long. WordPerfect solves this problem by printing the document to a temporary file on the disk. The program then sends that file to the printer and returns control of the computer back to you so that you can work on other files. When the file has been printed, the program automatically deletes the temporary file from the disk.

In effect, the computer does two things at the same time: It prints the file from the disk while you resume work without waiting for a printout to finish. However, it isn't really doing two things at the same time; it is just switching back and forth between the two jobs. You may notice this switching when you execute a command, for example, when moving the cursor from the beginning to the end of the file you are working on. The computer may take longer than usual to do this because it must switch from printing to editing before it can execute your command.

If while the first document is still being printed, you specify that additional documents be printed, they are stored in a ***print queue***, a line of up to 99 jobs waiting to be printed (Figure 38). The jobs appear in the queue in the order you specify, but you can manage the print queue by canceling jobs, pausing the printer and then resuming later, or changing the order in which jobs are printed.

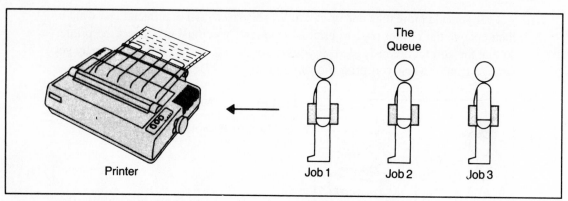

FIGURE 38   A Print Queue.   A print queue is simply a line of jobs waiting to be printed.

KEY/Strokes

MANAGING JOBS IN THE PRINT QUEUE

1. Either press **Shift-F7**

    Or   pull down the File menu and select *Print*

    The Print menu is displayed
2. Press **4** for *Control Printer* to display the Control Printer menu (Figure 39)
3. Select any of the choices described in Table 9
4. Either press **0** to return to the Print menu

    Or   press **F7** to return to the document screen

```
Print: Control Printer

Current Job

Job Number: 1                               Page Number:  1
Status:     Printing                        Current Copy: 1 of 1
Message:    Printer not accepting characters
Paper:      None
Location:   None
Action:     Check cable, make sure printer is turned ON


Job List

Job  Document          Destination       Print Options
 1   (Disk File)       LPT 1


Additional Jobs Not Shown: 0



1 Cancel Job(s); 2 Rush Job; 3 Display Jobs; 4 Go (start printer); 5 Stop: 0
```

FIGURE 39   The Control Printer Menu.   When you select *Control Printer* from the Print menu, a list of all jobs in the print queue is displayed along with a menu that you can use to manage the jobs. This screen also displays error messages, so if you have problems when printing, you should display it to see whether it identifies what the problem is. For example, here the message reads *Printer not accepting characters* and suggests *Check cable, make sure printer is turned ON*.

Table 9   Control Printer Menu Choices

1   *Cancel Job(s)* stops printing, removes the specified print jobs from the list, and advances the paper to the top of the new page. Selecting this option displays the prompt *Cancel which job? (*=All Jobs)*.
   • To cancel a single job, type the number of the job to be canceled, and then press **Enter**.
   • To cancel all jobs, type *, and then press **Enter**. The prompt reads *Cancel all print jobs? (Y/N) No*. Press **Y**. (You may need to press **Enter** again if the printer does not respond.)
   When you cancel print jobs, the Action part of the Control Printer screen displays the prompt *Press C to cancel job immediately* or a warning message is displayed at the bottom of the screen, asking *Are you sure?* WordPerfect recommends that you press **C** or **Y** only if the printer is not accepting input. If you do so at other times, you have to reset the printer, align forms, and download any soft fonts that were previously downloaded. You will also have to press **4** for *Go (start printer)* to resume printing.

2   *Rush Job* displays the prompt *Rush which job?* Type the number of the job listed in the first column of the Job List (press **3** for *Display Jobs* to list additional jobs, if any), and then press **Enter**. The prompt reads *Interrupt current job? (Y/N) No*. Either press **N** to print the job when the current job is finished printing or press **Y** to interrupt the current job. If you interrupt a job, it resumes printing at the top of the page you interrupted it on when the rushed job is finished.

3   *Display Jobs* displays all jobs in the print queue. When you are finished looking at the list, press **Enter** to return to the Control Printer menu. You need to use this command only when more than three print jobs are in the queue and the screen displays a number other than zero following the message *Additional jobs not shown*. Only three print jobs can be displayed on the screen without using this command.

4   *Go (start printer)* resumes printing a document when you have used the Stop command. The document resumes printing at the top of the page. If you stopped printing a multipage document after printing one or more pages and then use this command to continue, the prompt reads *Restart on page:* Type the number of the page you want to resume printing on, and then press **Enter**.

5   *Stop* stops printing so that you can resume printing later by pressing **4** for *Go (start printer)*. You might want to stop printing if you discover that you have set the wrong margins or font, have a paper jam, or need to change printer ribbons or toner. Before resuming printing, adjust the paper in your printer so that it is at the top of a form (usually you take it off line and press the Form Feed button). After selecting the Go command, specify the page number to resume on (if prompted to enter it), and then press **Enter**.

BINDING OFFSET

The Binding Offset command adds to the width of the margin on odd and even pages when you want to bind them back to back (Figure 40). On even-numbered pages, the right margin is increased. On odd numbered pages, the left margin is increased. There are two Binding Offset options you might want to consider.

   • When you use the command, you can keep margins even on both odd and even pages. To do so, select a binding offset distance and divide it by 2. Enter the result as the binding offset measurement, and add the same amount to the left and right margin settings (see Topic 18). For example, if you want a binding offset of ½ inch and 1-inch margins, set the binding offset to .25″ and the left and right margins to 1.25″. When you print the document, it will be shifted .25″ on the page so that the binding margin is ½ inch and the opposite margin is 1 inch.
   • You can add a binding margin to the top of the page rather than at the sides. To do so, press **Shift-F8** and then press **2** for *Page*, or pull down the Layout

menu and select *Page* to display the Page Format menu. Press **7** for *Page Size*, highlight the form you are using, and then press **5** for *Edit*. Press **7** for *Binding Edge* and then **1** for *Top*. Press **F7** three times to return to the document screen.

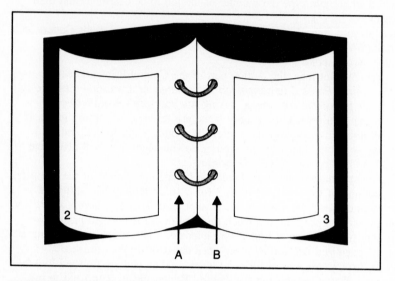

FIGURE 40   Binding Offset.   The Binding Offset command adds to the width of the margin on odd and even pages when you want to bind them back to back. On even-numbered pages, the right margin is increased (a). On odd-numbered pages, the left margin is increased (b).

TROUBLESHOOTING PRINTING PROBLEMS

When printing documents, you may occasionally run into problems. If you do, here are some points to consider.

- Before you can print, you must first select a printer.
- If the computer beeps when you try to print a document, press **Shift-F7** and then press **4** for *Control Printer* to display a message that tells you how to proceed.
- When you print a document, you may see the message *Disk Full*. The program first prints the document on the screen to a disk file, and this message appears if there is not enough room on the disk for it to do so. If this happens, delete some unneeded files from the disk. You can also use the Document on Disk command to print the file from the disk.
- If you have previously canceled a print job, you may have to press **4** for *Go (start printer)* from the Control Printer menu to send the next job to the printer.
- If you have entered font change codes in your text (see Topic 16), some fully formed character printers stop when they encounter them so that you can change print wheels. To resume printing after changing the print wheel, press **Shift-F7** or pull down the File menu and select *Print* to display the Print menu, press **4** for *Control Printer*, and then press **4** for *Go (start printer)*. Press **F7** to return to the document screen.
- If your document contains graphics, and they do not print completely on a laser printer, you might need to add memory to your printer. A full page of graphics requires at least one megabyte of memory in the printer.
- If you are printing on a network, your document is first sent to a print spooler before it is sent to the printer. If it has already been sent to the spooler from

your computer, you cannot cancel it. The same is true if you are using a laser printer. If the document has been sent to the printer, you cannot cancel it.

- When you cancel or stop a print job, your printer may continue printing for a while if it has a buffer. To empty the buffer, turn the printer off and then back on again unless you have downloaded fonts or unless paper is passing through the printer. Once you turn the printer off, all print jobs in the buffer are lost.

▼ TIPS

➤ **When you specify print options** listed on the bottom half of the Print menu, the changes are saved along with the document and remain in effect when you retrieve it again. The only exceptions to this rule are the *Number of Copies* and *Multiple Copies Generated by* choices. These two choices are automatically restored to their default values when you retrieve a document. All of the settings are restored to their default settings when you exit a document.

➤ **The** *View Document* **command first displays the section of the text in which the cursor is positioned**. If you want to view a specific page, move the cursor there before executing the View Document command.

➤ **When you print selected pages, a single page, or a block**, all footnotes for the pages print regardless of how long they are.

➤ **You can print a document that has been formatted for another printer** using the Document on Disk choice on the Print menu. When you do so, a message tells you it has been formatted for another printer, and a prompt asks if you want to continue.

➤ **To print on paper other than 8½ by 11 inches**, you must enter a code that specifies the paper type (see Topic 18).

▼ TUTORIALS

TUTORIAL 8A Printing Files

In this tutorial, you explore printing a file displayed on the screen and stored in a file on the disk. To begin this tutorial, you must load the program or clear the screen of any other document. You must also have completed Tutorial 7A, where you revised and saved the file named ENTER2.WP5.

Step 1 **Retrieve the Document.** Insert the disk on which you saved the ENTER2.WP5 document into one of the disk drives, and then retrieve the document.

Step 2 **Print the Document on the Screen.** Now send the document on the screen to the printer.

To print the document on the screen
Press   **Shift-F7** to display the Print menu
Press   **1** for *Full Document*

Result: The printer immediately begins printing.

Step 3 **Clear the Screen.** Clear the current document from the screen but remain in the program. When prompted *Save document? Yes (No)*, press **N** (for *No*), since you have previously saved this document.

Step 4 **Print the Document on the Disk.** Now let's print the same file, but this time from the disk.

To print the document on the disk

Press   **Shift-F7** to display the Print menu

Press   **3** for *Document on Disk*, and the prompt reads *Document name:*

Type   **ENTER2.WP5** and then press **Enter**. The prompt reads *Page(s): (All)*

Press   **Enter** to print the entire document

Result: The printer immediately begins printing the file from the disk.

Step 5 **Continue or Exit.** You have now completed this tutorial. You may either continue with your own work or exit WordPerfect and return to the operating system. If you are quitting for the day, remove your program and data disks, and then turn off the computer.

TUTORIAL 8B   Using List Files to Print a Document

In this tutorial, you practice using the List Files screen and menu. To begin this tutorial, you must first load the program. You should insert your data disk into one of the disk drives. If necessary, clear any existing document from the screen.

Step 1 **Change the Default Drive and Display the List Files Screen and Menu.** Now change the default drive to B on a floppy disk system or A on a hard disk system.

To change the default drive

Press   **F5** and the message reads *Dir* followed by the current directory

Press   **=** (the equal sign), and the prompt reads *New directory =* followed by the current directory

Type   **B:** on a floppy disk system or **A:** on a hard disk system, and then press **Enter**. The message reads *Dir* followed by the path of the new default drive and directory

Press   **Enter** again to display the list of files on the new default drive and directory

Result: The default drive is now drive B on a floppy disk system or drive A on a hard disk system, and a list of·the files in that drive is displayed.

Step 2 **Use List Files to Print a Document.** You can print a file on the disk by pointing to its name on the List Files screen. Be sure that the printer is on and has paper in it and that the paper is aligned.

To print a file

Press   the arrow keys to move the highlight over the desired file, in this case, *ENTER2.WP5*

Press   **4** for *Print*, and the prompt reads *Page(s): (All)*

Press   **Enter** to print the entire document

Result: The document is printed out on the printer, and the List Files screen and menu remain displayed.

Step 3 **Continue or Exit.** You have now completed this tutorial. You may either continue with your own work or exit WordPerfect and return to the operating system. If you are quitting for the day, remove your program and data disks, and then turn off the computer.

▼EXERCISES

EXERCISE 8A Preview a Document

In this exercise, you explore WordPerfect's View Document feature. With this command, you can preview your document on the screen before you print it. Although you cannot edit this file, you can scroll through it to check its layout before you print it. Follow the commands given here to preview the documents you created in the tutorials in Topics 3 though 6. Begin by retrieving the document you want to preview. Then press **Shift-F7** to display the Print menu. Press **6** for *View Document*.

The document appears on the screen looking just as it did when you printed it. Press **1** though **4** to see how you can change the size of the document. When you are finished, press **F7** to return to the original document. Finally, clear the screen and view another document, continue, or quit.

EXERCISE 8B Preview the PRINTER.TST Document

Retrieve the file named PRINTER.TST on the disk labeled *WordPerfect 1* (or in the same directory as your WordPerfect files on a hard disk system).

1. View the document using the View Document command.
2. When the document is being viewed, select each of the menu choices to see its effect.
3. When you are finished, exit View Document to return to the Print menu.
4. Print the document.
5. Read the document to see what features are supported by your printer.
6. Clear the screen without saving the document.

EXERCISE 8C Print Multiple Copies of a Document

Retrieve the PRINTER.TST file from the *WordPerfect 1* disk.

1. Use the Print menu to specify two copies, and then print them.
2. Change the number of copies back to 1. Otherwise, the change will remain in effect until you exit WordPerfect.

EXERCISE 8D Change Print Quality

Retrieve the PRINTER.TST document, and then display the Print menu. Notice the default settings for *Text Quality* and *Graphics Quality*.

1. Change the settings, and print the PRINTER.TST document to see the change.
2. Change the default settings back to their original settings.

▼QUESTIONS

1. What does it mean to say that a printer is on line or off line?
2. What happens when you turn a printer off and then back on while a job is printing?
3. If you wanted to print just pages 3 and 4 and 6 through 8, would you print the document from the screen or from a file on the disk? How would you specify pages to be printed?
4. List some typical printer options and describe them.
5. What is the purpose of the View Document command?
6. What command do you use to mark individual files on the List Files screen? All files?

As you type a document, only the letters and numbers you type are displayed on the document screen. However, you often enter invisible *codes* (also called printer control codes or format codes) into the document. You enter these codes whenever you press **Enter**, **Tab**, or **Spacebar**. You also enter them when you use formatting commands, for example, to center, indent, or underline text.

The function of these codes is to override the default formats and control how your text is printed on a page. When you print out the document, the codes arrive at the printer and give it instructions. For example, a code might tell the printer to advance to the top of the next page after printing 9 inches of text, print a page number at the bottom of the page, or indent a paragraph ½ inch from the left margin.

Although these codes are not displayed on the screen, you sometimes sense their presence. When you move the cursor through formatted text, pressing the arrow keys sometimes does not move the cursor. Although the cursor does not appear to be moving on the screen, it is moving through the codes in the document.

REVEALING CODES

WordPerfect allows you to reveal the hidden codes in a document. This makes editing much easier. You can see where carriage returns and other formatting codes are located, which makes it simple to delete or change them.

To reveal codes, press **Alt-F3** or **F11** or pull down the Edit menu and select *Reveal Codes*. The lower half of the Reveal Codes screen shows the text with codes, while the upper half shows the same text without codes (Figure 41). The ruler that divides the screen indicates margins with the symbols [and] and tabs with ▲ symbols. If the margins and tab stops fall at the same position, the symbols { and } are displayed instead.

The cursor appears in the top screen as a flashing underscore and in the lower screen as a reverse-video rectangle. Table 10 describes the codes that might be displayed on the Reveal Codes screen. They are usually displayed in a different intensity or color so that they stand out from the rest of the text. With the codes displayed, you can scroll through the document using any of the cursor movement keys and edit as you desire with any of the editing commands. When you are finished, press **Alt-F3** or **F11** to return to the document screen.

When you press Alt-F3 to reveal codes, the screen splits into two
parts.

1. The document is displayed on the top half of the screen just
   as it is on the document screen.

2. The lower half of the screen displays the same lines as the
   top half, but all codes are revealed.

```
                                         Doc 1 Pg 1 Ln 1" Pos 1"
{   ▲   ▲   ▲   ▲   ▲   ▲   ▲   ▲   ▲   ▲   }   ▲   ▲
When you press [BOLD]Alt[bold][-][BOLD]F3[bold] to reveal codes, the screen spli
ts into two[SRt]
parts.[HRt]
[HRt]
1.[→Indent]The document is displayed on the top half of the screen just[SRt]
as it is on the document screen.[HRt]
[HRt]
2.[→Indent]The lower half of the screen displays the same lines as the[SRt]
top half, but all codes are revealed.


Press Reveal Codes to restore screen
```

FIGURE 41   Revealing Codes.   You can press **Alt-F3** to reveal codes that are normally hidden.
The ruler line between the two windows indicates tab stops, indents, and margin settings at the
cursor's position.

KEY/Strokes

REVEALING CODES

1. Either press **Alt-F3** or **F11**

   Or   pull down the Edit menu and select *Reveal Codes*

2. Edit or revise the document as needed

3. Either press **Alt-F3** or **F11**

   Or   pull down the Edit menu and select *Reveal Codes*

TABLE 10   WordPerfect Codes

Code	Description
[ ]	Hard space
■	Current position of cursor
[-]	Hyphen character
-	Soft hyphen
[/]	Hyphenation canceled
[Adv]	Printer advance
[Bline]	Baseline position
[Block]	Beginning of block
[BlockPro]	Block protection
[Bold]	Bold
[Box Num]	Graphics box caption
[Cell]	Table cell
[Center]	Center
[Center Pg]	Text centered vertically on page
	(Continued)

TABLE 10   WordPerfect Codes *(Continued)*

Code	Description
[Cndl EOP]	Conditional end of page
[Cntr Tab]	Centered tab stop
[CNTR TAB]	Hard centered tab
[Col Def]	Column definition
[Col On:] [Col Off:]	Text columns begin/end
[Color]	Print color
[Comment]	Document comment
[Date]	Date/time function
[Dbl Und]	Double underline
[Dec Tab]	Decimal tab stop
[DEC TAB]	Hard decimal tab stop
[Decml/Algn Char]	Decimal character or thousands separator
[Def Mark:Index]	Index definition
[Def Mark:Listn]	List definition
[Def Mark:ToA]	Table of authorities definition
[DefMark:ToC]	Table of contents definition
[Dorm HRt]	Dormant hard return
[DSRt]	Default soft return (entered by the program in some situations)
[End Def]	End of index, list, table of authorities, or table of contents
[End Mark]	End of marked text
[End Opt]	Endnote options
[Endnote]	Endnote
[Endnote Placement]	Endnote placement
[Equ Box]	Equation box
[Equ Opt]	Equation options
[Ext Large]	Extra large print
[Fig Box]	Figure box
[Fig Opt]	Figure options
[Fine]	Fine print
[Flsh Rgt]	Flush right
[Font]	Base font change
[Footer]	Footer
[Footnote]	Footnote
[Force]	Force odd/even pages
[Ftn Opt]	Footnote/endnote options
[Full Form]	Table of authorities
[Header]	Header
[Hline]	Horizontal line
[HPg]	Hard page break
[Hrd Row]	Hard row
[HRt]	Hard carriage return
[HRt-SPg]	Hard carriage return and soft page break
[Hyph Off]	Hyphenation ends
[Hyph On]	Hyphenation begins
[HZone]	Change in hyphenation zone
[→Indent]	Indent begins
[→Indent←]	Left/right indent begins
[Index]	Index mark
[Insert Pg Num]	Inserted page number
[ISRt]	Invisible soft return
[Italc]	Italic
[Just]	Right justification
[Just Lim]	Word/letter spacing justification limits

(Continued)

TABLE 10   **WordPerfect Codes** *(Continued)*

Code	Description
[Kern]	Kern
[L/R Mar]	Left and right margin settings
[Lang]	Language
[Large]	Large print
[Leading Adj]	Leading adjustment
[Link]	Link to spreadsheet file
[Link End]	End of link to spreadsheet
[Ln Height]	Line height
[Ln Num]	Line numbering
[Ln Spacing]	Line spacing
[←Mar Rel]	Left margin release
[Mark:List]	List entry
[Mark:ToA]	Table of authorities entry
[Mark:ToC]	Table of contents entry
[Math Def]	Math columns definition
[Math Off]	Math ends
[Math On]	Math begins
[!]	Formula calculation
[t]	Subtotal entry
[+]	Calculate subtotal
[T]	Total entry
[=]	Calculate total
[*]	Calculate grand total
[N]	Negate
[New End Num]	New endnote number
[New Equ Num]	New equation number
[New Fig Num]	New figure number
[New Ftn Num]	New footnote number
[New Tbl Num]	New table number
[New Txt Num]	New text box number
[New Usr Num]	New user box number
[Note Num]	Footnote/endnote reference
[Outline Lvl]	Outline style
[Outline Off]	Outline off
[Outline On]	Outline on
[Outln]	Outline attribute
[Ovrstk]	Overstrike character
[Paper Sz/Typ]	Paper size and type
[Par Num]	Paragraph number
[Par Num Def]	Paragraph numbering definition
[Pg Num]	New page number
[Pg Num Style]	Page number style
[Pg Numbering]	Page numbering
[Ptr Cmnd]	Printer command
[RedLn]	Redlining begins/ends
[Ref]	Automatic reference
[Rgt Tab]	Right aligned tab stop
[RGT TAB]	Hard right aligned tab stop
[Row]	Table row
[Shadw]	Shadow
[Sm Cap]	Small caps
[Small]	Small print
[SPg]	Soft page break
[SRt]	Soft carriage return
[StkOut]	Strikeout
[Style Off]	Style off
	(Continued)

```
    The paired codes at the beginning and end of this
    sentence turn boldfacing on and off.

    The paired codes at the beginning and end of this
    sentence turn underlining on and off.




                                        Doc 1 Pg 1 Ln 1" Pos 1"
{    ▲    ▲    ▲    ▲    ▲    ▲    ▲    }    ▲    ▲    ▲    ▲    ▲    ▲
[BOLD]The paired codes at the beginning and end of this[SRt]
sentence turn boldfacing on and off.[bold][HRt]
[HRt]
[UND]The paired codes at the beginning and end of this[SRt]
sentence turn underlining on and off.[und][HRt]




    Press Reveal Codes to restore screen
```

FIGURE 44   Paired Codes.   Here paired codes have been entered to boldface and underline sentences. The first code in the pair turns the format on. The second code in the pair turns the format off. (The way the formatted text is displayed on your screen depends on your system and the way WordPerfect has been set up.)

There are two ways to enter paired codes, depending on whether you are formatting new or existing text.

- To format new text, you enter a beginning code, type text, and then enter an ending code. There is also a shortcut you can use. When you enter a beginning code, the off code is also automatically entered. After typing the text, you can press → to move the cursor to the right of the off code so that the rest of the text that you type isn't affected.
- To format existing text, you select a block of existing text (see Topic 14) and then execute a format command that automatically inserts codes at the beginning and end of the selected block.

If you insert text into a document containing paired codes, the position of the cursor determines the format of the text that you insert.

- If the cursor is between the codes, the text is formatted just like the other text between the code.
- If the cursor is outside of the codes, the text is not affected.

The number to the right of *Pos* in the status line at the bottom of the screen indicates when the cursor is inside of the codes and when it is outside of them. The way the number is displayed varies. For example, on some computers, the number changes color or intensity.

EDITING AND DELETING CODES

Codes that you enter into a document affect its format. You can return the affected sections to their default format by deleting the codes that you entered to change the formats. For example, if you have indented, boldfaced, superscripted, or centered text, or if you have changed margins, tab stops, or page numbers, you can restore them to their default settings by deleting the codes you entered. When deleting paired codes, you usually have to delete only one, and the other is deleted automatically. The way you delete codes depends on whether you are in Reveal Codes or not.

When Codes Are Revealed

The easiest way to delete codes is to use the Reveal Codes command so that you can see them on the screen. When you look at codes in the Reveal Codes screen, some of them can be quite long. However, when you move the cursor through them or delete them, they are like single characters. You only have to press one of the arrow keys twice to move from one side of the code to the other. To delete them, you only have to press **Backspace** or **Del** once.

When Codes Are Not Revealed

The codes you enter to format text are not normally displayed on the screen. If you try to delete one of these codes with **Backspace** or **Del**, a prompt may be displayed, for example, *Delete [BOLD]? No (Yes)*. Press **Y** if you want to delete the code, or press **N** if you do not. These prompts appear only when deleting the code will not change the way the document is displayed on the screen. These prompts also do not appear if you select and then delete a block that includes the codes (see Topic 14); instead, the codes are deleted along with the selected text.

▼ Joining Lines of Text Separated by Carriage Returns

When editing, you often want to delete blank lines, join two lines, or join paragraphs that were separated by hard carriage returns. Though not necessarily displayed on the screen, hard carriage returns are much like other characters you enter in a document; therefore, you delete them as you would other characters. To do this accurately, it helps if you can see them. To display hard carriage returns, press **Alt-F3** or **F11** to display the Reveal Codes screen.

To join two paragraphs, use the arrow keys to position the cursor on or to the right of a hard carriage return code, *[HRt]*. Either press **Del** to delete the highlighted code or press **Backspace** to delete the code to the left of the cursor so that the line or paragraph below jumps up to join the line above. If necessary, press **Spacebar** to insert spaces between the last word of the first paragraph and the first word of what was the second paragraph. Press **Alt-F3** or **F11** to return to the document screen.

(Continued)

```
The two paragraph codes [HRt] below this first paragraph indicate
where hard carriage returns have been entered.

To join the two paragraphs, you delete these hard carriage return
codes. If necessary, you then enter a space to separate the two
sentences in the new paragraph.




                                   Doc 1 Pg 1 Ln 1" Pos 1"
[ ▲   ▲   ▲   ▲   ▲   ▲   ▲   ▲   ▲   ▲   ▲   ▲   ]   ▲   ▲
The two paragraph codes [HRt] below this first paragraph indicate[SRt]
where hard carriage returns have been entered.[HRt]
[HRt]
To join the two paragraphs, you delete these hard carriage return[SRt]
codes. If necessary, you then enter a space to separate the two[SRt]
sentences in the new paragraph.



Press Reveal Codes to restore screen
```

Here, two paragraphs have been separated by two hard carriage returns (indicated by the *[HRt]* codes in the Reveal Codes screen). The *[SRt]* codes are soft carriage return codes.

Deleting the *[HRt]* codes joins the two paragraphs.

```
The two paragraph codes [HRt] below this first paragraph indicate
where hard carriage returns have been entered. To join the two
paragraphs, you delete these hard carriage return codes. If
necessary, you then enter a space to separate the two sentences in
the new paragraph.




                                   Doc 1 Pg 1 Ln 1.17" Pos 5.7"
[ ▲   ▲   ▲   ▲   ▲   ▲   ▲   ▲   ▲   ▲   ▲   ▲   ]   ▲   ▲
The two paragraph codes [HRt] below this first paragraph indicate[SRt]
where hard carriage returns have been entered. To join the two[SRt]
paragraphs, you delete these hard carriage return codes. If[SRt]
necessary, you then enter a space to separate the two sentences in[SRt]
the new paragraph.



Press Reveal Codes to restore screen
```

TIPS

➤ **You can adjust the size of the Reveal Codes screen** while it is displayed by pressing **Ctrl-F3**, then **1** for *Window*. Press ↑ or ↓ to change its size; then press **Enter**.

➤ **To remove several identical codes**, use the Search and Replace commands (see Topic 20).

➤ **If you inadvertently delete codes** and then press **F1** to undelete them, you cannot see the restored codes unless you use Reveal Codes.

> **The position of many open format codes is important**. Generally, line format codes should be entered at the beginning of a line and page format codes at the top of the page.

> **When you enter an open code to change a format, the settings specified in that code affect the text to the end of the document or the next code**. If you insert a code of the same type below the first code, the default settings displayed while executing the command are those specified in the first code. For example, let's say you enter a code to change tab stops so that they are every 1 inch instead of every ½ inch. If you then repeat the same command farther down in the document, the ruler line initially shows the tab stops set every 1 inch. This is very useful if you want to make slight adjustments in any settings you have made. Do not delete the first code until you have made the adjustments. Instead, move the cursor to the right of the first code, change the settings, and then delete the first code.

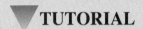 **TUTORIAL**

TUTORIAL 9A   Editing Codes

In this tutorial, you reveal codes when editing a document. To begin this tutorial, you must first load the program. You should insert your data disk into one of the disk drives and make that drive the default. If necessary, clear any existing document from the screen.

Step 1 **Enter the Document.** Enter the document shown in Figure 45. Press **F6** before typing the first sentence, then again at the end of the sentence. Press **F8** before typing the second sentence, then again at the end of the sentence.

> **The paired codes at the beginning and end of this sentence turn boldfacing on and off.**
>
> <u>The paired codes at the beginning and end of this sentence turn underlining on and off.</u>

FIGURE 45   **The CODES Document.**   You enter this document in this tutorial.

Step 2 **Save the Document.** Now that you have finished the document, save it under the filename CODES.WP5 so that you can retrieve it later.

Step 3 **Reveal Codes.** Now reveal codes so that you can see them on the screen.

To reveal codes
Press **Alt-F3**

Result: The screen splits horizontally into two parts. The lower half of the screen shows the text with codes. The upper half shows the same text without codes (see Figure 44).

Step 4 **Delete the Bold Codes.** Let's delete the codes that boldface the first sentence.

To delete the bold codes
Press **Home** three times, then press ↑ to move the cursor to the top of the document. The *[BOLD]* code is highlighted. (If it isn't, use the arrow keys to highlight it.)
Press **Del** to delete the code

Result: When you delete the beginning code in the lower part of the screen, the second code is automatically deleted and the sentence is no longer boldfaced.

Step 5 **Delete the Underline Codes.** Let's delete the codes that underline the second sentence.

To delete the underline codes
Move the cursor to highlight the *[UND]* code at the beginning of the second sentence
Press **Del** to delete the code

Result: When you delete the beginning code in the lower part of the screen, the second code is automatically deleted and the sentence is no longer underlined.

Step 6 **Join Paragraphs.** Now delete the *[HRt]* codes that separate the two paragraphs to make one complete paragraph.

To join lines separated by carriage returns
Move the cursor to highlight the first *[HRt]* code at the end of the first paragraph
Press **Del** until the two paragraphs are joined
Press **Spacebar** (if necessary) to insert a space between the joined sentences
Press ↓ to realign the paragraph

Result: When you delete the codes, the paragraphs are joined.

Step 7 **Split a Paragraph into Two Paragraphs.** To split a paragraph in two, you enter hard carriage returns.

To break a paragraph into two paragraphs
Move the cursor to under the *T* in *The paired codes* at the beginning of the second sentence
Press **Enter** twice to insert a blank line between the two paragraphs

Result: The paragraph is now split in two. The first *[HRt]* ends the paragraph, and the second inserts a blank line to separate it from the next paragraph. Press **Alt-F3** to return to the document screen.

Step 8 **Print the Document.** Be sure that the printer is on and has paper in it and that the paper is aligned. Then make a printout of the document.

Step 9 **Clear the Screen.** Clear the current document from the screen without saving your changes but remain in the program. When prompted *Save document? Yes*

(No) press **N** (for *No*), since you have previously saved this document and do not want to save your changes.

Step 10 **Continue or Exit.** You have now completed this tutorial. You may either continue with your own work or exit WordPerfect and return to the operating system. If you are quitting for the day, remove your program and data disks, and then turn off the computer.

▼EXERCISES

EXERCISE 9A   Edit Codes in the ENTER1 Document

Retrieve the ENTER1.WP5 document that you created in Tutorial 6A.

1. Reveal codes and practice editing by making each sentence its own paragraph. Then make a printout.
2. Delete the hard carriage return codes to rejoin the sentences into a single paragraph, and make another printout.
3. Clear the screen without saving your revisions.

EXERCISE 9B   Edit Codes in the BOLD1 Document

Retrieve the BOLD1.WP5 document that you created in Tutorial 6B.

1. Reveal codes and delete the codes that you entered to boldface and underline words.
2. Delete the code you entered to change the underlining style.
3. Print the document, then clear the screen without saving your revisions.

▼QUESTIONS

1. What is the purpose of the codes that you enter in a document?
2. What command do you use to reveal the codes in the document?
3. How do you override default formats in a document? How would you then remove your changes so that the document returns to its original format?
4. What is the difference between an open code and a paired code?
5. When you enter an open code, what part of the document is affected?
6. When you enter a paired code, what part of the document is affected?
7. If two lines or paragraphs were separated by a carriage return, how would you join them?

You can control where page breaks fall when you print a document. A ***page break*** is where the printer stops printing lines on the current sheet of paper, advances the paper to the top of the next page, and resumes printing on that page. The way the printer advances to the next page depends on your printer and the kind of paper you are using.

- If you are printing on continuous-form paper, the printer stops printing at a page break, advances the paper to the top of the next page, and then resumes printing.
- If you are printing on single sheets of paper on a printer with an automatic sheet feeder, the printer does not pause at a page break; rather, it ejects the current sheet, automatically feeds another sheet, and resumes printing.
- If you are hand-feeding the printer single sheets of paper, the printer ejects the current sheet and pauses at a page break. You then insert a new sheet and press a designated key to resume printing.

Controlling where page breaks occur is important when printing multipage documents because there are certain places where you want to avoid page breaks.

- Letters should not end with the closing of the letter alone at the top of the second page.
- Reports, term papers, and other important documents should often have major sections begin at the top of a new page.
- Tables should be kept together so that they do not break with one part on one page and the rest on the next page.

To control where page breaks occur, you should understand WordPerfect's three kinds of page breaks: soft, hard, and conditional. You should also understand widows and orphans and how to prevent them.

SOFT PAGE BREAKS

Soft page breaks are automatically entered and adjusted as you enter or delete text. Soft page breaks are indicated on the screen with single dashed lines (-------) and on the Reveal Codes screen with *[SPg]* or *[HRHt-SPg]* codes (Figure 46). If you edit the document so that the length of one or more pages changes, the soft page breaks are relocated automatically. You cannot directly change the position of a soft page break, and you cannot delete it. To move it, you have to change the amount or format of the text above it. For example, if you change top or bottom margins, line height or spacing, or the size of fonts, the soft page breaks will shift.

HARD PAGE BREAKS

Normally, page breaks occur automatically when a page is full, but you can also force them to fall at selected points in a document. To force a page break, you insert a hard page break. To do so, you move the cursor to where you want a page to break and then press **Ctrl-Enter**. (On enhanced keyboards, you can also press

Ctrl-Ins.) Hard page breaks are indicated on the screen with double dashed lines (=====) and on the Reveal Codes screen with *[HPg]* codes. To change a hard page break, you must delete the code you entered to create it.

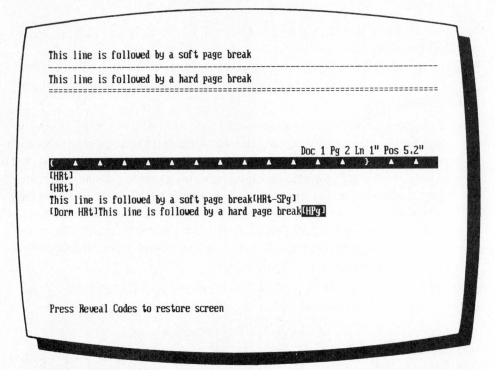

```
This line is followed by a soft page break
-----------------------------------------------------------------------
This line is followed by a hard page break
=======================================================================



                                          Doc 1 Pg 2 Ln 1" Pos 5.2"
{   ▲    ▲    ▲    ▲    ▲    ▲    ▲    ▲    ▲    ▲   }   ▲    ▲
[HRt]
[HRt]
This line is followed by a soft page break[HRt-SPg]
[Dorn HRt]This line is followed by a hard page break[HPg]



Press Reveal Codes to restore screen
```

FIGURE 46   Page Breaks.   Soft page breaks are indicated by a single dashed line and hard page breaks by a double dashed line.

CONDITIONAL PAGE BREAKS

You can prevent unwanted soft page breaks with a conditional page break. This command tells the printer, "If this section fits in the remaining space on this page, print it here; otherwise, advance the paper and begin printing it at the top of the next page." If the section is too long for a single page, it breaks as necessary and continues printing on subsequent pages. This command is extremely useful when you want to:

- Keep the lines of a table on the same page as the table headings.
- Keep an illustration on the same page as the text that refers to it.
- Keep a heading and at least the first two lines of the following text on the same page.

WordPerfect offers two ways to enter a conditional page break: You can select the block (see Topic 14) and then protect it, or you can specify the number of lines to be protected. You usually protect a block when you want to keep it together on the same page if you add or delete text above it. You specify lines when you want to keep a certain element with another. For example, you can use this command to keep a heading with at least the first two lines in the following paragraph.

KEY/Strokes

PROTECTING A BLOCK FROM A SOFT PAGE BREAK

1. Move the cursor under the first character in the block to be protected
2. Press **Alt-F4** or **F12** to enter block mode, and the status line flashes *Block on*
3. Press the cursor movement keys to highlight the block to be protected
   - If you protect a block beginning or ending in the middle of a line, the entire line is protected
   - Do not include the hard carriage return code at the end of the last paragraph
4. Press **Shift-F8** and the prompt reads *Protect block? No (Yes)*
5. Press **Y** to protect the block

KEY/Strokes

ENTERING A CONDITIONAL PAGE BREAK

1. Count the number of lines to be protected from a soft page break
2. Move the cursor to the line above the lines to be protected, even if that line has text on it
3. Either press **Shift-F8** and then press **4** for *Other*

   Or   pull down the Layout menu and select *Other*
4. Press **2** for *Conditional End of Page* and the prompt reads *Number of Lines to Keep Together*:
5. Type the number of lines to be protected from a page break, and then press **Enter**
6. Press **F7** to return to the document screen

WIDOWS AND ORPHANS

When printing documents longer than a single page, you can turn widow and orphan protection on so that at least two lines at the beginning or end of paragraphs are kept together at the bottom and top of each page. This command prevents the first line of a paragraph from printing by itself at the bottom of a page (called an orphan) and the last line of a paragraph from printing by itself at the top of the next page (called a widow).

If WordPerfect calculates that the first or last line of a paragraph is to print at the bottom or top of a page by itself, it moves another line to accompany it. Since single lines are prevented, no three-line paragraphs will be split; the entire paragraph will move to the next page if it will not print on the current page.

KEY/Strokes

TURNING WIDOW AND ORPHAN
PROTECTION ON OR OFF

1. Move the cursor to where you want to turn widow and orphan protection on or off
2. Either press **Shift-F8** and then press **1** for *Line*

    Or   pull down the Layout menu and select *Line*
3. Press **9** for *Widow/Orphan Protection*
4. Either press **Y** to turn protection on

    Or   press **N** to turn protection off
5. Press **F7** to return to the document screen

▼ **TIPS**

➤ **You can also affect where page breaks fall by changing the paper size**, for example, when printing on legal-size paper or on forms (see Topic 18).

➤ **Dormant hard carriage returns**. When a page is filled, WordPerfect automatically inserts a page break. This is shown on the screen as a dashed line (------). If the first line on the new page contains just a *[HRt]* code, that code is automatically converted to a dormant hard return indicated by a *[Dorm Hrt]* code. Lines with this dormant hard return code do not print. This prevents a blank line from being printed at the top of the page. If you edit the document so that the dormant hard return code is no longer the first line on a page, it is automatically converted back into a hard carriage return.

➤ **When you specify lines in the Conditional End of Page command, you must take line spacing into consideration if you have changed it**. For example, to protect three lines that have been double-spaced, specify 6 lines.

▼ **TUTORIAL**

TUTORIAL 10A   Specifying Page Breaks

In this tutorial, you control page breaks. To begin this tutorial, you must first load the program. You should insert your data disk into one of the disk drives and make that drive the default. If necessary, clear any existing document from the screen.

Step 1   **Enter a Document.** Enter the document shown in Figure 47. Press **Enter** at the end of each line.

This line is on page 1
This line is on page 2

FIGURE 47   The PAGES Document.   You enter this document in this tutorial.

Step 2   Enter a Hard Page Break. Now enter a hard page break so that the second line prints on page 2.

To enter a hard page break

Move	the cursor to under the *T* in *This line is on page 2*
Press	**Ctrl-Enter**

Result: A hard page break code is inserted in front of the line. The hard page break is indicated by the double dashed line on the screen. The status line now indicates that the cursor is on *Pg 2*.

Step 3   Protect a Block from a Page Break. No blocks in this document are large enough to require protecting, but execute the command anyway to see how it is done.

To protect a block from a soft page break

Move	the cursor to under the *T* in *This line is on page 1*
Press	**Alt-F4** to turn block on, and then press **Enter** to select the line
Press	**Shift-F8** and the prompt reads *Protect block? No (Yes)*
Press	**Y** to protect the block

Result: The block is protected. Use the Reveal Codes command to see the codes.

Step 4   Turn on Widow and Orphan Protection. Again, this document does not require widow and orphan protection, but execute the command anyway to see how it is done.

To turn widow and orphan protection on

Move	the cursor to the top of the second page
Press	**Shift-F8** to display the Format menu
Press	**1** for *Line* to display the Line Format menu
Press	**9** for *Widow/Orphan Protection*
Press	**Y** to turn protection on
Press	**F7** to return to the document screen

Result: Protection is now turned on from the position of the code to the end of the document.

Step 5   **Save the Document.** Now that you have finished the document, save it under the filename PAGES.WP5 so that you can retrieve it later.

Step 6   **Print the Document.** Be sure that the printer is on and has paper in it and that the paper is aligned. Then make a printout of the document. The document is printed on two pages.

Step 7   **Continue or Exit.** You have now completed this tutorial. You may either continue with your own work or exit WordPerfect and return to the operating system. If you are quitting for the day, remove your program and data disks, and then turn off the computer.

EXERCISE

EXERCISE 10A   Add Page Breaks to the RIGHTS Document

Retrieve the RIGHTS.WP5 document that you created in Exercise 6B.

1. Scroll down the document to see if one of the amendments is split by a soft page break. If so, move the cursor to the line where the amendment begins, and then add a hard page break.
2. Print the document.
3. Clear the screen without saving the document because the hard page break code might cause problems in later exercises.

QUESTIONS

1. What is a page break? Why would you want to control page breaks?
2. What is the difference between a soft and a hard page break?
3. What is a conditional page break? Describe the two procedures you can use to enter one.
4. What are the differences between a hard page break and a conditional page break?
5. What are widows and orphans? How can you prevent them from occurring?

TOPIC 11
Page Numbers

You can specify if and where page numbers are printed when you print a document. The default setting for WordPerfect is for page numbers not to be printed. You can, however, turn page numbers on and then back off anyplace in a document. When you do so, you can also specify where on the page they will print relative to the margins. Figure 48 shows some of the page number positions you can specify. You can also enter page numbers in headers and footers (see Topic 23). Page numbers are not displayed on the document screen but are added as the document is printed. They can be seen with the View Document command, and their codes can be seen on the Reveal Codes screen.

You can start a new page number sequence anywhere in your document. When you do so, you can specify whether numbers are printed as Arabic numerals (1, 2, 3), lowercase Roman numerals (i, ii, iii), or uppercase Roman numerals (I, II, III). You can use Roman numerals, for example, to number the table of contents and then start the body of the document with an Arabic 1 on the first page.

TURNING PAGE NUMBERS ON AND OFF

Page number settings, like all other WordPerfect formats, take effect at the position where you enter a code to change the setting. They remain in effect until the end of the document or until you enter another page number code. For example, after you turn on page numbers, you can turn them off farther down in the document.

KEY/Strokes

TURNING PAGE NUMBERS ON OR OFF

1. Move the cursor to the beginning of the page where page numbers are to be turned on or off
2. Either press **Shift-F8** and then press **2** for *Page*
   Or   pull down the Layout menu and select *Page*
3. Press **6** for *Page Numbering* to display the Page Numbering menu
4. Make any of the choices described in Table 11

TABLE 11   Page Numbering Menu Choices

1   *New Page Number* specifies the page number that is to be printed on the page in which the cursor is positioned and the style it is to be printed in. All subsequent pages are numbered in sequence beginning with the specified number. Type the new page number in the style you want to use And then press **Enter**. For example
• Type **1**, **2**, or **3** for Arabic
• Type **i**, **ii**, or **iii** for lowercase Roman
• Type **I**, **II**, or **III** for uppercase Roman

2   *Page Number Style* allows you to combine the page numbers with text, for example, *Page 1 of 5*, *Page: 1*, *Page 1 of Chapter 1*. To do so, you enter text with the *^B* code (press **Ctrl-B** to enter it). To combine with text, for example to print **Page: #,** type **Page:**, press **Spacebar**, and then press **Ctrl-B**.

3   *Insert Page Number* inserts the *^B* code into the document at the cursor's position using the format specified in *2 Page Number Style*. You can also enter the code by pressing **Ctrl-B**. When the document is printed, this *^B* code is replaced with a page number. You can enter this code anywhere in the document and in headers, footers, footnotes, and endnotes.

4   *Page Number Position* specifies the position in which page numbers are printed or no page numbering (Figure 48).

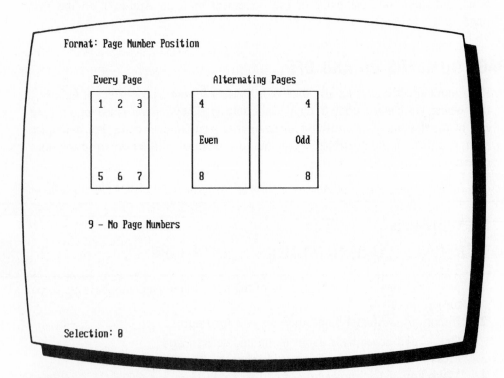

FIGURE 48   The Page Number Position Menu.   The Page Number Position menu illustrates your page number position choices. For example, selecting **1** prints page numbers in the upper left-hand corner of every page. Selecting **4** prints them in the upper left-hand corner of even-numbered pages and the upper right-hand corner of odd-numbered pages.

SUPPRESSING PAGE NUMBERS

You can turn numbers on and off anywhere in a document, but there is a special command you use to suppress them on single pages, like title pages or where illustrations will be inserted. For example, if your document has five pages and you suppress the page number on page 3, pages 1, 2, 4, and 5 are still numbered. You can then insert the page with the illustration following page 2.

KEY/Strokes

SUPPRESSING PAGE NUMBERS OR PRINTING THEM ON A SINGLE PAGE

1. Move the cursor to the beginning of the page where page numbers are to be suppressed or printed
2. Either press **Shift-F8** and then press **2** for *Page*
   Or   pull down the Layout menu and select *Page*
3. Press **8** for *Suppress (this page only)*
4. Either press **1** for *Suppress All Page Numbering, Headers and Footers*
   Or   press **3** for *Print Page Number at Bottom Center* and then press **Y** to print or **N** to not print
   Or   press **4** for *Suppress Page Numbering* and then press **Y** to suppress or **N** to print
5. Press **F7** to return to the document screen

▼TIPS

➤ **If you specify new page numbers anywhere in the document, those changes divide the document into sections**. To print selected pages when the prompt reads *Page(s): (All)*, see the box "Specifying Pages to Be Printed" in Topic 8.

➤ **If you change page numbers throughout a document**, the status line indicates the renumbered page sequence, not the consecutive page number beginning at the first page.

➤ **You can force an odd or even page number on a page**. When you do so, you move the cursor to the page and specify that it be odd or even. If necessary, the program then inserts a blank page in front of the page so that it prints as specified. For example, if you force an odd number on page 2, the page becomes page 3, and a blank page 2 is inserted when you print the document. To force an odd or even page break, move the cursor to the top of the page where you want the change to take effect, and then press **Shift-F8** to display the Format menu. Press **2** for *Page*, and then press **2** for *Force Odd/Even Page*. Press **1** for *Odd* or **2** for *Even*, and then press **F7** to return to the document screen.

▼TUTORIAL

TUTORIAL 11A   Specifying Page Numbers

In this tutorial, you add page numbers to a document. To begin this tutorial, you must first load the program. You should insert your data disk into one of the disk drives and make that drive the default. If necessary, clear any existing document from the screen.

Step 1   **Retrieve the PAGES Document.** Insert the disk you saved the PAGES.WP5 document on into one of the disk drives, and then retrieve the document.

Step 2 **Turn Page Numbers On.** Turn page numbers on by entering a code at the top of the document.

To turn page numbers on

Press   **Home** three times, and then press ↑ to move the cursor to the beginning of the document above all codes

Press   **Shift-F8** to display the Format menu

Press   **2** for *Page* to display the Page Format menu

Press   **6** for *Page Numbering* to display the Page Numbering menu

Press   **4** for *Page Number Position No page number* to display an illustration of page numbering options (Figure 48)

Press   **6** to enter page numbers at the bottom center of the page

Press   **F7** to return to the document screen

Result: No change is seen on the screen, but a page number code has been entered.

Step 3 **Start New Page Numbers.** Now let's specify that page numbers be printed in lowercase Roman on page 1 and in Arabic on page 2.

To start a new Roman page number

Press   **Alt-F3** to reveal codes

Move   the cursor to the right of the *[Pg Numbering:Bottom Center]* code on page 1

Press   **Shift-F8** to display the Format menu

Press   **2** for *Page* to display the Page Format menu

Press   **6** for *Page Numbering* to display the Page Numbering menu

Press   **1** for *New Page Number*

Type   **i** and then press **Enter**

Press   **F7** to return to the document screen

To start a new Arabic page number

Move   the cursor to the beginning of the line on page 2 following the hard page break *[HPg]* code

Press   **Shift-F8** to display the Format menu

Press   **2** for *Page* to display the Page Format menu

Press   **6** for *Page Numbering* to display the Page Numbering menu

Press   **1** for *New Page Number*

Type   **2** and then press **Enter**

Press   **F7** to return to the document screen

Result: The document now has codes for the page numbers and styles that you specified. Press **Alt-F3** to return to the document screen.

Step 4 **Save the Document.** Now that you have finished the document, save it so that you can retrieve it later.

Step 5 **Print the Document.** Be sure that the printer is on and has paper in it and that the paper is aligned. Then make a printout of the document. The document is printed on two pages. Page 1 is numbered at the bottom center with a Roman i, and page 2 is numbered in the same position with an Arabic 2.

Step 6 **Continue or Exit.** You have now completed this tutorial. You may either continue with your own work or exit WordPerfect and return to the operating system. If you are quitting for the day, remove your program and data disks, and then turn off the computer.

▼EXERCISE

EXERCISE 11A   Add Page Numbers to the RIGHTS Document

Retrieve the RIGHTS.WP5 document that you created in Exercise 6B.

1. Add page numbers so that they print at the bottom center of each page in uppercase Roman numerals.
2. Print the document.
3. Suppress the page numbers on page 1.
4. Save and then print the document.

▼QUESTIONS

1. Does WordPerfect normally print page numbers on each page of a document?
2. List and describe at least two options available for page numbering control.

You use tab stops to indent paragraphs or lists or to create tables with aligned columns. WordPerfect's tab stops are much like those on a typewriter. You can align text and numbers with these tab stops, indent text to them, or change them where needed. You can also display a ruler that indicates the positions of margins and tab stops (Figure 49). The indicators on the ruler change as you move through the document if you change tab stops or margins at any point. On the ruler, triangles (▲) indicate tab stops, brackets ([and]) indicate the left and right margins, and braces ({ and }) indicate a left or right margin and tab stop in the same position.

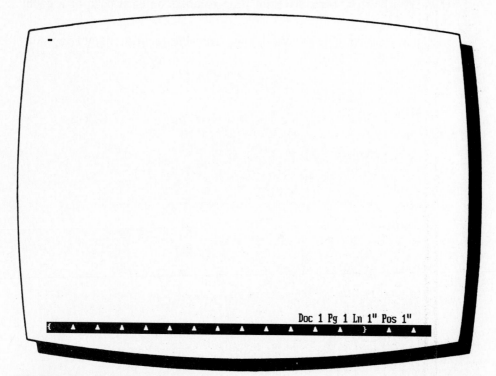

Doc 1 Pg 1 Ln 1" Pos 1"

FIGURE 49   The Ruler.   The ruler can be displayed to indicate tab stops (▲), left and right margins ([and]), and left or right margins that are in the same position as tab stops ({ and }).

Using tab stops to align text is critical. If you align text with the **Spacebar**, your document may print poorly (Figure 50). This is because many printers use proportionally spaced type, which means that each character occupies a different width-space. For example, the letter ''W'' takes up more space than the letter ''I.'' Columns that appear aligned on the screen are not aligned on a printout. If you use tab stops to align columns, they print correctly.

Item	Number	Price
Disks	200	5.95
Books	100	3.95
Cables	400	9.95

This table prints columns that are out of alignment because they were aligned with spaces rather than tabs.

Item	Number	Price
Disks	200	5.95
Books	100	3.95
Cables	400	9.95

This table prints correctly because tabs were used to align the columns.
FIGURE 50   Tabs.

KEY/Strokes
DISPLAYING AND REMOVING THE RULER

1. Either press **Ctrl-F3** and then press **1** for *Window*

   Or   pull down the Edit menu and select *Window*

   The prompt reads *Number of lines in this window:*
2. Either press ↑ once to display the ruler at the bottom of the screen. (Pressing it more than once divides the screen into two windows—see Topic 15.)

   Or   press ↓ to remove the ruler. (On most systems, the prompt should read *Number of lines in this window: 24*)
3. Press **Enter** to return to the document screen

ALIGNING TEXT WITH TAB STOPS

All tab stops are initially set every ½ inch, and text tabbed to these tab stops is left-aligned. You can align text or numbers with these tab stops as you enter the text or after you have entered it.

1. To align text with a tab stop as you enter the text, press **Tab** until the cursor is in the desired tab column, and then type the text. If you type enough text to reach past the right margin, the second and subsequent lines wrap back to and align with the left margin, not with the tab stop.
2. To align text with a tab stop after you have entered the text, position the cursor under the first character in the text to be aligned. When you then press **Tab** the cursor and all text to its right moves to the next tab stop. You must be in insert mode to do this. If you are in typeover mode, pressing **Tab** just moves the cursor through the text.

Tab Alignment Shortcuts

Although you can set decimal, center, and right-aligned tab stops, you can also align text using regular left-aligned tab stops.

- To align the decimal points in numbers like $10.95 with left-aligned tab stops, press **Ctrl-F6** instead of **Tab** to move the cursor to the tab stop. The status line then reads *Align char* = . Type the number and then press **Tab** or **Ctrl-F6** to move to the next tab stop, or press **Enter** to end the line.

- To center text on a left-aligned tab stop, press **Tab** to move the cursor to the tab, press **Shift-F6**, type the text, and then press **Tab** or **Shift-F6** to move to the next tab stop, or press **Enter** to end the line.
- You can right-align text with a left-aligned (or decimal) tab stop. To do so, press **Ctrl-F6** to move the cursor to the tab stop, and then type the text without entering an alignment character.

DECIMAL TABS AND ALIGNMENT CHARACTERS

Columns of numbers, including those containing decimal points, can be aligned with decimal tab stops (Figure 51). WordPerfect's default setting is to align decimal points (periods), but you can change the alignment character to any character on the keyboard including spaces. This is very useful when you want to align columns based on commas (,), pound signs (#), dollar signs ($), or a letter. For example, this is useful when you are writing to a country like France that uses commas where we use decimal points, and vice versa. Whereas we would write 1,000.50, in France they would write 1.000,50. To align numbers with decimal tabs:

1. Position decimal tab stops in the desired columns (see ''Setting Tab Stops'' in this topic).
2. Press **Tab** to move the cursor to the decimal tab position, and the status line reads *Align char* = . to indicate that you are in a decimal tab column.
3. Enter the part of the number preceding the decimal point. As you do so, the numbers you enter move to the left while the cursor remains in the decimal tab column.
4. Enter a decimal point using the period key (or other alignment character that you have specified).
5. Type the numbers that follow the decimal point. As you do so, the decimal remains fixed in place, and all numbers are entered to the right of it.

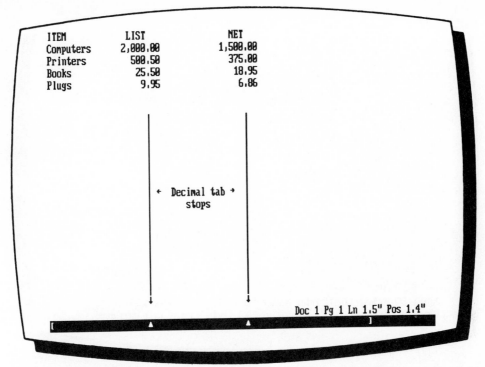

FIGURE 51   Decimal Tabs.   Numbers with decimals can be aligned with decimal tab stops so that all the decimals are aligned in the same column.

KEY/Strokes

CHANGING THE ALIGNMENT CHARACTER

1. Move the cursor to where you want the alignment character to change
2. Either press **Shift-F8** and then press **4** for *Other*

   Or   pull down the Layout menu and select *Other*
3. Press **3** for *Decimal/Align Character*
4. Enter the new alignment character using any key on the keyboard, including a space (the default is the period), and then press **Enter** twice
5. Press **F7** to return to the document screen

SETTING TAB STOPS

You can set up to 40 tab stops in a document and set them anywhere up to 54½ inches from the left edge of the page. The tab stops you enter remain in effect until the end of the document or until you enter another tab setting code below them. To change tab stops, you display the Tab Settings screen (Figure 52). With this screen displayed, you have a number of options.

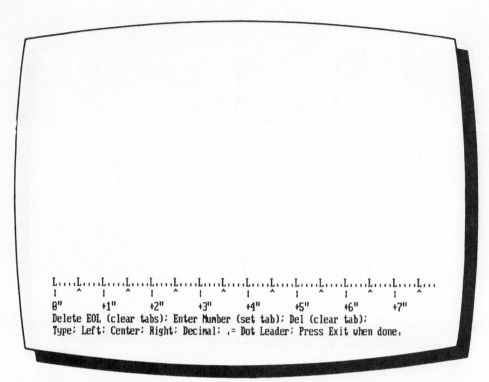

```
L....L....L....L....L....L....L....L....L....L....L....L....L....L....L....L....L...
  !    ^    !    ^    !    ^    !    ^    !    ^    !    ^    !    ^    !    ^    !    ^
  0"      +1"      +2"      +3"      +4"      +5"      +6"      +7"
Delete EOL (clear tabs); Enter Number (set tab); Del (clear tab);
Type; Left; Center; Right; Decimal; ,= Dot Leader; Press Exit when done,
```

FIGURE 52   The Tab Settings Screen.   The Tab Settings screen displays the tab stops in effect at the cursor's position. The instructions at the bottom of the screen tell you how to delete and set new tab stops.

- You can press **T** and specify if tab stops are relative (the default) or absolute.
  - Relative tab stops shift if you change the left margin so that they always stay the same distance from the margin. For example, if you have a relative tab stop ½ inch from the left margin and then increase the left margin by ½ inch, the tab stop shift to the right ½ inch. When you are setting relative tabs, the *0″* indicator shows where the left margin is positioned.
  - Absolute tab stops are set relative to the left edge of the paper you print on, so they do not shift when you change the left margin. When you are setting absolute tabs, the *0″* indicator shows where the left edge of the page is positioned.
- You can move the cursor along the ruler line and enter tab stop codes. Enter an **L** for a left-aligned tab, a **C** for a centered tab, an **R** for a right-aligned tab, or a **D** for a decimal tab stop (Figure 53).

Left-aligned
Centered
Right-aligned
Doc 1 Pg 1 Ln 2.16" Pos 6.1"

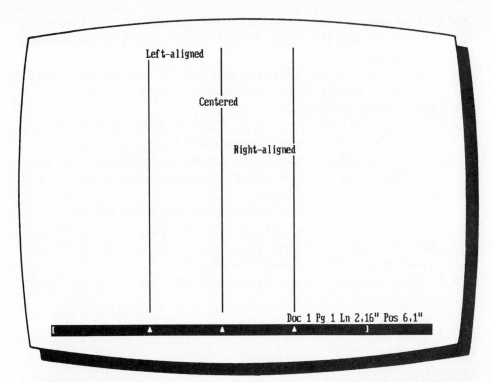

FIGURE 53 Tab Alignment. You can set tab stops so that text tabbed to them is left-aligned, right-aligned, or centered.

- You can highlight any tab stop code and press the period (.). This specifies that dot leaders be inserted whenever you press **Tab** to move the cursor to that tab stop in the document (Figure 54).

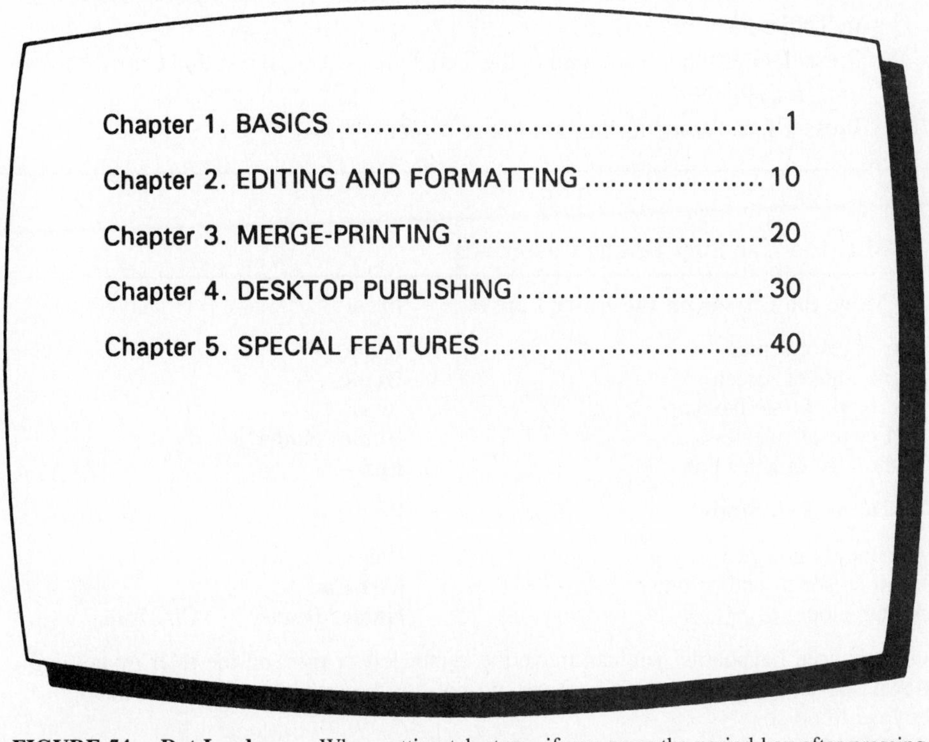

Chapter 1. BASICS 1
Chapter 2. EDITING AND FORMATTING 10
Chapter 3. MERGE-PRINTING 20
Chapter 4. DESKTOP PUBLISHING 30
Chapter 5. SPECIAL FEATURES 40

FIGURE 54 Dot Leaders. When setting tab stops, if you press the period key after pressing the letter **L**, **R**, or **C**, dot leaders are inserted whenever you press **Tab** to move the cursor to that tab stop in the document.

- You can move the cursor anywhere on the ruler line and press **Ctrl-End** to delete all tab stops to the cursor's right. This is helpful when you want to reset all tabs.
- To enter a single tab stop, type its position in inches, and then press **Enter**. If you enter a fractional tab stop position, like ½, enter it as **0.5**, and not **.5**, since a leading period indicates a dot leader.
- To enter tab stops at regular intervals, type the beginning position in inches, a comma, the interval in inches, and then press **Enter**. For example, type **1,1** and then press **Enter** to set tab stops every inch beginning at a left margin of 1 inch. The type of tab stop set with this command depends on the type of tab stop set in the beginning position.
  - If no tab is set there, this command enters left-aligned tabs (*L*).
  - To set another type, enter that type in the beginning position before using this command. For example, press **D** at 1 inch; then type **1,1** and press **Enter** to set decimal tab stops every 1 inch.
- To move a tab code, position the cursor under it, then hold down **Ctrl** and press → or ←.

KEY/Strokes
SETTING TAB STOPS

1. Move the cursor to where the new tab stops are to take effect
2. Either press **Shift-F8** and then press **1** for *Line*

   Or   pull down the Layout menu and select *Line*
3. Press **8** for *Tab Set* to display the Tab Settings screen (Figure 52)
4. Move the cursor to the desired position on the ruler, and then use the tab stop editing commands described in Table 12 to enter the tab stop codes described in Table 13

   Press **T** at any point to display the Tab Type menu, and press **1** for *Absolute* or **2** for *Relative*
5. Press **F7** to return to the document screen

TABLE 12   Tab Stop Editing Commands

To Move the Cursor on the Ruler Line to	Press
Left edge of screen	**Home**, ←
Right edge of screen	**Home**, →
Left or right one tab stop	↓ or ↑
Left edge of ruler line	**Home**, **Home**, ←
Right edge of ruler line	**End**
To Delete Tab Stops	**Press**
At cursor's position	**Del**
From cursor to end of line	**Ctrl-End**
All tab stops	**Home**, **Home**, ←, **Ctrl-End**

On enhanced keyboards, you can move the cursor left or right on the ruler by holding down **Alt** and press ← or →. However, do not use the arrow keys on the numeric keypad to do so.

TABLE 13   Tab Stop Codes

Alignment	Code
Text left-aligns	**L**
Text centers on tab stop	**C**
Text right-aligns	**R**
Text aligns with decimal or other specified alignment character	**D**
Text left-aligns (with dot leader)	**L** then . (period)
Text centers (with dot leader)	**C** then . (period)
Text right-aligns (with dot leader)	**R** then . (period)
Text aligns with decimal or other specified alignment character (with dot leader)	**D** then . (period)

▼**TIPS**

➤ **To align text with tab stops so that the alignment doesn't change if you change tab stop types, use hard tab codes.**
  - To enter a hard left-aligned tab code, press **Home, Tab**
  - To enter a hard centered tab code, press **Home, Shift-F6**
  - To enter a hard flush-right tab code, press **Home, Alt-F6**
  - To enter a hard decimal tab code, press **Ctrl-F6**

➤ **When aligning text in columns with the Tab key, you can change the distance between columns on the screen by changing the display pitch.** This is helpful if text overlaps on the screen where tabs, indents, and column margins have been entered. Changing the display pitch affects only the document on the screen. It does not affect printouts or other documents. To change the display pitch, press **Shift-F8** to display the Format menu. Press **3** for *Document*, and then press **1** for *Display Pitch*. Press **Y** to have the pitch adjusted automatically, or press **N** and then enter the pitch you want to use. Decreasing the pitch, for example, from .9″ to .7″, expands the lines horizontally; increasing it compresses them.

➤ **In typeover mode,** pressing **Tab** moves the cursor through the text in front of it without entering a tab code. In insert mode, pressing **Tab** inserts a tab code that moves the text in front of the cursor to the next tab stop.

▼**TUTORIAL**

TUTORIAL 12A   Using Tab Stops

In this tutorial, you change tab stops and then use them to align text and decimals. To begin this tutorial, you must first load the program. You should insert your data disk into one of the disk drives and make that drive the default. If necessary, clear any existing document from the screen.

Step 1   **Display the Ruler.** Begin by displaying the ruler so that you can get a better idea of what happens when you work with tab stops.

To display the ruler

Press   **Ctrl-F3** to display the Screen menu

Press   **1** for *Window*, and the prompt reads *Number of lines in this window: 24*

Press   ↑ once to display the ruler at the bottom of the screen

Press   **Enter** to return to the document

Result: The ruler is displayed at the bottom of the screen. Triangles (▲) indicate tab stops, brackets ([and]) indicate the left and right margins, and braces ({ and }), if any, indicate a left or right margin and tab stop in the same position.

Step 2   **Enter New Tab Stops.** The default tab stops are set every ½ inch, as the ruler shows. In this step, you change these tab stops.

To enter new tab stops

Press   **Home** twice and then press ↑ to move the cursor to the beginning of the document

Press   **Shift-F8** to display the Format menu

Press   **1** for *Line* to display the Line Format menu

Press   **8** for *Tab Set* to display the Tab Settings screen (Figure 52)

Press   **Home** twice and then press ← to move the cursor to the beginning of the line

Press   **Ctrl-End** to delete all tab stops

Press   → to move the cursor to *2"*

Press   **L** to enter a left-aligned tab stop

Press   → to move the cursor to *4"*

Press   **D** to enter a decimal tab stop

Press   → to move the cursor to *6"*

Press   **R** to enter a right-aligned tab stop

Press   **F7** twice to return to the document

Result: The new tab stops appear on the ruler at the bottom of the screen. Press **Alt-F3** to display the code that has changed the tab settings.

- Press ← to highlight *[Tab Set:Rel: +2", every 2"]* (the tab code may vary slightly depending on your program's initial font setting), and watch the ruler in the middle of the screen. The tabs to the left of (or above) the code are the original default tab stops.
- Press → to move the cursor to the right of the code, and watch the ruler. The tabs to the right of (or below) the code are the revised tab stops.
- Press **Alt-F3** to return to the document screen.
- Watch the ruler at the bottom of the screen while you press **Home** three times, and then press ↑ to move the cursor to the beginning of the document in front of all codes. The ruler shows tab stops every ½ inch.
- Now press → or ↓ to move the cursor to the right of the code. The ruler now displays the new tab stops.

Step 3   **Enter a Table.** Now that you have set tab stops, you can enter a table to see the way they work. When you enter the table, be sure that your cursor is to the right of the tab code so that the new tab settings are in effect on the ruler.

To enter the table

Type   **U.S. Prices** and then press **Enter**

Press   **Tab** to move the cursor to the first tab stop

Type   **Computer** and then press **Tab**. The status line reads *Align char* = . to indicate that the cursor is in a decimal tab column

As Figure 59 shows, you can indent paragraphs in many ways, and all indents are aligned with tab stops. To change the distance your text is indented from the left margin, change the tab stops (see "Setting Tab Stops" in Topic 12). The distance you indent is up to you, but the standard text indent is ½ inch.

- To indent the first line of a paragraph, move the cursor to the beginning of the first line, and then press **Tab**.
- To indent an entire paragraph, move the cursor to the beginning of the paragraph, and then press **F4** to indent it from the left margin or press **Shift-F4** to indent it from both margins. Each time you press these keys, the paragraph is indented one tab stop. When indenting existing text, the indent affects all text up to the next hard carriage return (press ↓ to realign the paragraph). If you do this with new text, all text that you enter is affected until you press **Enter**. This automatically ends the indent and returns the cursor to the left margin.

```
        When you indent paragraphs, you can indent just the first line
    or the entire paragraph. When indenting an entire paragraph, you
    can indent just the left side or both sides (called a double
    indent).

        When you indent paragraphs, you can indent just the first line
        or the entire paragraph. When indenting an entire paragraph,
        you can indent just the left side or both sides (called a
        double indent).

            When you indent paragraphs, you can indent
            just the first line or the entire paragraph.
            When indenting an entire paragraph, you can
            indent just the left side or both sides
            (called a double indent).

    1.  When you indent a paragraph, you can create a hanging indent
        by inserting an indent code in place of the space that follows
        the number.

    2.  This line was indented as it was being entered. The number is
        left hanging and the rest of the paragraph aligns with the
        first tab stop.

                                                    Doc 1 Pg 1 Ln 1" Pos 1"
```

FIGURE 59   Indents.   Indents can take several forms. You can indent the first line of a paragraph. You can indent an entire paragraph from the left margin. You can create double indents to indent a paragraph from both the left and right margins. You can create a hanging indent (also called a reverse indent or an outdent).

ENTERING HANGING INDENTS

One of the major applications of hanging indents is for numbered lists, called enumerations. There is more than one way to enter hanging indents in lists like these.

Hanging indents are especially useful when you are preparing numbered outlines or lists (Figure 60). The numbers in the list stand off by themselves, but the text following them is indented and aligned. When creating enumerations, the size of the largest number should be used to determine the amount of indent.

```
                          WRONG

  1.  The paragraphs in this list all have their own indent settings,
      so the list appears out of alignment.
  10.  The paragraphs in this list all have their own indent
      settings, so the list appears out of alignment.
  100.  The paragraphs in this list all have their own indent
      settings, so the list appears out of alignment.
  1000.  The paragraphs in this list all have their own indent
      settings, so the list appears out of alignment.

                          RIGHT

     1.  The paragraphs in this list have been indented based on the
         largest number in the list, so they look aligned.
    10.  The paragraphs in this list have been indented based on the
         largest number in the list, so they look aligned.
   100.  The paragraphs in this list have been indented based on the
         largest number in the list, so they look aligned.
  1000.  The paragraphs in this list have been indented based on the
         largest number in the list, so they look aligned.


                                            Doc 1 Pg 1 Ln 1" Pos 1"
```

FIGURE 60   Hanging Indents.   When you use hanging indents to create enumerations, the largest number you use determines the amount of the indent that you specify for all entries. Set the tab stop to a position so that there is room for the largest number followed by a period and one or more spaces. You can also set decimal tab stops to align the periods that follow the numbers.

To Create a Hanging Indent in New Text

There are two procedures you can use to enter a hanging indent as you enter text:

- Type the text to be left hanging; for example, type **1**, and then press **F4** to insert an indent code. Type the rest of the paragraph, and then press **Enter** to return the cursor to the left margin and end indenting.
- Press **F4** to move the cursor to the desired tab stop, and then press **Shift-Tab** to move the cursor back to the left margin. Type the text to be left hanging, press **Tab**, type the rest of the paragraph, and then press **Enter**. Pressing **Enter** moves the cursor to the left margin and end indenting.

To Create a Hanging Indent in Existing Text

Move the cursor to the place in the first line where you want text to begin indenting, press **F4** to insert an indent code, and then press ↓ to re-form the rest of the paragraph.

To Create a Hanging Indent with Margin Release

When words wrap or when you press **Enter**, the cursor always returns to the left margin. To enter text to the left of the left margin, you use the *Margin Release* command. To use this command, move the cursor to the left margin on the line you want entered or moved to the left of the left margin. Press **Shift-Tab** to move the cursor to the next tab stop to its left. Each time you press this command, the cursor moves one more tab stop to the left until it reaches the last tab stop. If you are entering new text, type it in, and then press **Enter** at the end of the line or paragraph. To control the distance the text moves to the left of the left margin, change the tab stop settings. Tab stops to the left of the 0″ on the Tab Settings screen are to the left of the left margin.

Creating Indents

- To indent the first line of a paragraph, move the cursor to the beginning of the first line, and then press **Tab**.
- To indent an entire paragraph, move the cursor to the beginning of the paragraph, and then press **F4**.
- To double-indent a paragraph, move the cursor to the beginning of the paragraph, and then press **Shift-F4**.
- To enter a hanging indent:
  - Type the text to be left hanging, for example, type **1**, and then press **F4** to insert an indent code. Type the rest of the paragraph, and then press **Enter** to return the cursor to the left margin and end indenting.
  - Press **F4** to move the cursor to the desired tab stop, and then press **Shift-Tab** to move the cursor back to the left margin. Type the text to be left hanging, and then press **Tab.** Type the rest of the paragraph, and then press **Enter** to move the cursor to the left margin and end indenting.
- To enter text to the left of the left margin, move the cursor to the left margin on the line you want entered or moved to the left of the left margin. Press **Shift-Tab** to move the cursor to the next tab stop to its left.

▼**TUTORIAL**

TUTORIAL 13A   Indenting Paragraphs

In this tutorial, you indent text. To begin this tutorial, you must first load the program. You should insert your data disk into one of the disk drives and make that drive the default. If necessary, clear any existing document from the screen.

Step 1   **Enter the Document.** Enter the document shown in Figure 61. Remember to press **Enter** twice at the end of paragraphs to insert a blank line between the paragraphs.

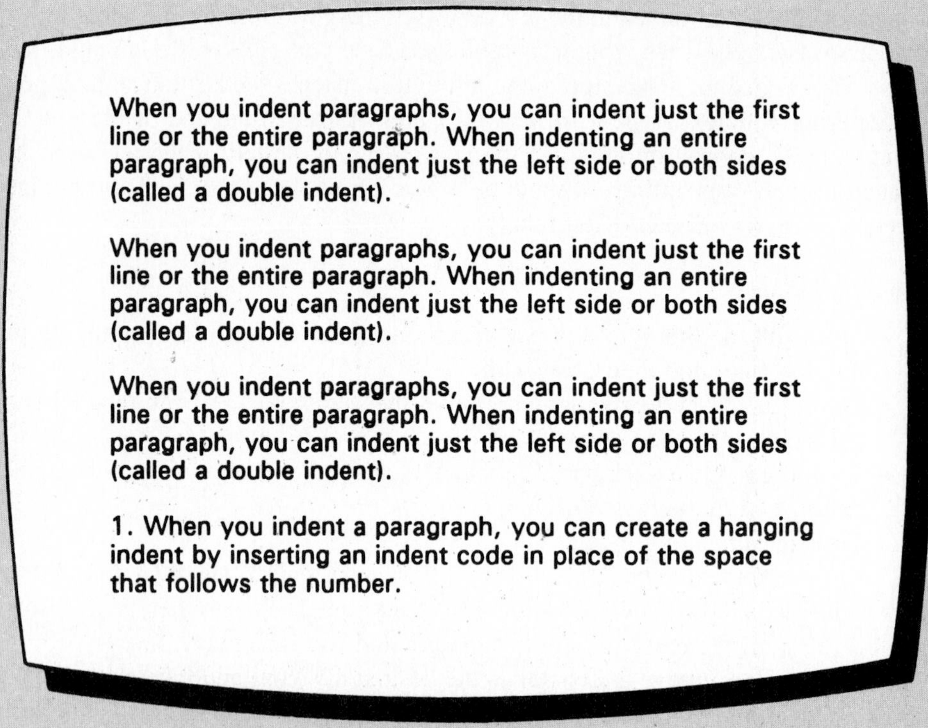

When you indent paragraphs, you can indent just the first line or the entire paragraph. When indenting an entire paragraph, you can indent just the left side or both sides (called a double indent).

When you indent paragraphs, you can indent just the first line or the entire paragraph. When indenting an entire paragraph, you can indent just the left side or both sides (called a double indent).

When you indent paragraphs, you can indent just the first line or the entire paragraph. When indenting an entire paragraph, you can indent just the left side or both sides (called a double indent).

1. When you indent a paragraph, you can create a hanging indent by inserting an indent code in place of the space that follows the number.

FIGURE 61   The INDENTS Document.   You enter this document in this tutorial.

Step 2 **Indent the First Line of a Paragraph.** Many documents have the first line of text in each paragraph indented ½ inch.

To indent the first line of a paragraph
Move   the cursor to the beginning of the first paragraph
Press   **Tab** to move the cursor to the desired tab stop
Press   ↓ to reform the existing text

Result: The first line of the paragraph is indented to the first tab stop.

Step 3 **Indent an Entire Paragraph.** You indent entire paragraphs to set them off from the main body of the text.

To indent an entire paragraph
Move   the cursor to the beginning of the second paragraph
Press   **F4** to move the cursor and the first line of the paragraph to the first tab stop
Press   ↓ to reform the existing text

Result: All lines in the paragraph are indented ½ inch from the left margin.

Step 4 **Double-Indent a Paragraph.** You can also indent both sides of a paragraph.

To double-indent a paragraph
Move   the cursor to the beginning of the third paragraph
Press   **Shift-F4** twice to move the cursor and the first line of the paragraph to the second tab stop
Press   ↓ to reform the existing text

Result: Both sides of the paragraph are indented 1 inch.

Step 5 **Enter Hanging Indents.** You can enter hanging indents after you enter text or while you enter it.

To enter a hanging indent in existing text

Move	the cursor to the space following the period in the numbered item
Press	**Del** to delete the space
Press	**F4** to indent the paragraph
Press	↓ to reform the rest of the paragraph

To enter a hanging indent in new text

Press	**Home** twice and then press ↓ to move the cursor to the end of the document
Press	**Enter** to insert a blank line
Type	**2.** and then press **F4**
Type	**This line was indented as it was being entered. The number is left hanging, and the rest of the paragraph aligns with the first tab stop.**
Press	**Enter**

Result: Both paragraphs now have hanging indents.

Step 6   **Enter Text to the Left of the Left Margin.** To enter text to the left of the left margin, you use the Margin Release command. This command moves the cursor left, from tab stop to tab stop.

To enter text to the left of the left margin

Press	**Home** twice and then press ↓ to move the cursor to the end of the document
Press	**Enter** to insert a blank line
Press	**Shift-Tab** to move the cursor to the next tab stop to its left (each time you press this command, the cursor, as well as the line, moves one more tab stop to the left)
Type	**3.** and then press **F4** to enter an indent code
Type	**This is a hanging indent with the number entered to the left of the left margin. The remainder of the paragraph aligns flush with the left margin.**
Press	**Enter**

Result: The number and period are left hanging.

Step 7   **Save the Document.** Now that you have finished the document, save it under the filename INDENTS.WP5 so that you can retrieve it later.

Step 8   **Print the Document.** Be sure that the printer is on and has paper in it and that the paper is aligned. Then make a printout of the document.

Step 9   **Continue or Exit.** You have now completed this tutorial. You may either continue with your own work or exit WordPerfect and return to the operating system. If you are quitting for the day, remove your program and data disks, and then turn off the computer.

▼ EXERCISES

EXERCISE 13A   Enter a Document on Computer Abuse

Enter the document shown in Figure 62.

1. Indent the numbered paragraphs as shown. Press **Enter** twice after entering the last line of the document.
2. Change the paragraph indent from .5″ to .4″.

3. Save the file as ABUSE.WP5 and make a printout.

4. Indent the numbers to .3″, and then change the indent for the text to .8″.

5. Print and then save the revised document.

THE FIVE MOST COMMON TECHNIQUES USED TO
COMMIT COMPUTER-RELATED FRAUD AND ABUSE

Computer-related Fraud

1. Entering unauthorized information
2. Manipulating authorized input information
3. Manipulating or improperly using information files and records
4. Creating unauthorized files and records
5. Overriding internal controls

Computer-related Abuse

1. Stealing computer time, software, information, or equipment
2. Entering unauthorized information
3. Creating unauthorized information files and records
4. Developing computer programs for nonwork purposes
5. Manipulating or improperly using computer processing

FIGURE 62   The ABUSE Document.

EXERCISE 13B   Indent Paragraphs

Enter the document shown in Figure 63.

1. Indent the bulleted items, and print the document.

2. Change the tab stops so that the indents are only .3″ and not .5″. To do this, you must change the first tab stop that falls to the right of the left margin.

3. Save the document as CVRLTR2.WP5, and make a printout.

In many fields of work, writing a letter of application is the customary way to ask for a personal interview.

This is particularly true in the following cases:

- When the employer you wish to contact lives in another city or town

- As a cover letter when you are mailing resumes

- When you are answering an ad

The following guidelines may help you write a letter of application:

- Type neatly; using care in sentence structure, spelling, and punctuation.

- Use a good grade of letter-sized white bond paper.

- Address your letter to a specific person, if possible (use city directories or other sources).

- State exactly the kind of position you are seeking and why you are applying to a particular firm.

- Be clear, brief, and businesslike.

- Enclose a resume.

Letters of application will vary considerably depending on the circumstances in which they are used.

FIGURE 63   The CVRLTR2 Document.

▼ QUESTIONS

1. List and describe three ways to indent text.
2. What is a hanging indent? What is it used for? Describe three ways to create a hanging indent.
3. What command do you use to enter text to the left of the left margin?

If you are revising typewritten copy, at some point you will likely take a pair of scissors and some glue and reorganize your work by cutting and pasting. With WordPerfect, you do this electronically. Blocks of text are the sections you cut or copy from one place in a document and then paste in at another place. You can also select blocks to format, sort, spell-check, or print, as described in the appropriate topics in this text.

TYPES OF BLOCKS

A block of text can be a character, a word, a phrase, a sentence, a paragraph, a group of paragraphs, or an entire document.

Line Blocks

When working with blocks of text, you usually copy, move, or delete lines of text, called a line block (Figure 64). The block can begin or end anywhere in the lines.

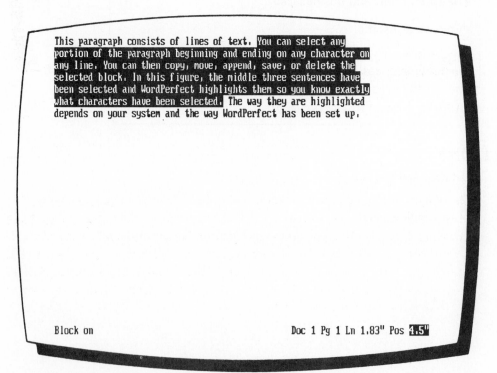

This paragraph consists of lines of text. You can select any portion of the paragraph beginning and ending on any character on any line. You can then copy, move, append, save, or delete the selected block. In this figure, the middle three sentences have been selected and WordPerfect highlights them so you know exactly what characters have been selected. The way they are highlighted depends on your system and the way WordPerfect has been set up.

Block on   Doc 1 Pg 1 Ln 1.83" Pos 4.5"

FIGURE 64   Line Block.   Line blocks can be characters, words, phrases, sentences, or paragraphs. A block can begin or end anywhere in the document.

Column Blocks

WordPerfect allows you to work with columns of text, called a column block (Figure 65). This feature is useful when revising or formatting tables or other text aligned in columns. For example, what if you want to reorganize a table by copying, moving, or deleting one of the columns? If the program works only with lines, you must painstakingly copy, move, or delete the entries in the selected column one line at a time. But with column mode, you can select a column and then copy, move, or delete it all at once. WordPerfect defines a column block as one or more columns separated from adjoining columns by codes for tabs, tab aligns, indents, or hard carriage returns (but not spaces).

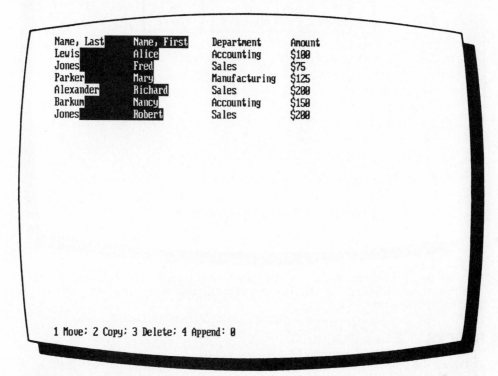

FIGURE 65   Column Block.   Using column mode, you can copy, move, or delete entire columns in one step. This figure shows the second column highlighted so that one of these operations can be performed on it.

Rectangular Blocks

Rectangular blocks are like column blocks, but they have no conditions; that is, you specify them by indicating an upper left-hand corner and a lower right-hand corner (Figure 66). You select this type of block when you copy or move parts of line drawings or formulas. When you delete or move a rectangular block, the remaining parts of the lines on either side of the rectangle close up individually like a column block. Thus deleting or moving a rectangular block from a paragraph of text turns it into nonsense. Each line reads correctly up to where the block was deleted or moved and then continues with the text that was on the same line on the other side of the deleted or moved block. It is much like tearing a lengthwise strip out of the middle of a page and pasting the two remaining halves together.

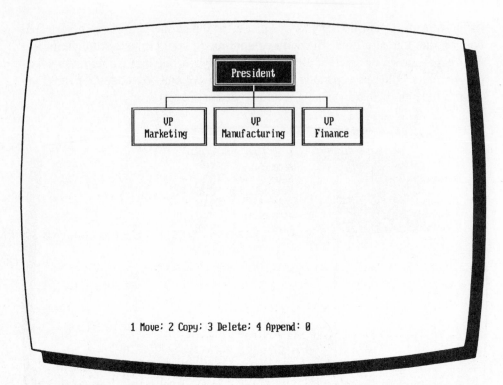

FIGURE 66   Rectangular Block.   A rectangular block is any portion of a document selected by specifying an upper left-hand corner and a lower right-hand corner. Here one part of the organization chart has been selected.

SELECTING BLOCKS

To work with blocks, you select them first. To do so, you can highlight them with the cursor movement keys. Usually, you move the cursor to the beginning of the block, turn on block mode, and then press cursor movement keys and execute block commands to highlight the block. When block is on, *Block on* flashes on the status line. A selected block appears highlighted so that it stands out from the text you have not selected. It may be in a different color or highlighted in ***reverse video*** (dark characters against a bright background). After selecting a block of text, you can copy, move, delete, save, or append it to the end of another file. You can also press **F1** to cancel the selection if you change your mind.

After selecting a block, you can change its size by pressing any of the cursor movement keys. Or, when the status line displays the message *Block on*, you can move the cursor with the following special commands:

- Type a character to highlight to the next occurrence of that character; for example, type a period to highlight to the end of the sentence.
- Press **Spacebar** to highlight the word and the trailing space.
- Press **Enter** to highlight up to the next hard carriage return.
- Use the Search command (**F2**) to expand the highlight to the specified string (see Topic 20).

When you select a block of text, any hidden codes in the block are also selected. Since you normally do not see these codes, you can encounter problems unless you reveal codes when selecting blocks in heavily formatted documents.

▼ Selecting Blocks with a Mouse

If you are using a mouse, you can use it to select a block.

1. Point to the beginning or end of the block.
2. Press the left button and drag the mouse to highlight the block, then release the button.

You can manipulate the block or change its size with any of the cursor movement keys or commands. To cancel the selection, click the middle button on a three-button mouse, or hold down either button on a two-button mouse and click the other button.

▼ Quick Copy and Quick Move

To copy a block quickly, select it, then press **Ctrl-Ins**. When the prompt reads *Move cursor; press Enter to retrieve*, move the cursor to where you want to insert a copy of the block, and then press **Enter**.

To move a block quickly, select it, then press **Ctrl-Del**. When the prompt reads *Move cursor; press Enter to retrieve*, move the cursor to where you want to insert the block, and then press **Enter**.

WORKING WITH SELECTED BLOCKS

After selecting a block, you can perform a number of functions on it.

- Copying a block leaves the existing block intact and inserts a copy in the new location. When you copy a line block, the text moves over and down to make room for the new copy. When you copy a column block into other columns, the columns to the right move over to make room for it.
- Moving a block deletes the block in the original position and then inserts it in the new location. When you move a line block, the block is moved to the new position and is deleted from the original position. All text closes up to fill the space the block was moved from. When you move a selected column, the columns originally arranged in one order are arranged in a different order.
- Deleting a block deletes the selected block from the screen but not from the computer's memory. When you delete a line block, all text closes up to fill the space the block was deleted from. When you delete a column block, all columns close up to fill the space the column was deleted from. The block is moved into a separate undelete buffer so that you can undo the deletion by pressing **F1**. The Delete command does not replace text in the copy and move buffer. For example, you can move a block, then delete a block, and then retrieve the first block if you want to.
- Appending a block copies it to the end of an already existing file on the disk. When appending a block, you specify the name of the file you want the block appended to. If the filename you enter does not exist, a file by that name is created. The block on the screen is not affected.
- Saving a block copies the selected block to its own file on the disk. You can retrieve the new file and edit it just like any other document file. It can also be retrieved into another position in the document you saved it from or into any other document. Moving blocks to their own files is often used to break

large documents into smaller, more manageable files. Working on smaller documents has several advantages:

- You can get around them more easily.
- You can save and retrieve them faster.
- You are less likely to run out of memory.
- You are less likely to lose your entire document if you make a catastrophic mistake.

    To save a selected block into its own file, select the block, press **F10,** and the prompt reads *Block name*: Type the name of the new file, and then press **Enter**.

- Printing a block sends the selected block to the printer. To print a selected block, press **Shift**-**F7** and the prompt reads *Print block? No (Yes)*. Press **Y** to print the block. The block is printed in the same position on the page as if it had been printed with the rest of the text on that page. If you select and print a block at the bottom of the page, it will print at the bottom of the page.

KEY/Strokes

MOVING, COPYING, DELETING, OR APPENDING A BLOCK

1. Begin by positioning the cursor
    - If selecting a line block, move the cursor to the first character to be included in the block
    - If selecting a column block, move the cursor to under any character in the first line in the desired column
    - If selecting a rectangle, move the cursor to the upper left-hand corner of the block
2. Press **Alt-F4** or **F12** to enter block mode, and the status line flashes *Block on*
3. Highlight the block
    - To select a line block, use the cursor movement keys to highlight the block, or use the special commands described in the box ''Selecting Blocks''
    - To select a column block, position the cursor anywhere on the last line of the desired column
    - To select a rectangle block, move the cursor to the lower right-hand corner of the block
4. Press **Ctrl-F4** to display the Move menu and make one of the choices described in Table 14
5. Make any of the choices listed on the Move submenu, and then take the action suggested in Table 15

TABLE 14   The Move Menu for Selected Blocks

Choices	Description
1	*Block* selects the highlighted block
2	*Tabular Column* selects the column positioned between tabs on the selected lines
3	*Rectangle* selects the block indicated by the starting and ending position of the highlight

TABLE 15   The Move Submenu

Choices	Description
1	*Move* displays the prompt *Move cursor; press Enter to retrieve.* Move the cursor to where you want the block moved, and then press **Enter**. If you are moving a column block, move the cursor to the first line of the column you want to move the column to, and then press **Enter**.
2	*Copy* displays the prompt *Move cursor; press Enter to retrieve.* Move the cursor to where you want the block moved, and then press **Enter**. If you are copying a column block, move the cursor to the first line of the column you want to copy the column to, and then press **Enter**.
3	*Delete* deletes the block. (You can also delete a block by selecting it and then pressing **Del**.)
4	*Append* displays the prompt *Append to:* if you selected **1** for *Block* in the previous step. Type the name of the file you want to append the block to, and then press **Enter**.

WORKING WITH PREDEFINED BLOCKS

If you press **Ctrl-F4** without first selecting a block of text, a second version of the Move menu is displayed. This menu provides choices that allow you to move, copy, or delete sentences, paragraphs, and pages—the most frequent line blocks.

- A sentence begins with a capital letter and ends with a period (.), question mark (?), or exclamation point (!) followed by up to three spaces.
- A paragraph begins and ends with a hard carriage return code *[HRt]*.
- A page ends with a hard or soft page break code, *[HPg]* or *[SPg]*. Hard page break codes are moved or copied along with the rest of the page.

KEY/Strokes

MOVING, COPYING, DELETING, OR APPENDING A PREDEFINED BLOCK

1. Move the cursor to anywhere in the sentence, paragraph, or page
2. Press **Ctrl-F4** to display the Move menu
3. Make one of the choices described in Table 16, and the Move submenu is displayed
4. Make any of the choices listed on the Move submenu, and then take the action suggested in Table 15

Press	**Ctrl-F4** to display the Move menu
Press	**2** for *Tabular Column*, and the menu reads *1 Move; 2 Copy; 3 Delete; 4 Append:*
Press	**1** for *Move*, and the prompt reads *Move cursor; press Enter to retrieve*
Press	**Home** twice press ↑ , and then press **End** to move the cursor to the right of the number *300* in the first row
Press	**Enter** to copy the column from the buffer

Result: When you move the column into the buffer, the column is deleted, and all other columns move over to fill the space. When you then copy it back in from the buffer, it appears as the rightmost column in the table.

Step 3   **Copy a Column.** When you copy or move columns, you also include the tab code that you originally inserted to align the columns. In this step, you select the column of numbers 200, 500, and 800, and the tab codes to their left.

To copy a column

Move	the cursor to under any digit in the number *200* in the first row
Press	**Alt-F4** to turn block on, and the status line flashes *Block on*
Press	↓ and → as needed to expand the highlight over any character in the number *800* in the last row
Press	**Ctrl-F4** to display the Move menu
Press	**2** for *Tabular Column*, and the menu reads *1 Move; 2 Copy; 3 Delete; 4 Append:*
Press	**2** for *Copy*, and the prompt reads *Move cursor; press Enter to retrieve*
Move	the cursor to the *3* in the number *300* in the first row
Press	**Enter** to copy the column from the buffer

Result: The first column is now copied so that there are two identical columns side by side. The other columns moved to the right to make room for the copied column.

Step 4   **Copy a Line.** You can also copy lines, just as you copied columns of text.

To copy a line

Move	the cursor to the line labeled *A*
Press	**Home** and then press ← to move the cursor to the beginning of the line
Press	**Alt-F4** to turn block on, and the status line flashes *Block on*
Press	**End** to highlight the entire line
Press	**Ctrl-F4** to display the Move menu
Press	**1** for *Block*, and the menu reads *1 Move; 2 Copy; 3 Delete; 4 Append:*
Press	**2** for *Copy*, and the prompt reads *Move cursor; press Enter to retrieve*
Press	**Home** twice and then press ↓ to move the cursor to the end of the document
Press	**Home** and then press ← to move the cursor to the beginning of the line
Press	**Enter** to copy the block from the buffer

Result: The first line is now copied so that there are two identical lines, one at the top of the document and one at the bottom.

Step 5   **Delete a Block and Then Undo the Deletion.** Now delete two of the lines in the document, and then undo both deletions.

To delete the first block

Move	the cursor to the *A* line at the top of the screen
Press	**Home** and then press ← to move the cursor to the beginning of the line
Press	**Alt-F4** to turn block on, and the status line flashes *Block on*
Press	**End** to highlight the entire line
Press	**Del** and the prompt reads *Delete Block? No (Yes)*
Press	**Y** to delete the block

To delete the second block

Move	the cursor to the *B* line
Press	**Home** and then press ← to move the cursor to the beginning of the line
Press	**Alt-F4** to turn block on, and the status line flashes *Block on*
Press	**End** to highlight the entire line
Press	**Del** and the prompt reads *Delete Block? No (Yes)*
Press	**Y** to delete the block

To undo the last deletion

Move	the cursor to the beginning of the second blank row. (Text is restored at the cursor's position.)
Press	**F1** to display the Undelete menu and show the most recent deletion in reverse video
Press	**1** for *Restore*

To undo the first deletion

Press	**Home** twice and then press ↑ to move the cursor to the beginning of the document
Press	**F1** to display the Undelete menu and show the most recent deletion in reverse video
Press	**2** for *Previous Deletion* repeatedly to cycle through up to three previous deletions
Press	**1** for *Restore* to restore the desired deletion

Result: Both deleted blocks are restored, and the document is now as it was.

Step 6   **Work with Predefined Blocks.** WordPerfect has a shorthand approach to copying or moving sentences, paragraphs, and pages—the most frequent line blocks. A sentence ends with a period (.), question mark (?), or exclamation point (!); a paragraph ends with a hard carriage return; and a page ends with a hard or soft page break.

To copy a paragraph

Move	the cursor to anywhere in the last line of the document
Press	**Ctrl-F4** to display the Move menu
Press	**2** for *Paragraph*, and the entire line ending in a hard carriage return is highlighted
Press	**2** for *Copy*, and the prompt reads *Move cursor; press Enter to retrieve*
Press	**Home** twice and then press ↓ to move the cursor to the end of the document
Press	**Enter** to copy the block from the buffer

Result: The paragraph is copied at the end of the document. If it isn't in a row by itself, press **Enter**.

Step 7   **Save the Document.** Now that you have finished the document, save it under the filename BLOCKS.WP5 so that you can retrieve it later.

Step 8 **Print the Document.** Be sure that the printer is on and has paper in it and that the paper is aligned. Then make a printout of the document.

Step 9 **Continue or Exit.** You have now completed this tutorial. You may either continue with your own work or exit WordPerfect and return to the operating system. If you are quitting for the day, remove your program and data disks, and then turn off the computer.

TUTORIAL 14B Using Boldfacing and Underlining

In this tutorial, you boldface and underline text. To begin this tutorial, you must first load the program. You should insert your data disk into one of the disk drives and make that drive the default. If necessary, clear any existing document from the screen.

Step 1 **Enter the Document.** Enter the sentence in the following instruction.

To enter the document

Type	**You can boldface and underline text as you enter it or after you enter it.**
Press	**Enter**

Step 2 **Boldface Text.** Now boldface text that has already been entered.

To boldface existing text

Move	the cursor to under the *b* in *boldface*
Press	**Alt-F4** to turn block on, and the status line flashes *Block on*
Press	**Spacebar** once to highlight the word
Press	**F6** to boldface the word

Result: The word you boldfaced should stand out from the rest of the text. If not, adjust your screen's brightness and contrast. If that doesn't work, press **Alt-F3** to see the codes on either side of the words. Press the same keys to return to the document screen.

Step 3 **Underline Text.** Now underline text that has already been entered.

To underline existing text

Move	the cursor to under the *u* in *underline*
Press	**Alt-F4** to turn block on, and the status line flashes *Block on*
Press	**Spacebar** once to highlight the word
Press	← to position the cursor one space to the right of the letter *e* (so that you do not underline the space following the word)
Press	**F8** to underline the word

Result: The word you underlined should stand out from the rest of the text.

Step 4 **Boldface and Underline Text.** Now you both boldface and underline text.

To boldface and underline existing text

Move	the cursor to under the first *t* in *text*
Press	**Alt-F4** to turn block on, and the status line flashes *Block on*
Press	**t** four times to highlight the phrase *text as you enter it*
Press	**F6** to boldface the text
Press	**Alt-F4** to turn block on, and the status line flashes *Block on*
Press	**Ctrl-Home** twice to highlight the same block again
Press	**F8** to underline the text

Result: The words you boldfaced and underlined should stand out from the rest of the text.

Step 5 **Change the Type of Underlining.** You can specify whether the spaces between words are underlined or not when you use the underline format. Let's change the setting so that spaces are not underlined.

To change the kind of underline

Press **Home** twice then press ↑ to move the cursor to the top of the document

Press **Shift-F8** to display the Format menu

Press **4** for *Other* to display the Other Format menu

Press **7** for *Underline*, and the prompt reads *Spaces*

Press **N** for *No*, and the prompt reads *Tabs*

Press **N** for *No*

Press **F7** to return to the document screen

Result: If your screen displays underlining, spaces are no longer underlined. If not, you will see that they are not when you print out the document.

Step 6 **Save the Document.** Now that you have finished the document, save it under the filename BOLD2.WP5 so that you can retrieve it later.

Step 7 **Print the Document.** Be sure that the printer is on and has paper in it and that the paper is aligned. Then make a printout of the document. The words you boldfaced should be darker than the rest of the text, and the words you underlined should have a line under them. The spaces between the underlined words should not be underlined if your printer supports this option.

Step 8 **Continue or Exit.** You have now completed this tutorial. You may either continue with your own work or exit WordPerfect and return to the operating system. If you are quitting for the day, remove your program and data disks, and then turn off the computer.

▼**EXERCISES**

EXERCISE 14A Reorganize the RIGHTS Document

Retrieve the RIGHTS.WP5 document that you created in Exercise 6B.

1. Rearrange the paragraphs so that the clauses are in numerical order. Be sure to check the spacing between the clauses. There should be only one blank line between them.

2. Add the heading **BILL OF RIGHTS** to the top of the document; then center and boldface it.

3. Save the document under the same name.

4. Print the revised document.

EXERCISE 14B Save Bill of Rights Clauses in Their Own Files

Retrieve the RIGHTS.WP5 document that you reorganized in Exercise 14A.

1. Copy each of the ten amendments into its own file on the disk. Use the filenames A1.WP5, A2.WP5, A3.WP5, and so on.

2. Clear the screen without saving the document.

EXERCISE 14C Append a Block to the ABUSE Document

Append a paragraph to the ABUSE.WP5 document that you created in Exercise 13A. To begin, enter the paragraph shown in Figure 68.

1. Print the document.
2. Save the document as APPEND.WP5, but leave it on the screen.
3. Select the entire document, and then append it to the ABUSE.WP5 document.
4. Clear the screen, and then retrieve ABUSE.WP5.
5. Print the document, and then clear the screen without saving the document.

This paragraph was created and saved as APPEND.WP5. The paragraph was then selected and appended to the ABUSE.WP5 file on the disk.

FIGURE 68   The APPEND Document.

EXERCISE 14D Enter a Document with Columns

Enter the document shown in Figure 69. (Press **Tab** once or twice between entries to align them in columns.)

1. Save the document as COLUMN.WP5 and make a printout.
2. Move column B to the right of column C.
3. Copy column D to the right of column E.
4. Delete column D.
5. Print the document, and then clear the screen without saving the document.

A	B	C	D	E
1	2	3	4	5
6	7	8	9	10
11	12	13	14	15

FIGURE 69   The COLUMN Document.

▼QUESTIONS

1. What is a block of text? What kinds of blocks can you work with?
2. What is column mode? When would you use it?
3. What is a rectangular block? When would you select one?
4. What operations can you perform on blocks?
5. When selecting a block, what keys do you press to turn block on? List and describe three keys (other than the cursor movement keys) that you can press to expand the highlight.
6. What is the difference between moving and copying a block of text?
7. What are the advantages of being able to save a block to a file on the disk?

WordPerfect has two document screens that you use to display different documents so that you can compare, copy, or move text between them. You can switch back and forth between these two screens or display them both on the screen at the same time.

- When the two screens are displayed back to back, pressing **Shift-F3** switches you back and forth between them. The *Doc* indicator on the status line reads *Doc 1* or *Doc 2* to indicate which of the two documents is currently displayed.
- When you split the screen, it is split with a tab ruler (Figure 70). When the cursor is in the upper window, the triangles indicating tab stop positions point up; when the cursor is in the lower window, the triangles point down. Pressing **Shift-F3** moves the cursor back and forth between the two halves of the screen.

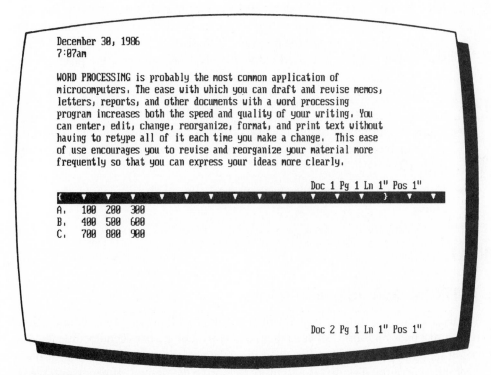

FIGURE 70　Windows.　You can use WordPerfect's two windows to display different documents. This makes it easy to compare documents or copy and move text from one document to another.

KEY/Strokes

DISPLAYING TWO DOCUMENTS ON THE SAME SCREEN

1. Either press **Ctrl-F3** and then **1** for *Window*

   Or   pull down the Edit menu and select *Window*

   The prompt reads *Number of lines in this window: 24*

2. Either type the number of lines (0 or any number greater than 23 returns you to full-screen display), and then press **Enter**

   Or   press ↑ and ↓ to move the tab ruler to the desired position, and then press **Enter**

3. Press **Shift-F3** to move the cursor between the windows

TIP

> ➤ **If you have a document on both windows,** when you exit from the first one, you are asked if you want to exit that document. If you answer Yes, the other document in the other window appears on the screen. You then have to exit that document to quit the program. If there is no document on the second screen, the window is closed automatically when you exit the program.

**SUMMARY**

> ➤ Windows allow you to display two different files so that you can compare, copy, or move text. To move the cursor between the windows, you press **Shift-F3**.

> ➤ You can display windows back to back or on the screen at the same time.

▼**TUTORIAL**

TUTORIAL 15A Using Windows

In this tutorial, you retrieve two documents onto WordPerfect's two screens. You then move back and forth between them and copy a block between documents. To begin this tutorial, you must first load the program. You should insert your data disk into one of the disk drives and make that drive the default. If necessary, clear any existing document from the screen.

Step 1   **Retrieve the Document.** Insert the disk on which you saved the ENTER2.WP5 document into one of the disk drives, and then retrieve the document.

Step 2   **Switch Screens.** Now switch to the other screen.

To switch screens

   Press   **Shift-F3** to switch to the other screen

Result: The other document screen appears, and the status line reads *Doc 2.* The screen is blank at the moment.

Step 3   **Retrieve the BLOCKS Document.** Retrieve the file named BLOCKS.WP5.

Step 4 **Switch Back and Forth between Screens.** Now practice switching back and forth between the two screens. To do so, press **Shift-F3**. When you are finished, be sure the status line reads *Doc 2*.

Step 5 **Copy a Block between Windows.** Now copy a block from the document on screen 2 to the document on screen 1.

To copy a block

Move	the cursor to the first character in any line
Press	**Home**, ← to move the cursor to the beginning of the line
Press	**Alt-F4** to turn block on, and the status line flashes *Block on*
Press	**Enter** to highlight the entire line
Press	**Ctrl-F4** to display the Move menu
Press	**1** for *Block*
Press	**2** for *Copy*, and the prompt reads *Move cursor; press Enter to retrieve*
Press	**Shift-F3** to display the other screen, and the status line reads *Doc 1*
Press	**Home** twice and then ↓ to move the cursor to the end of the document
Press	**Enter** to copy the block

Result: The block is copied from one document to the other.

Step 6 **Display Both Windows on the Same Screen.** You do not have to display the two screens back to back. You can also display them on the same screen so that you can see both documents at the same time.

To display two documents on the same screen

Press	**Ctrl-F3** to display the Screen menu
Press	**1** for *Window*, and the prompt reads *Number of lines in this window: 24*
Press	↑ until the prompt reads *Number of lines in this window: 12*, and then press **Enter**

Result: The two documents are now displayed on the same screen (Figure 70). Press **Shift-F3** to move the cursor between the windows. When you are finished, be sure the status line reads *Doc 1*. To return the display to a single screen, repeat the same commands you used to divide it, but press ↓ until the prompt reads *Number of lines in this window: 24*, and then press **Enter**.

Step 7 **Continue or Exit.** You have now completed this tutorial. Either continue on your own document or another tutorial, or exit WordPerfect and return to the operating system.

To clear both screens or exit without saving either document

Press	**F7** and the prompt reads *Save document? (Y/N) Yes*
Press	**N** and the prompt reads *Exit doc 1? (Y/N) No*
Press	**Y**
Press	**F7** and the prompt reads *Save document? (Y/N) Yes*
Press	**N** and the prompt reads *Exit WP? (Y/N) No*
Press	**Y** to quit the program, or press **N** to clear the screen and work on your own document

Result: If you did not exit the program, the document screen is now blank so that you can enter your own document. If you did exit the program, the command prompt is displayed on the screen. If you are quitting for the day, remove your program and data disks, and then turn off the computer.

▼EXERCISE

EXERCISE 15A   Use Both Document Screens

Retrieve documents that you have previously created onto both document screens.

1. Move blocks from one document to the other, and make a printout of the results.
2. Split the screen so that both documents are displayed at the same time.
3. Clear both screens without saving either document.

▼QUESTIONS

1. List and describe two advantages of being able to display two documents at the same time.
2. Describe two ways in which two documents can be displayed.
3. What command do you use to move between the two document screens?

The ways you could emphasize text on a word processing program were once limited to boldface, underline, italic, and pitch. Today, a much wider selection is available because of fonts. To use fonts successfully, all you have to understand is how you can change their appearance and size. (All font choices are listed on the Font pull-down menu shown in Figure 71.)

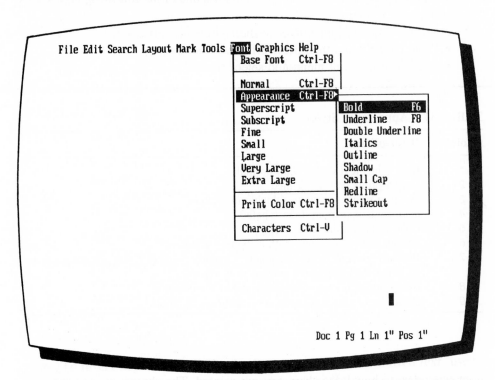

FIGURE 71   Font Appearances and Sizes.   You can assign font appearances and sizes by selecting the text and using the choices on the pull-down Font menu.

FONT APPEARANCE

Font appearance refers to the way the formatted text is printed (Figure 72). The choices range from underlining to boldfacing, and they are listed in Table 17.

Bold

<u>Underline</u>

<u>Double Underline</u>

Italic

SMALL CAPS

FIGURE 72   Font Appearance.   Fonts can be printed in a range of styles, including those shown here.

➤ **Some fully formed character printers stop when they encounter font change codes in a document** so that you can change print wheels. To resume printing after changing the print wheel, press **Shift-F7** to display the Print menu, press **4** for *Control Printer*, and then press **4** for *Go (start printer)* to resume printing. Press **F7** to return to the document screen.

▼ TUTORIALS

Note: The tutorials and exercises in this topic are printer-dependent. For example, if your printer does not support italic type, your italicized words may be underlined. You didn't make a mistake; it's just that printers without italics substitute underlining automatically. In other cases, changing fonts has no effect on the printout. This is because not all printers can change fonts when instructed to do so.

TUTORIAL 16A   Entering Superscripts and Subscripts

In this tutorial, you superscript and subscript characters. To begin this tutorial, you must first load the program. You should insert your data disk into one of the disk drives and make that drive the default. If necessary, clear any existing document from the screen.

Step 1   **Enter a Document.** Enter the document in Figure 74. Press **Enter** twice at the end of each line to insert a blank line.

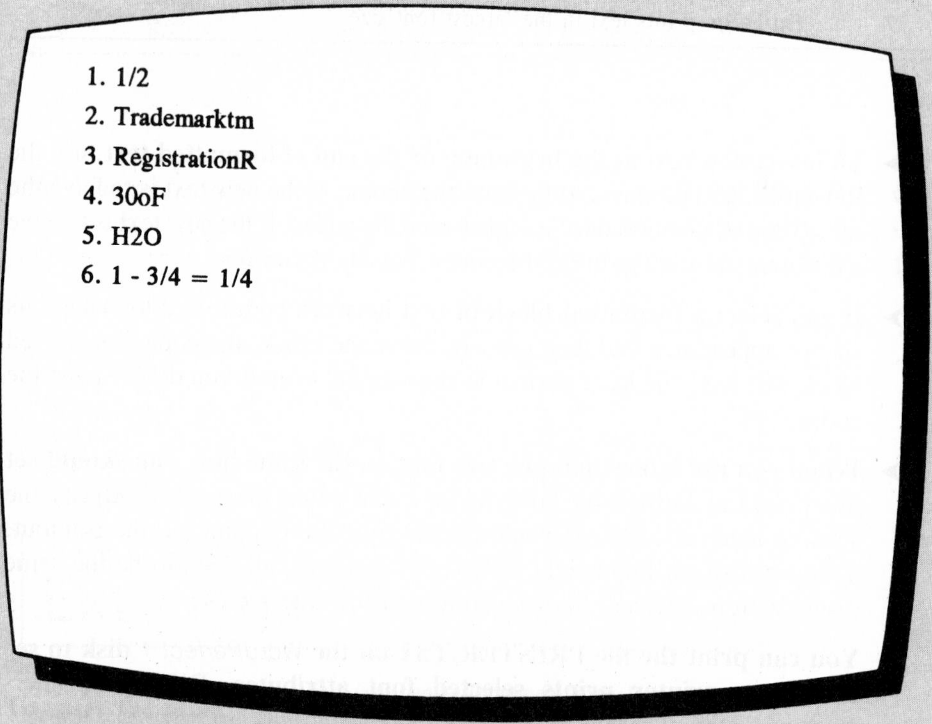

```
1. 1/2
2. Trademarktm
3. RegistrationR
4. 30oF
5. H2O
6. 1 - 3/4 = 1/4
```

FIGURE 74   The SCRIPTS Document.   You enter this document in this tutorial.

Step 2   **Superscript Characters.** Now select and superscript all characters that are to print above the line.

To superscript existing text

Move	the cursor to under the *1* in *1/2* on line 1
Press	**Alt-F4** or **F12** to turn block on, and the status line flashes *Block on*
Press	→ to highlight the number *1*
Press	**Ctrl-F8** to display the Font menu
Press	**1** for *Size*
Press	**1** for *Suprscpt*

Result: No change is seen on the screen (unless you have a color display), but as you move the cursor to the left, back under the *1*, the format may be indicated on the *Pos* indicator on the status line. Now select each of the other characters to be superscripted, and use the same command to superscript them. They are the *tm* at the end of line 2, the *R* at the end of line 3, the *o* following the 30 on line 4, and the *3* in *3/4* and the *1* in *1/4* on line 6.

Step 3 **Subscript Characters.** Now select and subscript all characters that are to print below the line.

To subscript existing text

Move	the cursor to under the *2* in *1/2* on line 1
Press	**Alt-F4** or **F12** to turn block on, and the status line flashes *Block on*
Press	→ to highlight the number *2*
Press	**Ctrl-F8** to display the Font menu
Press	**1** for *Size*
Press	**2** for *Subscpt*

Result: No change is seen on the screen but you will see the effects in your printout. Now select each of the other characters to be subscripted, and use the same command to subscript them. They are the *2* in *H2O* on line 5 and the two *4*s on line 6.

Step 4 **Save the Document.** Now that you have finished the document, save it under the filename SCRIPTS.WP5 so that you can retrieve it later.

Step 5 **Print the Document.** Now that you have completed the document, make a printout to see how it looks. Be sure that the printer is on and has paper in it and that the paper is aligned. Your printed document should look similar to the one in Figure 75.

1. $^1/_2$
2. Trademark^{tm}
3. Registration^R
4. 30°F
5. H$_2$O
6. 1 - $^3/_4$ = $^1/_4$

FIGURE 75   The Printed SCRIPTS Document.   When you print your SCRIPTS document, your results should be similar to these.

Step 6 Continue or Exit. You have now completed this tutorial. You may either continue with your own work or exit WordPerfect and return to the operating system. If you are quitting for the day, remove your program and data disks, and then turn off the computer.

TUTORIAL 16B   Changing Font Sizes and Appearance

In this tutorial, you change font appearances and sizes. To begin this tutorial, you must first load the program. You should insert your data disk into one of the disk drives and make that drive the default. If necessary, clear any existing document from the screen.

Step 1 Enter the Document. Enter the document shown in Figure 76.

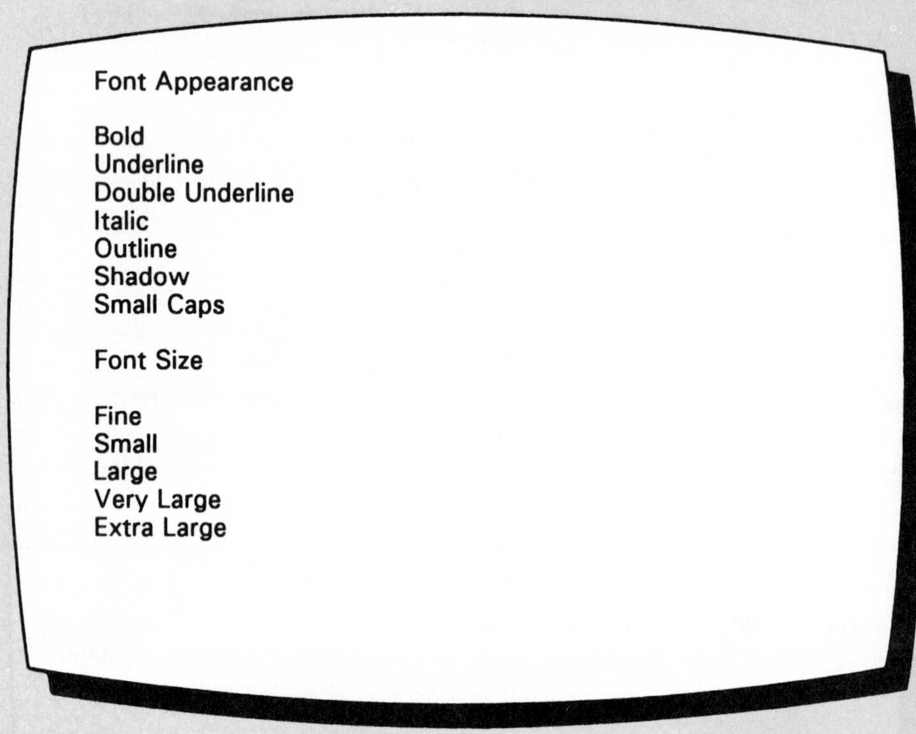

Font Appearance

Bold
Underline
Double Underline
Italic
Outline
Shadow
Small Caps

Font Size

Fine
Small
Large
Very Large
Extra Large

FIGURE 76   The FONTS Document.   You enter this document in this tutorial.

Step 2 Change Font Appearance. You boldfaced and underlined text in previous tutorials using the function keys. Here you format text with these formats and others using the Font Appearance menu.

To change font appearance

Move   the cursor to under the *B* in *Bold*

Press   **Alt-F4** or **F12** to turn block on, and the status line flashes *Block on*

Press   **End** to highlight the line

Press   **Ctrl-F8** to display the Font menu

Press   **2** for *Appearance*

Press   **1** for *Bold*

Result: The first word is now boldfaced. Repeat the same instructions to change the font appearance of the other terms using the appropriate menu command.

Step 3 **Change Font Size.** Besides changing the appearance of a font, you can change its size for selected text.

To change font size

Move the cursor to under the *F* in *Fine*

Press **Alt-F4** or **F12** to turn block on, and the status line flashes *Block on*

Press **End** to highlight the line

Press **Ctrl-F8** to display the Font menu

Press **1** for *Size*

Press **3** for *Fine*

Result: The first word is now formatted to be printed in the fine font size. Repeat the same instructions to change the font size of the other terms using the appropriate menu command.

Step 4 **Print the Document.** Be sure that the printer is on and has paper in it and that the paper is aligned. Then make a printout of the document. The results you obtain depend on what fonts are supported by your printer. If your text appears normal, your printer does not support the appearance or size you specified. Avoid those formats in later documents when using the same printer.

Step 5 **Save the Document.** Now that you have finished the document, save it under the filename FONTS.WP5 so that you can retrieve it later.

Step 6 **Continue or Exit.** You have now completed this tutorial. You may either continue with your own work or exit WordPerfect and return to the operating system. If you are quitting for the day, remove your program and data disks, and then turn off the computer.

EXERCISES

EXERCISE 16A   Format with Superscripts and Subscripts

Enter the document shown in Figure 77.

1. Subscript and superscript the appropriate characters in each fraction.
2. Superscript the registration symbol following WordPerfect.
3. Save the file as SUPERSUB.WP5 and then print the document.

---

1 + 1/2 = 1 1/2

WordPerfectR is a registered trademark of the
WordPerfect Corporation.

FIGURE 77   The SUPERSUB Document.

EXERCISE 16B   Enter a Document on Italics

Enter the document shown in Figure 78.

1. Italicize the same words as those shown in the figure.
2. Save the file under the name ITALIC.WP5 and then print the document.

Use *italics* in the following instances:

1. For a term being defined.

Spallation denotes a nuclear reaction induced by high-energy bombardment and involving the ejection of more than two or three particles.

Of a sinusoidal function, the *epoch angle* is the phase angle at the reference time $t = 0$.

2. For a term introduced by *called* or *known as*.

...is called the *quotient*.

...is known as *factoring*.

3. For emphasis of a word, a phrase, or a sentence. To maintain emphasis, use italics sparingly.

4. All letter symbols used in mathematical equations or used to designate angles, curves, coordinate points, and so forth are set in italics.

the curve *ABC*

the equations $x = 1$ and $z = 2 - w$

When the context is italic, letter symbols are also set in italic, but all numerals and all abbreviations are set in roman, for example, *Solve the equation for* 2*x* - 2*y*.

FIGURE 78   The ITALIC Document.

EXERCISE 16C   Boldface Headings in the CVRLTR1 Document

Retrieve the CVRLTR1.WP5 document that you created in Exercise 6A. It contains four headings, called run-in heads, that open the last four paragraphs. These headings are "Salutation," "Opening," "Body," and "Closing."

1. Boldface the run-in heads.
2. Save and then print the document.

EXERCISE 16D   Underline Headings in the COLUMN Document

Retrieve the COLUMN.WP5 document that you created in Exercise 14D.

1. Underline the letter headings at the top of the document.
2. Print the document.
3. Change the underlining style for tabs. If they were underlined in the first printout, turn them off. If they were not underlined, turn them on.
4. Save and then print the document.

▼ QUESTIONS

1. List and briefly describe three font appearances you can use.
2. Describe a superscript and a subscript.

Among the most useful features of word processing programs are those you use to align text within the margins. You have four choices when aligning text with the left and right margins (Figure 79): You can justify it so that it is flush or even with both margins, align it flush with the left margin, align it flush with the right margin, or center it between the margins.

WordPerfect's default setting is for justified text. Justified text aligns with both the left and right margins. If you turn justification off, text is left-aligned with a ragged right margin. You can also align text with the right margin so that the left margin is ragged, or you can center it between the margins.

(a)

WordPerfect's default setting is for justified text. Justified text aligns with both the left and right margins. If you turn justification off, text is left-aligned with a ragged right margin. You can also align text with the right margin so that the left margin is ragged, or you can center it between the margins.

(b)

WordPerfect's default setting is for justified text. Justified text aligns with both the left and right margins. If you turn justification off, text is left-aligned with a ragged right margin. You can also align text with the right margin so that the left margin is ragged, or you can center it between the margins.

(c)

WordPerfect's default setting is for justified text. Justified text aligns with both the left and right margins. If you turn justification off, text is left-aligned with a ragged right margin. You can also align text with the right margin so that the left margin is ragged, or you can center it between the margins.

(d)

FIGURE 79 Aligning Text with the Left and Right Margins. You can full-justify text (a), or align it left (b), right (c), or centered (d).

JUSTIFYING TEXT

WordPerfect has changed the meaning of a standard term that can cause confusion. To use both WordPerfect and other programs that use the term correctly, you should understand both uses. The term *justified text* universally means text that is aligned flush with both the left and right margins. To justify text so that it aligns with both margins, the program inserts spaces of varying width between words to expand the lines. WordPerfect has used this term to refer to codes that align text in four possible combinations: justified, flush left, flush right, and centered. They then use the term *full justification* to distinguish true justified text from the other three alignments.

- Text that is fully justified is aligned flush with both the left and right margins.

167

VERTICALLY CENTERED TEXT

WordPerfect has a command that centers text vertically on the page between the top and bottom margins (Figure 81). This command is useful when you are formatting title pages for documents. The effects of vertical alignment are seen only on the printout of the document or when using the View Document command on the Print menu; the effects are not displayed on the screen.

WordPerfect 5.1

Procedures Manual

Final Manuscript

April 6, 1992

FIGURE 81   Text Centered Vertically.   You can center text vertically on the page. This is useful when you are printing title pages for documents.

KEY/Strokes

CENTERING TEXT VERTICALLY ON THE PAGE

1. Move the cursor to the beginning of the page to be centered vertically (press **Ctrl-Home** and then ↑)
2. Either press **Shift-F8** and then **2** for *Page*
    Or   pull down the Layout menu and select *Page*
3. Press **1** for *Center Page (top to bottom)*
4. Press **1** to change *No* to *Yes*. (To change *Yes* back to *No*, you must delete the *[Center Pg]* code entered into the document when you changed it to *Yes*.)
5. Press **F7** to return to the document screen

▼ **TIPS**

➤ **You can right-align text with a left-aligned or decimal tab stop**. To do so, see the box ''Tab Alignment Shortcuts'' in Topic 12.

➤ **If you type text in front of a code that you entered to center or align text flush right, the text might not be displayed on the screen** (although it will print out). If this happens, press **Alt-F3** or **F11** to reveal codes and the missing text.

➤ **When using justified text**, hard spaces prevent the program from inserting unwanted soft spaces in formulas and computer commands. To enter a hard space, press **Home** and then press **Spacebar**.

▼ **TUTORIAL**

TUTORIAL 17A   Aligning Text with Margins

In this tutorial, you align text with the margins. To begin this tutorial, you must first load the program. You should insert your data disk into one of the disk drives and make that drive the default. If necessary, clear any existing document from the screen.

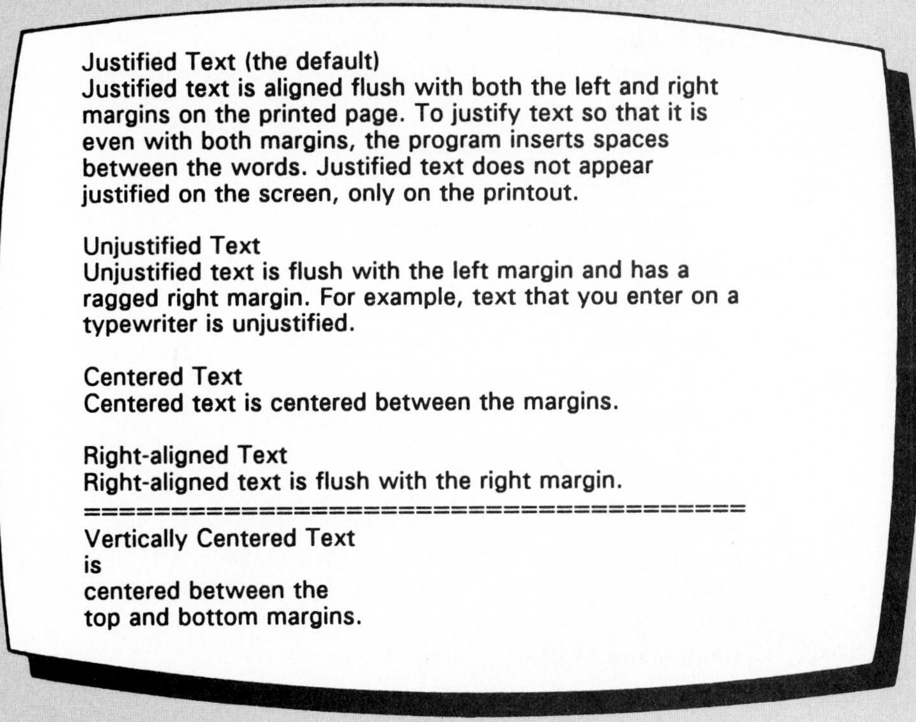

Justified Text (the default)
Justified text is aligned flush with both the left and right
margins on the printed page. To justify text so that it is
even with both margins, the program inserts spaces
between the words. Justified text does not appear
justified on the screen, only on the printout.

Unjustified Text
Unjustified text is flush with the left margin and has a
ragged right margin. For example, text that you enter on a
typewriter is unjustified.

Centered Text
Centered text is centered between the margins.

Right-aligned Text
Right-aligned text is flush with the right margin.
==
Vertically Centered Text
is
centered between the
top and bottom margins.

FIGURE 82   The ALIGN Document.   You enter this document in this tutorial.

Step 1   **Enter the Document**. Enter the document shown in Figure 82. Remember to press **Enter** once at the end of each line that does not reach the right margin (like the headings) and twice at the end of a paragraph to insert a blank line. The double-dashed line (=====) in the figure indicates a hard page break. Type the text above the hard page break, press **Ctrl-Enter** to enter the hard page break, and then type the four lines of text below it. Press **Enter** at the end of the last line.

Step 2   **Turn Justification Off.** The default setting is for fully justified text. Let's leave the first paragraph justified but turn justification off for the second paragraph so that it is flush left.

To turn full justification off

Move	the cursor to under the *U* in the heading *Unjustified Text*
Press	**Shift-F8** to display the Format menu
Press	**1** for *Line* to display the Line Format menu
Press	**3** for *Justification*
Press	**1** for *Left*
Press	**F7** to return to the document screen

Result: No change is obvious on the screen because justified text is not shown on the screen.

Step 3   **Horizontally Center Text.** Now center a line of text between the margins.

To center text between the margins

Move	the cursor to under the *C* in *Centered* in the sentence below the heading *Centered Text*
Press	**Shift-F6** to center the text
Press	↓ to align the line

Result: The line is now centered between the margins.

Step 4   **Right-align Text.** Now align a line of text with the right margin.

To right-align single lines of text

Move	the cursor to under the *R* in *Right* in the sentence below the heading *Right-aligned Text*
Press	**Alt-F6** to right-align the text
Press	↓ to align the line

Result: The line aligns with the right margin.

Step 5   **Center a Block of Text Vertically.** Now center text between the top and bottom margins. Since the block is simulating a title page, you also center it horizontally by selecting the entire block before executing the center command.

To center text vertically on the page

Press	**Ctrl-Home** and the prompt reads *Go to*
Type	**2** and then press **Enter** to move the cursor to the top of the second page
Press	**Shift-F8** to display the Format menu
Press	**2** for *Page* to display the Page Format menu
Press	**1** for *Center Page (top to bottom)* to center the text vertically
Press	**Y** for *Yes*
Press	**F7** to return to the document screen

To center a block of text horizontally

Move	the cursor to under the *V* in *Vertically* at the top of the second page
Press	**Alt-F4** or **F12** to turn block on, and the status line flashes *Block on*
Press	**Enter** four times to highlight the entire block. (If you did not press **Enter** at the end of the last line, press **End** to highlight the line.)
Press	**Shift-F6** and the prompt reads *[Just:Center]? No (Yes)*
Press	**Y** for *Yes*

Result: The block is centered horizontally and vertically, but vertical centering will be seen only when you print out the document.

Step 6   **Center Text on a Column.** You can center text on columns instead of between the margins.

To center new text in a column

Press	**Home** twice and then press ↓ to move the cursor to the end of the document
Press	**Enter** to insert a blank line
Press	**Ctrl-Enter** to insert a hard page break
Press	**Spacebar** until the status line reads *Pos 4″* (or as close to 4 inches as you can get on your system)
Press	**Shift-F6**
Type	**Centered in column** and then press **Enter** to end centering and return the cursor to the left margin

Result: The text is centered in the column 4 inches from the left margin.

Step 7   **Save the Document.** Now that you have finished the document, save it under the filename ALIGN.WP5 so that you can retrieve it later.

Step 8   **Print the Document.** Be sure that the printer is on and has paper in it and that the paper is aligned. Then make a printout of the document. The first paragraph is fully justified, the second has a ragged right margin, the third is centered, and the fourth is aligned with the right margin. On the second page, the text is centered both vertically and horizontally. On the third page, the line is centered on the specified column.

Step 9   **Continue or Exit.** You have now completed this tutorial. You may either continue with your own work or exit WordPerfect and return to the operating system. If you are quitting for the day, remove your program and data disks, and then turn off the computer.

▼EXERCISES

EXERCISE 17A   Center Headings on the RIGHTS Document

Retrieve the RIGHTS.WP5 document that you created in Exercise 6B.

1. Center the heading at the top of the document if it is not already centered.
2. Center the headings for each amendment.
3. Save and then print the document.
4. Left justify each amendment (but not the centered headings), and then print the document.
5. If you like the look of the unjustified version better than the justified one, save the document; otherwise, clear the screen without saving it.

EXERCISE 17B   Enter and Center a Poem

Enter the poem shown in Figure 83.

1. Center the poem both vertically and horizontally on the page.
2. Add the centered title THE NEW COLOSSUS to the top of the document, and then insert a blank line below the heading.

3. Specify an extra-large font size and a bold appearance for the heading.
4. Italicize the entire poem.
5. Boldface the poet's name.
6. Save the document under the filename POEM.WP5.
7. Print the document.

Not like the brazen giant of Greek fame,
With conquering limbs astride from land to land,
Here at our sea-washed, sunset gates shall stand
A mighty woman with a torch, whose flame
Is the imprisoned lightning, and her name
Mother of Exiles. From her beacon-hand
Glows world-wide welcome; her mild eyes command
The air-bridged harbor that twin cities frame.
"Keep, ancient lands, your storied pomp!" cries she
With silent lips. "Give me your tired, your poor,
Your huddled masses yearning to breathe free,
The wretched refuse of your teaming shore.
Send these, the homeless, tempest-tost to me,
I lift my lamp beside the golden door!"

Emma Lazarus

FIGURE 83   The POEM Document.

▼ QUESTIONS

1. List four ways in which you can align text, and give some examples of when you might want to use the alignments.
2. What does it normally mean to say that text is justified? In what four ways can you "justify" text with WordPerfect?
3. What is a ragged margin?

As you have seen, WordPerfect's default settings print a document single-spaced on 8½-by-11-inch paper with 1-inch margins. You can, however, change both the margins and the size of the paper that you print on.

CHANGING MARGINS

You can change margins at any point in a document by entering a margin code. The code is an open code, so it affects all text following it until the end of the document or another margin code. All margins are set in inches and are automatically retained regardless of the size of the font or paper that you use to print the document.

- Left and right margin settings determine where the first and last characters on a line are printed. The left and right margin settings determine the length of lines printed. On an 8½-by-11-inch sheet, if you set the left and right margins to 1 inch, the line length is 6½ inches (8½ minus 2).
- The top and bottom margins are measured from the top and bottom of the page and determine the space left blank above and below the first and last lines of text on a page.

KEY/Strokes

CHANGING THE LEFT AND RIGHT MARGINS

1. Move the cursor to where the new margins are to begin. (If it is not at the left margin, the program automatically inserts a hard return code, *[HRt]*, in front of the margin code.)
2. Either press **Shift-F8** and then **1** for *Line*

   Or   pull down the Layout menu and select *Line*
3. Press **7** for *Margins* and the prompt reads *Left*
4. Type the left margin setting in inches, and then press **Enter**. The prompt reads *Right*
5. Type the right margin setting in inches, and then press **Enter**
6. Press **F7** to return to the document screen

KEY/Strokes

CHANGING THE TOP AND BOTTOM MARGINS

1. Move the cursor to the top of the page where the new setting is to begin (press **Ctrl-Home** then ↑)
2. Either press **Shift-F8** and then **2** for *Page*

    Or   pull down the Layout menu and select *Page*
3. Press **5** for *Margins* and the prompt reads *Top*
4. Type the top margin setting in inches, press **Enter**, and the prompt reads *Bottom*
5. Type the bottom margin setting in inches, and then press **Enter**
6. Press **F7** to return to the document screen

PAGE SIZE AND TYPE

Occasionally you need to print on a paper that measures other than 8½ by 11. For example, you may need to print on legal-size paper, executive stationary, or forms. To do so, you enter a code in the document where you want the paper size or type to change. You select the desired paper size from a menu that lists a variety of forms. The forms that are listed are those that have been defined for the printer that you are using. When you select a paper size and type, the definition for that form tells the computer the size of the paper, where the paper is located in the printer, and how the paper is fed to the printer. If the form on which you want to print isn't listed, you can select *[ALL OTHERS]* from the list and then select a paper size from the list that appears. When you use the *[ALL OTHERS]* code, you can print without defining a form and the document can also be easily printed on other printers.

The form you select also affects the way the text is displayed on the screen and where page breaks fall. For example, if you select a wide form, your text is displayed wider than normal, so that you may have to scroll the screen sideways to edit the document.

KEY/Strokes

CHANGING PAPER SIZE AND TYPE

1. Move the cursor to where you want to change the paper size or type
2. Either press **Shift-F8** and then **2** for *Page*

    Or   pull down the Layout menu and select *Page*
3. Press **7** for *Paper Size* to display a list of paper sizes from which you can choose (Figure 84)
4. Highlight the desired size, and then press **1** for *Select*
5. Press **F7** to return to the document screen

```
Format: Paper Size/Type
                                                    Font  Double
Paper type and Orientation   Paper Size   Prompt Loc   Type  Sided  Labels

Envelope - Wide              9.5" x 4"     No   Manual  Land  No
Legal                        8.5" x 14"    No   Contin  Port  No
Legal - Wide                 14" x 8.5"    No   Contin  Land  No
Standard                     8.5" x 11"    No   Contin  Port  No
Standard                     8.5" x 11"    No   Contin  Port  No
Standard                     8.5" x 11"    No   Contin  Port  No
Standard - Wide              11" x 8.5"    No   Contin  Land  No
[ALL OTHERS]                 Width ≤ 8.5"  Yes  Manual        No




1 Select; 2 Add; 3 Copy; 4 Delete; 5 Edit; N Name Search: 1
```

FIGURE 84   Paper Sizes and Types.   The Paper Size/Type menu lists a number of forms on which you can print. (Your menu may vary because the list depends on the printer you are using.)

▼TIPS

➤ **If you change the top margin to print the first line below a letterhead**, be sure to reset it to its original position for the second and subsequent pages.

➤ **When entering margin settings you can enter fractions**. For example, to set a margin to 1½ inches, you can type **1.5** or **1 1/2**.

➤ **If you print a document so that it will be copied on both sides of the paper and bound**, you can change the gutter margin with the Binding command (see Topic 8).

▼TUTORIAL

TUTORIAL 18A   Changing Margins

In this tutorial, you change margins. To begin this tutorial, you must first load the program. You should insert your data disk into one of the disk drives and make that drive the default. If necessary, clear any existing document from the screen.

Step 1   **Enter a Document.** Enter the document shown in Figure 85. Remember to press **Enter** twice at the end of each paragraph to insert a blank line. The double-dashed line (= = = = =) across the figure indicates a hard page break. Type the text above the hard page break; then press **Enter** to end the paragraph. Press **Ctrl-Enter** to enter the hard page break, and then type the text below it.

This tutorial introduces you to page layout. It includes changing the left and right margins, line height, line spacing, and the top margin.

Left and right margins can be changed for the entire document or for selected sections. This paragraph has had its margins changed.

Line height can also be changed for the entire document or just sections. You can choose between Auto (the default) and Fixed. This paragraph has been printed at a fixed setting of .25".

Line spacing, like the other settings in this tutorial, can be changed for the entire document or just sections. This paragraph is printed double-spaced.

==

The top margin can be changed for the entire document or just for selected pages. The top margin on this page is changed from 1 inch (the default) to 2 inches.

FIGURE 85   The LAYOUT Document.   You enter this document in this tutorial.

Step 2 **Change the Left and Right Margins**. You can change margins for the entire document or just sections of it. Here, change the margins at the beginning of the second paragraph, and then restore them to their original settings at the end of the paragraph.

To change the left and right margins

Move	the cursor to under the *L* in *Left* at the beginning of the second paragraph
Press	**Shift-F8** to display the Format menu
Press	**1** for *Line* to display the Line Format menu
Press	**7** for *Margins* and the prompt reads *Left*
Type	**2** and then press **Enter**. The prompt reads *Right*
Type	**2** and then press **Enter**
Press	**F7** to return to the document screen
Press	↓ to reform the paragraph

To restore the left and right margins

Move	the cursor to the blank line between the second and third paragraphs
Press	**Shift-F8** to display the Format menu
Press	**1** for *Line* to display the Line Format menu
Press	**7** for *Margins* and the prompt reads *Left*
Type	**1** and then press **Enter**. The prompt reads *Right*
Type	**1** and then press **Enter**
Press	**F7** to return to the document screen
Press	↓ to reform the paragraph

Result: The second paragraph is indented 1 inch from both the left and right margins. The following paragraphs are aligned with the original 1-inch margins.

Step 3 **Change the Top Margin.** Finally, change the top margin on the second page to 2 inches.

To change the top margin

Move	the cursor to under the *T* in *The top margin* at the top of the second page
Press	**Shift-F8** to display the Format menu
Press	**2** for *Page* to display the Page Format menu
Press	**5** for *Margins* and the prompt reads *Top*
Type	**2** and then press **Enter** twice
Press	**F7** to return to the document screen

Result: No change is seen on the screen, but the new top margin will appear on the printout.

Step 4 **Save the Document.** Now that you have finished the document, save it under the filename LAYOUT.WP5 so that you can retrieve it later.

Step 5 **Print the Document.** Be sure that the printer is on and has paper in it and that the paper is aligned. Then make a printout of the document.

Step 6 **Continue or Exit.** You have now completed this tutorial. You may either continue with your own work or exit WordPerfect and return to the operating system. If you are quitting for the day, remove your program and data disks, and then turn off the computer.

▼EXERCISE

EXERCISE 18A   Change the CVRLTR1 Document's Margins

Retrieve the CVRLTR1.WP5 document that you created in Exercise 6A.

1. Change the left and right margins to 1.5 inches.
2. Save and then print the document.

▼QUESTIONS

1. List and describe at least three things you can change that affect page formats.
2. If you want 6-inch lines of text and even left and right margins, what should the margin settings be?
3. If you change the top margin so you print below a letterhead on the first page of a letter, what should you do if the document is more than one page?

A document's margin settings determine how much of the page is used for the document. Within the margins, you also have a great deal of control over the document's appearance. For example, you can change the default settings to vary line height, line spacing, and leading. When you make these changes, WordPerfect automatically retains the margins that you specified.

- The number of characters printed on a line is determined by the left and right margin settings and the font being used.
- The number of lines printed on a page is based on the length of the paper, the settings for the top and bottom margins, the size of the fonts used on the page, the line height and line spacing, and the number of lines occupied by headers and footers.

LINE HEIGHT

Line height sets the distance from the bottom of one line to the bottom of the next. You can set this to Auto to have the program adjust line spacing if you change font sizes. You can also set it to a fixed height if you want all lines to be the same distance from adjacent lines regardless of the type size. However, if you use a fixed line height setting and change font sizes, lines may overlap if the font size is too large for the specified line height.

KEY/Strokes

CHANGING THE LINE HEIGHT

1. Move the cursor to where you want the line height to change
2. Either press **Shift-F8** and then **1** for *Line*

   Or   pull down the Layout menu and select *Line*
3. Press **4** for *Line Height*
4. Either press **1** for *Auto*

   Or   press **2** for *Fixed*, type a line height measurement (for example, **.25** for ¼ inch or **.5** for ½ inch between the bottom of one line and the bottom of the next), and then press **Enter**
5. Press **F7** to return to the document screen

LINE SPACING

Line spacing is based on the line height setting. Setting line spacing to 1 sets line spacing to the same distance as the line height setting; setting line spacing to 2 doubles the line height; 3 triples it; and so on. To make fine adjustments in line spacing, enter decimals like 1.1 or 1.2. You can change line spacing for an entire document or for individual paragraphs (Figure 86). WordPerfect displays line spacing on the screen to the nearest whole number. For example, 1.5 spacing is displayed as double spacing. When you print the document, the line spacing is whatever you have specified.

Line spacing can be changed throughout a document. Here, one paragraph is single-spaced and another is double-spaced.

Line spacing can be changed throughout a document.

Here, one paragraph is single-spaced and another is

double-spaced.

FIGURE 86   Line Spacing. Line spacing can be changed throughout a document. Here, one paragraph is single-spaced and another is double-spaced.

KEY/Strokes

CHANGING LINE SPACING

1. Move the cursor to where you want the line spacing to change
2. Either press **Shift-F8** and then **1** for *Line*

   Or   pull down the Layout menu and select *Line*
3. Press **6** for *Line Spacing*
4. Type the desired spacing; for example, type **.5** for half spacing to **2** for double spacing, and then press **Enter**
5. Press **F7** to return to the document screen

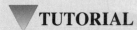▼**TUTORIAL**

TUTORIAL 19A   Changing Page Formats

In this tutorial, you change line heights and line spacing. To begin this tutorial, you must first load the program. You should insert your data disk into one of the disk drives and make that drive the default. If necessary, clear any existing document from the screen.

Step 1   **Retrieve the Document.** Insert the disk on which you saved the LAYOUT.WP5 document into one of the disk drives and then retrieve the document.

Step 2   **Change the Line Height.** Now change the line height from Auto to Fixed, printing lines .25″ apart. Then reset line height to its Auto setting at the end of the paragraph.

To change the line height

Move   the cursor to under the *L* in *Line height* at the beginning of the third paragraph

Press   **Shift-F8** to display the Format menu

Press   **1** for *Line* to display the Line Format menu

Press	**4** for *Line Height*
Press	**2** for *Fixed*
Type	**.25** and then press **Enter**
Press	**F7** to return to the document screen

To restore the line height to Auto

Move	the cursor to the blank line between the third and fourth paragraphs
Press	**Shift-F8** to display the Format menu
Press	**1** for *Line* to display the Line Format menu
Press	**4** for *Line Height*
Press	**1** for *Auto*
Press	**F7** to return to the document screen

Result: No change is seen on the screen, but the results will be seen in your printout if your printer supports this feature.

Step 3 **Change the Line Spacing.** Now change the line spacing for the fourth paragraph from single spacing to double spacing.

To change the line spacing

Move	the cursor to under the *L* in *Line spacing* at the beginning of the fourth paragraph
Press	**Shift-F8** to display the Format menu
Press	**1** for *Line* to display the Line Format menu
Press	**6** for *Line Spacing*
Type	**2** and then press **Enter**
Press	**F7** to return to the document screen

To restore the line spacing

Move	the cursor to the space following the period at the end of the fourth paragraph
Press	**Shift-F8** to display the Format menu
Press	**1** for *Line* to display the Line Format menu
Press	**6** for *Line Spacing*
Type	**1** and then press **Enter**
Press	**F7** to return to the document screen

Result: All text in the fourth paragraph is double-spaced.

Step 4 **Save the Document.** Now that you have finished the document, save it so that you can retrieve it later.

Step 5 **Print the Document.** Now that you have completed the document, make a printout to see how it looks. The second paragraph is indented from both margins, the third paragraph is printed with ¼ inch between the bottom of one line and the bottom of the next, and the fourth paragraph is printed double-spaced. The top margin on the second page is 2 inches instead of 1 inch.

Step 6 **Continue or Exit.** You have now completed this tutorial. You may either continue with your own work or exit WordPerfect and return to the operating system. If you are quitting for the day, remove your program and data disks, and then turn off the computer.

▼EXERCISE

EXERCISE 19A   Change the CVRLTR1 Document's Line Spacing

Retrieve the CVRLTR1.WP5 document that you created in Exercise 6A.

1. Change the line spacing to 2.
2. Change the top margin to 2 inches.
3. Save and then print the document.

▼QUESTIONS

1. List and describe at least three things you can change that affect page formats.
2. What does changing the line height do?
3. What does changing the line spacing do?

TOPIC 20
Searching and Replacing

When you want to find text in a document, you use the Search command. If you want to find text and replace it with new text, you use the Replace command. You can search or replace any string of characters. Strings are simply letters, words, numbers, symbols, sentences, codes, or the like that appear in sequence. Table 19 lists some examples of strings.

TABLE 19   Examples of Strings

Character	Example
Letters	**a**
Words	**president**
Numbers	**$100.00**
Symbols	**--->**
Numbers and letters	**100 Elm Street**
Sentences	**Thank you for your consideration.**
Codes	*[Date:3 1, 4]*, *[HRt]*

SEARCH

When you press **F2** or pull down the Search menu and select *Forward* or *Backward* to search a document, you are prompted to enter the string you want to find. If the specified string is found, the program moves the cursor to the character or space immediately following it. The search then ends automatically; you then press **F2** twice to continue the search. You might search for strings for several reasons.

- You can use the command to find a section of a document. Just enter a keyword that appears in the section's title or contents, and the Search command finds it.
- You can use the command to check words that you frequently misspell, especially those you misspell in more than one way. For example, using wildcards (see the "Search and Replace Options" section later in this topic), you can find all occurrences of the word *similar* even if they have been misspelled *similar, simelar,* and *similer.*

184

KEY/Strokes
SEARCHING FOR STRINGS

1. Move the cursor to where you want to begin the search
2. Either press **F2** to search toward the end of the document or press **Shift-F2** to search toward the beginning of the document

   Or   pull down the Search menu (Figure 87) and select *Forward* or *Backward*

   The prompt reads *-> Srch:* or *<- Srch:* (The arrows indicate the direction of the search, and you can press ↑ or ↓ to change the direction.)
3. Type the string you want to find
4. Press **F2** (or **Esc**) to begin the search and move the cursor to the first occurrence of the specified string
5. Repeat Step 2, but press the keys twice or pull down the Search menu and select *Next* or *Previous*

   When no occurrence is found, a message reads ** Not found **

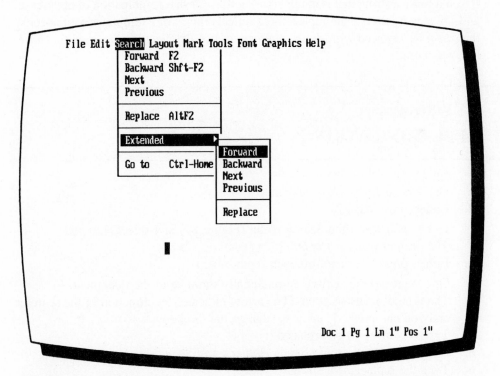

FIGURE 87   The Search Menu.   The search menu lists all of WordPerfect's Search and Replace commands.

REPLACE

The Replace command is begun by pressing **Alt-F2** and has many useful applications. You can use it to replace misspelled words with their correct spelling or to save typing time. If a word or phrase appears repeatedly in a document, you can substitute an unusual character (or characters) that is unlikely to appear elsewhere in the document instead of repeatedly entering the word or phrase. Later, you can replace the character with the actual word or phrase. For example, if you often refer to a book title in a long report, you can enter an abbreviation wherever the title is to appear. Then you can replace the abbreviation with the actual title.

You can make dramatic (and sometimes unwanted) changes to a document with the Replace command. You should always save your document first, in case something goes wrong.

When you use the Replace command, you are prompted *w/Confirm? No (Yes)*.

- If you respond *Yes* to this prompt, each time a string is found, a prompt asks if you want to replace it or not.
- If you answer *No* to this prompt, the command finds all occurrences of a string and automatically replaces them with the new string. You are not prompted to confirm the replacement. Be careful with commands that affect the entire document in this way. Sometimes the command will not differentiate between whole words or parts of words, for example, *row* and *arrow*. This command also ignores context. For example, if the document contains the sentences *He can read very well* and *She read the book just before class*, and you replace *read* with *write*, the second sentence would end up as *She write the book just before class* and would no longer make sense.

If you replace a string that is in uppercase letters (or in a combination of uppercase and lowercase letters), the replacement reflects this. For example, if you specify that *them* be replaced with *those*, any occurrence of *Them* is converted to *Those* and not *those*.

KEY/Strokes
REPLACING STRINGS

1. Either move the cursor to where you want to begin
   Or   select a block of text
2. Either press **Alt-F2**
   Or   pull down the Search menu (Figure 87) and select *Replace*
   The prompt reads *w/Confirm? No (Yes)*
3. Either press **Y** to confirm each replacement
   Or   press **N** to replace automatically throughout the document
   The prompt reads -> *Srch:* (The arrow indicates the direction of the search, and you can press ↑ or ↓ to change the direction.)
4. Type the string to be replaced
5. Press **F2** and the prompt reads *Replace with:*
6. Type the replacement string
7. Press **F2** to begin the replace operation
   - If you answered No to the prompt *w/Confirm?* all strings are replaced automatically
   - If you answered Yes to the prompt *w/Confirm?* the cursor flashes following the string when the first occurrence is found, and the prompt reads *Confirm? No (Yes)*. Press **Y** to replace, or press **N** to leave unchanged. The cursor immediately jumps to the next occurrence
   After all occurrences of the string have been found, the prompt no longer appears
8. Hold down **Ctrl** and then press **Home** twice to return to where you were when you began

SEARCH AND REPLACE OPTIONS

Both search and replace are powerful editing tools. Wildcards and other options make them even more so.

- You can change the direction of search when the prompt reads *Srch:* by pressing ↑ or ↓.
- To find whole words only, for example, *the* but not *there*, enter spaces before and after the word when you enter it. Using this procedure avoids the problem of replacing parts of words when you intended to replace only whole words. For example, searching and replacing *row* with *column* converts *arrow* into *arcolumn* and *rowboat* into *columnboat*. When you specify this option, you should be aware that searching for a singular will not find plurals or possessives; for example, searching for *row* will not find *rows*. You will also not find the string if it ends with a period or other punctuation mark. To do so, you must repeat the procedure, this time specifying *(space)row*.
- To find all occurrences, regardless of case, enter the search string in lowercase letters. This is useful because a word falling at the beginning of a sentence is capitalized, whereas the same word falling elsewhere in a sentence may not be.
- To find strings that match your case, enter the appropriate characters in uppercase when specifying the string to be searched for; for example, *The* finds *The* and *THE* but not *the*, whereas *THE* finds only *THE*.
- To delete strings, enter the string to be deleted when prompted for the string to search for, but leave the replacement string blank. When the replace operation is completed, all the specified strings are deleted.
- Replace can be used to replace format codes in a document. When the prompt reads *Srch:* or *Replace with:* just press the keys you used originally to enter the code you want to find or replace (you cannot just type the codes). For example, press **F6** to locate boldface codes *[BOLD]*. You can also use menus to enter codes following the prompt. For example, to search for margin change codes, press **Shift-F8**, then press **1** for *Line*, and then press **7** for *Margins*.
- You can use wildcards to substitute for any characters. To enter a wildcard, press **Ctrl-V** at the appropriate spot in the search string, and the prompt reads *Key =*. Press **Ctrl-X** and the ^X wildcard is displayed on the screen. Do not use this wildcard as the first character or when searching for codes.
- You can search for codes and when one is found, the cursor stops one space to its right. To delete the code, press **Backspace**. Often, a prompt appears asking if you want to delete the code. Press **Y** to do so, or press any other key to cancel the command. To eliminate the prompt when searching for codes, press **Alt-F3** or **F11** to reveal codes before beginning the search.
- You can search for soft and hard carriage returns and page breaks. To do so when the prompt reads *Srch:*, press **Ctrl-V** to display the prompt *Key =*. Enter one of the codes listed below, and then press **F2** to continue.
  - Press **Ctrl-M** to find a soft carriage return.
  - Press **Ctrl-J** to find a hard carriage return.
  - Press **Ctrl-K** to find a soft page break. (This will not find a *[HRt-SPg]* code; to do so, use **Ctrl-J** instead.)
  - Press **Ctrl-L** to find a hard page break.

Press   **F2** to search toward the end of the document, and the prompt reads -> *Srch: the*

Type   **THEM** and then press **F2**

To search for strings toward the beginning of the document

Press   **Home** twice and then press ↓ to move the cursor to the end of the document

Press   **Shift-F2** to search toward the beginning of the document, and the prompt reads <- *Srch: THEM*

Press   **F2** to begin the search using the suggested string

Result: Both commands highlight the same word but find it searching from opposite ends of the document.

Step 5   **Replace All Strings.** When you want to replace all occurrences of a string, you tell the program to replace all occurrences without asking you to confirm each replacement.

To replace strings

Press   **Home** twice and then press ↑ to move the cursor to the beginning of the document

Press   **Alt-F2** and the prompt reads *w/Confirm? No (Yes)*

Press   **N** to replace the string automatically throughout the document, and the prompt reads -> *Srch: THEM*

Type   **the** and then press **F2**. The prompt reads *Replace with:*

Type   **she** and then press **F2** to begin the replace operation

Result: Since you specified the search string in lowercase and answered No to the prompt *w/Confirm?*, all strings are replaced automatically. Obviously, you can create havoc with this combination of commands. Press **Home** twice and then press ↑ to move the cursor to the beginning of the document and repeat the command, but specify *she* as the string to search for and *The* as the string to replace with. This partially restores the file, but the second and third characters in each word in the first section are no longer uppercased.

Step 6   **Replace Strings One at a Time.** You can confirm replacements so that you do not make serious mistakes like those demonstrated here. Now selectively replace *The* with *THE* to restore the words in the first section to all uppercase.

To replace strings

Press   **Home** twice and then press ↑ to move the cursor to the beginning of the document

Press   **Alt-F2** and the prompt reads *w/Confirm? No (Yes)*

Press   **Y** to confirm each replacement, and the prompt reads -> *Srch: she*

Type   **The** and then press **F2**. The prompt reads *Replace with:*

Type   **THE** and then press **F2** to begin the replace operation

Result: Since you answered Yes to the prompt *w/Confirm?*, the command finds the string and pauses. The cursor flashes under the second character, and the prompt reads *Confirm? No (Yes)*. To replace the string, press **Y**. The cursor then immediately jumps to the next occurrence, and the prompt is displayed again. Replace only the strings in the first section. After all occurrences of the string have been found, the prompt no longer appears. When you are finished, your document should look as it did originally (Figure 88).

Step 7 **Replace Strings in a Selected Block.** When you do not want to replace throughout the entire document, you can select just the part of the text in which you want to replace. Here you replace the pairs of asterisks with a book title.

To replace strings in a block

Move	the cursor under the first asterisk in the fourth section
Press	**Alt-F4** or **F12** to turn block on
Press	**Enter** twice to highlight the last two lines of the list
Press	**Alt-F2** and the prompt reads *w/Confirm? No (Yes)*
Press	**N** to replace automatically throughout the document, and the prompt reads *-> Srch: the*
Type	****** and then press **F2**. The prompt reads *Replace with:*
Type	**WordPerfect User's Manual** and then press **F2**

Result: Both pairs of asterisks are immediately replaced with the title.

Step 8 **Delete Strings.** To delete strings, enter the string to be deleted when prompted for the string to search for, but leave the replacement prompt blank. Here, delete all occurrences of the string *their* regardless of case.

To delete strings

Press	**Home** twice and then press ↑ to move the cursor to the beginning of the document
Press	**Alt-F2** and the prompt reads *w/Confirm? No (Yes)*
Press	**N** to replace the string automatically throughout the document, and the prompt reads *-> Srch: ***
Type	**their** and then press **F2**. The prompt reads *Replace with:*
Press	**F2** to begin the replace operation without specifying a replacement string

Result: Since you specified the search string in lowercase, did not enter a replacement string, and answered No to the prompt *w/Confirm?* all *their* strings are deleted automatically.

Step 9 **Use Wildcards.** When searching for strings or searching and replacing them, you can use wildcards. To match any character, press **Ctrl-V** and then press **Ctrl-X** at the appropriate spot in the search string. The ^X wildcard is displayed on the screen. Do not use this wildcard as the first character or when searching for format codes.

To search with wildcards

Press	**Home** twice and then press ↑ to move the cursor to the beginning of the document
Press	**F2** to search toward the end of the document, and the prompt reads *-> Srch: their*
Type	**th**
Press	**Ctrl-V** and the prompt reads *Key =*
Press	**Ctrl-X** and the prompt reads *-> Srch: th^X*
Type	**m** and then press **F2**

Result: The cursor moves to the end of the first string beginning with *th* and ending with *m*. Press **F2** twice to find the next occurrence.

Step 10 **Replace Codes.** When editing a document, you frequently want to find formatting codes so that you can delete or change them. With WordPerfect, you can specify many codes in the search and replace strings. To experiment with this command, you replace hard carriage returns with asterisks and then replace the asterisks with hard carriage returns.

To search for hard carriage returns and replace them with asterisks

Press	**Home** twice and then press ↑ to move the cursor to the beginning of the document
Press	**Alt-F2** and the prompt reads *w/Confirm? No (Yes)*
Press	**N** to make all replacements automatically, and the prompt reads *-> Srch: th^Xm*
Press	**Enter** and the prompt reads *-> Srch: [HRt]*
Press	**F2** and the prompt reads *Replace with:*
Type	* and then press **F2** to begin the replace operation

To search for asterisks and replace them with hard carriage returns

Press	**Home** twice and then press ↑ to move the cursor to the beginning of the document
Press	**Alt-F2** and the prompt reads *w/Confirm? No (Yes)*
Press	**N** to make all replacements automatically, and the prompt reads *-> Srch: [HRt]*
Type	* and then press **F2**. The prompt reads *Replace with:*
Press	**Enter** and then press **F2** to begin the replace operation

Result.   The first set of commands replaced all hard carriage returns with asterisks. The second set replaced the asterisks with hard carriage returns.

Step 11   **Print the Document**. Be sure that the printer is on and has paper in it and that the paper is aligned. Then make a printout of the document.

Step 12   **Continue or Exit**. You have now completed this tutorial. You may either continue with your own work or exit WordPerfect and return to the operating system. In either case, do not save the document since you did so in Step 2 and you do not want to save the changes you made in subsequent steps. If you are quitting for the day, remove your program and data disks, and then turn off the computer.

▼EXERCISES

EXERCISE 20A   Replace in a New Document

Enter the document as shown in Figure 89.

1. Search for *[series]* and replace with *Information Processing on Microcomputers Series*.
2. Search for *[title]* and replace with *WordPerfect 5.1 Procedures Manual*.
3. Save the document under the name SEARCH2.WP5.
4. Print the document and clear the screen.

This [title] is part of an integrated series, [series]. One of the key features of the series is a standard organization that correlates all components by a parallel numbering system. Because all components use the same numbering system, you can easily find the information you need. This [title] and all other texts in the [series] use the same conventions for keys, commands, and prompts. The publisher has also developed several supplements for the [series] that are free on adoption.

FIGURE 89   The SEARCH2 Document.

EXERCISE 20B Replace in the RIGHTS Document

Retrieve the RIGHTS.WP5 document that you created in Exercise 6B.

1. Search for the heading *Clause* and replace with *Amendment*.
2. Save and then print the document.

EXERCISE 20C Search the KYSTROKE File

Retrieve the KYSTROKE.WP5 document that is on the *WordPerfect 5.1 Student Resource Disk*. This file contains a listing of all KEY/Stroke boxes in this text. You can use this file like an on-line index to locate information you need to find.

1. Search for any information in which you might be interested and list its page number. For example, search for the terms *Loading*, *Exiting*, *Printing*, *Undeleting*, *Widow*, *Page Numbers*, and so on.
2. Clear the screen without saving the document.

▼QUESTIONS

1. What is a string? Give some examples.
2. What is the Search command, and what is it used for?
3. What is the Replace command, and what is it used for?
4. What is a wildcard used for?
5. List and describe three options available when you want to search or replace.

WordPerfect includes a spelling checker, an especially valuable aide when you are editing important documents. The spelling checker compares words in your document to a list of words stored in the dictionary file WP{WP}US.LEX. Words are also checked against a supplemental dictionary, WP{WP}US.SUP, that contains words you add to the dictionary while spell-checking documents.

Any words not found in the dictionaries are highlighted, and a list of suggested replacement words is displayed along with the Not Found menu. The spelling checker also looks for words that contain numbers, words that are repeated twice in succession, and words with irregular case, like *HellO* or *washington*. You can select a replacement word from the list, use a menu command to ignore the word, or add the word to your dictionary.

Spelling checkers are nice, but you cannot rely on them entirely. They check only for spelling, not usage. For example, spelling checkers would find no problems in the sentences *Eye wood like two except you invitation, butt can not. Unfortunately, their are another things i half too due* or *Too bee oar know two Bee.* These may be exceptionally fine examples of bad grammar, but each word is spelled correctly. Also, even the best spelling checkers are not 100% accurate. Because of these limitations, you must proofread documents carefully for content and context.

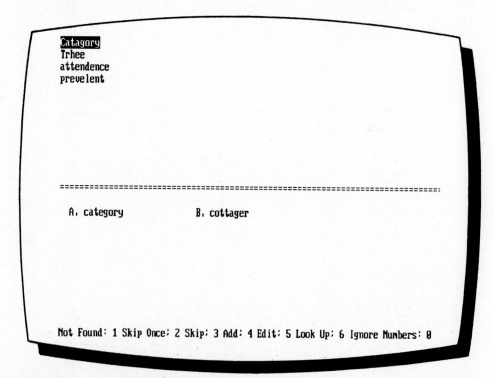

FIGURE 90   The Not Found Screen and Menu.   If a word in the document is not found in the dictionary during a spell check, a list of possible replacement words and the Not Found menu are displayed on the bottom half of the screen.

KEY/Strokes
SPELL-CHECKING A DOCUMENT

1. Either leave the cursor anywhere in the document to check the entire document

   Or move the cursor to a page if you want to spell-check a specific page

   Or move the cursor to the beginning of a word to be checked

   Or select a block

2. Either press **Ctrl-F2** to display the Spell Check menu

   Or pull down the Tools menu and select *Spell*

3. Select one or more of the choices described in Table 20

   When you press **1** for *Word*, **2** for *Page*, or **3** for *Document*, the program displays the message ** Please wait ** and compares the words in the document to the words in its word lists. (You can press **F1** at any point to cancel spell-checking.)

   If a word not in the word lists is found, the word is displayed in reverse video, and the Not Found menu and a list of words appear (Figure 90)

   ▪ To replace the word in the document with one of the words on the displayed list, press the letter that precedes the replacement

   ▪ If a list of suggested replacement words does not appear, or if the list does not contain a choice you like, press **4** for *Edit*, and then type in your corrections. When you are finished, press **F7** to resume spell-checking

   ▪ If the list of words is longer than the screen, press **Enter** to display more

   ▪ If you do not want to replace the word with a listed word, you select one of the Not Found menu commands. The menu choices vary somewhat depending on the situation. Table 21 describes all the menu choices that might appear and explains what each is used for

   After you spell-check a word, the cursor moves to the next word not found in the dictionaries, and the Not Found menu is displayed again. When spell-checking is complete, a message tells you the number of words in the document, and the prompt reads *Press any key to continue*. When you do so:

   ▪ If you spell-checked a page or a word, the document screen reappears

   ▪ If you spell-checked a page, the cursor moves to the next page, and the Spell Check menu remains on the screen so that you can check the next page or press **F7** to return to the document screen

TABLE 20   Spell Check Menu Choices

1   *Word* spell-checks the word containing the cursor.

2   *Page* spell-checks the page containing the cursor.

3   *Document* spell-checks the entire document.

4   *New Sup. Dictionary* specifies a different supplemental dictionary. The prompt reads *Supplemental dictionary name:*. Type a new supplemental dictionary (the default is WP{WP}US.SUP), or press **Enter** to accept the default and return to the Spell Check menu.

5   *Look Up* looks up words that sound like the one you enter (see the description in Table 21).

6   *Count* counts the words in the document. This command is useful when preparing documents with strict length limitations. Typical applications are when typing assigned reports and other school-related projects or when preparing articles for magazines and newspapers.

TABLE 21   Not Found and Double Word Menu Choices

1   *Skip Once* skips the word, and spell checking continues. If the same word is encountered again, it is highlighted.

2   *Skip* skips the word, and spell checking continues. If the same word is encountered again, it is not highlighted.

3   *Add* saves the word in the supplemental dictionary WP{WP}US.SUP.

3   *Delete 2nd* deletes the second word when repeating words are encountered.

4   *Edit* moves the cursor to the word so that you can correct it. (You can also press ← or → to do the same.) When you are finished, press **F7**. If your correction does not match a word in the dictionary, the word remains highlighted.

5   *Disable Double Word Checking* turns off double word checking so that no further double words are highlighted.

5   *Look Up* displays the prompt *Word:* or *word pattern:*. Type the word you want to confirm the spelling of. You can use wildcards to display a list of words that match a specified pattern.
  • The question mark (?) substitutes for a single letter.
  • The asterisk (*) substitutes for zero or more characters in sequence.
    For example, if you want to find how to spell *category*, you can enter *cat** to display all words beginning with those three letters or *cat?gory* if you are unsure of only a single character. If you enter a word without a wildcard, the program displays words that sound like the word you enter. When you are finished looking up words, press **F7** to return to the document screen.

6   *Ignore Numbers* turns off the spell checking of subsequent words that contain a number, for example, F3 or 3D.

 Using the Spell Checker on a Floppy Disk System

WordPerfect's spelling checker is on a separate disk and is not loaded along with the program. Before executing the Spell Check command, you should save the file you are working on. If you are working on a floppy disk system, you should also insert the *Speller* disk into drive B. After completing the procedure (and not before), remove the *Speller* disk from drive B, and then reinsert your data disk.

If you execute the Spell Check command without inserting the *Speller* disk, a message reads *WP{WP}US.LEX not found:*, and a menu offers the following choices: *1 Enter Path; 2 Skip Language; 3 Exit Spell*. If this menu appears, insert the *Speller* disk into drive B, and then press **1** for *Enter Path*. The prompt reads *Temporary dictionary path:*. Type **B:** and then press **Enter** to display the Spell Check menu.

TUTORIAL

TUTORIAL 21A Spell-checking a Document

In this tutorial, you use WordPerfect's spelling checker. To begin this tutorial, you must first load the program. You should insert your data disk into one of the disk drives and make that drive the default. If necessary, clear any existing document from the screen. If you are working on a floppy disk system, you must also have a copy of the WordPerfect *Speller* disk.

Step 1 **Enter Words.** Enter the list of misspelled words and the sentence shown in Figure 91. Remember to press **Enter** after each word in the list so that your list matches the one in the illustration.

> Catagory
> Trhee
> attendence
> prevelent
> definitly
> affirmitive
>
> Eye wood like two except you invitation, butt can not.
> Unfortunately, their are other things I half too due.

FIGURE 91   The SPELL Document.   You enter this document in this tutorial.

Step 2 **Spell-check the List.** Now check the spelling of the words. If you are working on a floppy disk system, remove your data disk from drive B, and then insert the *Speller* disk.

To spell check a document

Press   **Ctrl-F2** to display the Spell menu
Press   **3** for *Document*

Result: The screen displays the message * *Please wait* * while the Spell Check program is loaded into memory. If a word on the screen, like *Catagory*, isn't found in the program's word list, the word is displayed in reverse video, and the Not Found menu and list of words appear (Figure 90).

To replace the word in the document with one of the words on the displayed list, type the letter that precedes the replacement. When you correct a word, the next misspelled word is displayed. Correct each word until the prompt reads *Word count: 25 Press any key to continue.* Press any key to return to editing the document. Notice the following about the spell-checked list:

- The case of a corrected word remains unchanged. If it began with an upper-case letter, it is replaced with an uppercase letter. If it was all uppercase, it remains all uppercase.
- The program finds no spelling errors in the sentence because the program checks only your spelling, not usage or grammar. The words in the sentences are all spelled correctly; they are just used incorrectly.

Step 3 **Count Words.** When you spell-check a document, WordPerfect displays the number of words in the document. There is also a separate command that does the same thing; it counts the words in a document or in a selected block of text.

To count words
Press   **Ctrl-F2** to display the Spell Check menu
Press   **6** for *Count* to count all the words in the document

Result: In a moment, the status line reads *Word count: 25 Press any key to continue*. Press any key to return to the Spell Check menu, and then press **F7** to return to the document screen.

Step 4 **Print the Document.** Be sure that the printer is on and has paper in it and that the paper is aligned. Then make a printout of the document.

Note: If you are using a floppy disk drive system, remove the *Speller* disk from drive B and insert your data disk.

Step 5 **Save the Document.** Now that you have finished the document, save it under the filename SPELL.WP5 so that you can retrieve it later.

Step 6 **Continue or Exit.** You have now completed this tutorial. You may either continue with your own work or exit WordPerfect and return to the operating system. If you are quitting for the day, remove your program and data disks, and then turn off the computer.

EXERCISES

EXERCISE 21A   Spell-check Your Documents

Retrieve and spell-check any document you entered in a previous exercise.

- If you are working from your own floppy disks and any words are highlighted that you know are spelled correctly, add them to your dictionary. (Do not do this if you are working on the school's hard disk.)
- Save any document in which you correct errors under its original filename.
- If you spell-check any documents and do not find errors, clear the screen without saving the document.

EXERCISE 21B   Count Words

Retrieve any document you have entered, and count the words in the document without spell-checking it. When you are finished, clear the screen without saving the document.

▼QUESTIONS

1. What is the purpose of a spelling checker?

2. If the spell checker stops at a word that is not in its dictionary but is spelled correctly, what choices do you have?

3. If the spell checker stops at a word that is spelled incorrectly, but no suggested substitute word is acceptable, what do you do?

WordPerfect includes a thesaurus that you can use to look up synonyms and antonyms. When using a thesaurus, you position the cursor anywhere in the word and request the thesaurus to display a list of synonyms and antonyms. For example, when the word *wicked* is highlighted, the thesaurus may display the synonyms *bad*, *corrupt*, *evil*, *sinful*, *vile*, *hateful*, and *malevolent* and the antonyms *good*, *benevolent*, and *mild*. You can then select one of the suggested words to replace the word in the document, look up another word, or quit the thesaurus and return to the document.

The thesaurus contains 10,000 headwords (words that can be looked up) and many references, including synonyms and antonyms (Figure 92).

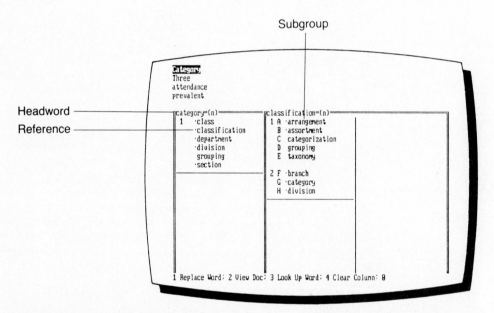

FIGURE 92   The Thesaurus Screen.   When you use the thesaurus, the word you looked up (the headword) is displayed on the screen border. Often, nouns (n), verbs (v), adjectives (a), and antonyms (ant) are listed under separate categories. The words displayed for each form of the headword are called references and are identified by letters. References preceded by dots are also headwords, so that you can press the letter in front of them to look up additional words. References with the same connotation are grouped into numbered subgroups.

KEY/Strokes
LOOKING UP A WORD IN THE THESAURUS

1. Move the cursor to any position in the word to be looked up
2. Either press **Alt-F1**

   Or   pull down the Tools menu and select *Thesaurus*
   The Thesaurus menu and list of words appears (see Figure 92)
   - If the word you highlight is not in the thesaurus, the prompts read *Word not found* and then *Word:*. Enter a new word, and then press **Enter** to continue, or press **F7** to return to the document
   - If the word you highlight is in the thesaurus, the Thesaurus screen and menu are displayed
3. Use the menu commands described in Table 22 and the cursor movement keys described in Table 23 to move the numbers and lists displayed on the Thesaurus screen
4. Either press **F7** when you are finished to return to the document screen

   Or   press **Spacebar** to return to your document without making changes

TABLE 22   **Thesaurus Menu Choices**

1   *Replace Word* replaces the word in the document with one of the words displayed on the list. Before using, press → or ← to move the reference menu selection letters (*A*, *B*, *C*, and so on) to the column containing your choice, if necessary. (Table 23 describes other keys you can use to move the cursor through a long list.) Then press **1** and the prompt reads *Press letter for word*. Press the letter preceding the desired replacement, and the document screen reappears.

2   *View Doc* returns the cursor to the document so that you can scroll through the document to see the word in context before choosing a replacement. Press **F7** to return to the Thesaurus menu.

3   *Look Up Word* displays the prompt *Word:* so that you can enter a word to be looked up.

4   *Clear Column* clears subgroups from the Thesaurus screen. (You can also press **Backspace** or **Del** to do the same.)

TABLE 23   **Thesaurus Screen Cursor Movement Keys**

Code	Press
Move the menu selection letters between columns	← or →
View subgroups too long to fit on the screen	↑ or ↓
Move column up or down	**PgUp** or **PgDn** **+** or **-** on the numeric keypad
Move to the first subgroup	**Home, Home,** ↑
Move to the last subgroup	**Home, Home,** ↓
Move to a specific subgroup	**Ctrl-Home**, subgroup number, **Enter**

Using the Thesaurus on a Floppy Disk System

WordPerfect's thesaurus is on a separate disk and is not loaded along with the program. Before executing the Thesaurus command, you should save the file you are working on. If you are working on a floppy disk system, you should also insert the *Thesaurus* disk into drive B. After completing the procedure (and not before), remove the *Thesaurus* disk from drive B, and then reinsert your data disk.

If you execute the Thesaurus command without inserting the *Thesaurus* disk and changing the default drive to B, a message reads *ERROR: File not found—WP{WP}US.THS*, and a document screen reappears. Insert the disk, and then execute the command again.

 TUTORIAL

TUTORIAL 22A   Looking Up Words in the Thesaurus

In this tutorial, you use WordPerfect's thesaurus. To begin this tutorial, you must first load the program. You should insert your data disk into one of the disk drives and make that drive the default. If necessary, clear any existing document from the screen. If you are working on a floppy disk system, you must also have a copy of the WordPerfect *Thesaurus* disk.

Step 1 **Retrieve the SPELL Document.** Insert the disk on which you saved the SPELL.WP5 document into one of the drives and retrieve it.

Step 2 **Find Synonyms.** Now let's use the thesaurus to look up synonyms and antonyms. Before you execute the Thesaurus command on a floppy disk system, insert the *Thesaurus* disk into drive B.

To look up words in the thesaurus

Move the cursor to any position in the word *Category*
Press **Alt-F1** to display the Thesaurus menu and a list of words (Figure 93)
Press **B** for *classification* to see additional possibilities branching from that word (see Figure 92)
Press **B** again for *assortment* to see additional possibilities branching from that word
Press **4** for *Clear Column* twice to remove the last two columns
Press **1** for *Replace Word*, and the prompt reads *Press letter for word*
Press **B** for *classification* to replace *Category* with *Classification*

Result: The word in the document is replaced, and the document screen reappears.

Step 3 **Continue Looking Up Words.** Continue experimenting by moving the cursor to any word and repeating the steps described. Replace each word with a synonym or an antonym.

Step 4 **Print the Document**. Be sure that the printer is on and has paper in it and that the paper is aligned. Then make a printout of the document.

Note: If you are using a floppy disk drive system, remove the *Thesaurus* disk from drive B and reinsert your data disk.

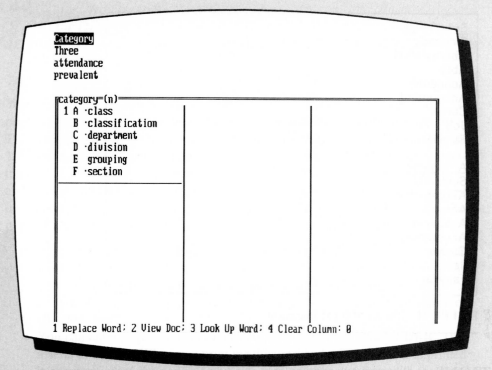

FIGURE 93   The Thesaurus Screen and Menu.   When you press **Alt-F1**, a list of words in the thesaurus is displayed along with a menu.

Step 5   Save the Document. Now that you have finished the document, save it so that you can retrieve it later.

Step 6   Continue or Exit. You have now completed this tutorial. You may either continue with your own work or exit WordPerfect and return to the operating system. If you are quitting for the day, remove your program and data disks, and then turn off the computer.

▼**EXERCISE**

EXERCISE 22A   Find Synonyms and Antonyms

Enter the document shown in Figure 94. (You can enter the first part and then copy it.)

1. Save the document as SYNONYM.WP5 and make a printout.
2. Use WordPerfect's Thesaurus command to replace each word in the first part with a synonym and each of the words in the second part with an antonym.
3. Make a printout, and clear the screen.

• When you enter headers and footers, the program normally aligns them flush left. To change the alignment (Figure 95), use the commands to center or align them flush left or right (see Topic 17). For example, if you enter two headers or two footers so that they print on the same pages, keep them short, and use the Flush Right command (**Alt-F6**) to align one ·of them with the right margin so that they do not overlap.

You can have as many headers and footers as you want in a document, as long as there are only two of each on a page. To change headers or footers, enter new ones where you want them to change.

KEY/Strokes

ENTERING HEADERS OR FOOTERS OR DISCONTINUING THEM

1. Move the cursor to the top of the page where you want the headers or footers to begin (**Ctrl-Home** and then ↑)
2. Either press **Shift-F8** and then **2** for *Page*

    Or   pull down the Layout menu and select *Page*
3. Either press **3** for *Headers*

    Or   press **4** for *Footers*
4. Select the header or footer type described in Table 24
5. Press the number indicating the occurrence of the header or footer (see Table 24), and the blank header/footer screen appears
6. Type the header or footer text (you can enter up to one full page of text), press **Shift-F5** to enter the date or time, or press **Ctrl-B** to enter a code to number pages
7. Press **F7** twice to save the header or footer text and return to the document screen

KEY/Strokes

EDITING HEADERS OR FOOTERS

1. Move the cursor to below where the header code is in the text. (The program searches from the cursor toward the top of the document for the next header or footer code, and that is the header or footer displayed.)
2. Either press **Shift-F8** and then **2** for *Page*

    Or   pull down the Layout menu and select *Page*
3. Either press **3** for *Headers*

    Or   press **4** for *Footers*
4. Select either header or footer type, and then press **5** for *Edit* to display the next header or footer above the cursor
5. Edit the header or footer text
6. Press **F7** twice to save the header or footer text and return to the document screen

Press	**5** for *Edit* to display the header text
Edit	the header text so that it reads *This is an edited header*
Press	**F7** to save the revised header text and return to the Page Format menu
Press	**F7** to return to the document screen

Result: The revised header is saved, and no change is seen on the screen.

Step 6 **Save the Document.** Now that you have finished the document, save it under the filename HEADERS.WP5 so that you can retrieve it later.

Step 7 **Print the Document.** Be sure that the printer is on and has paper in it and that the paper is aligned. Then make a printout of the document. The header prints at the top of the page and is aligned with the left margin. The page numbers print in the upper right-hand corner of the document. The footer prints both the date and page number using the codes you entered.

Step 8 **Continue or Exit.** You have now completed this tutorial. You may either continue with your own work or exit WordPerfect and return to the operating system. If you are quitting for the day, remove your program and data disks, and then turn off the computer.

EXERCISE

EXERCISE 23A Add Headers and Footers to the RIGHTS Document

Retrieve the RIGHTS.WP5 document that you created in Exercise 6B.

1. Add a footer that prints *Bill of Rights* flush left and the date flush right at the bottom of every page.

2. Save and then print the document. If your footer does not print out on the first page, the code you entered in a previous exercise to suppress page numbers is the wrong code. Reveal Codes and delete the *[Suppress:..]* code and make a new printout.

QUESTIONS

1. What are headers and footers? Why are they used?

2. What are headers and footers that appear on more than one page called?

3. List and describe some options you have when printing headers and footers.

4. Assume that your document is to be printed on both sides of the page and then bound. How do you align headers and footers so that they are on the outside edge of each page?

Footnotes are numbered references printed at the bottom of the page. The numbers in the footnotes match the numbers in the text that refer to the footnotes. Endnotes are just like footnotes, but instead of printing at the bottom of the same page as the reference number, they are printed at the end of the document.

You can enter footnotes and endnotes anywhere in a document by entering codes. They are automatically numbered when you enter them, and the numbers change automatically to reflect any added or deleted notes. You can also specify options that include changing the spacing between or within notes, changing starting numbers, or changing the line that separates the notes from the document portion of the page.

After entering footnotes or endnotes, you can edit them. When you use the command to edit a footnote or an endnote, the program searches for the next note following the cursor and asks if you want to edit that note. You can either accept it or enter a new number. Since the program moves the cursor to the note, it is usually faster to move the cursor in front of the note you want to edit before using the edit commands.

KEY/Strokes

ENTERING OR EDITING FOOTNOTES OR ENDNOTES OR CHANGING OPTIONS

1. Move the cursor to where you want the footnote or endnote reference to appear in the document or above where you want to change the style of all footnotes and endnotes
2. Either press **Ctrl-F7** and then **1** for *Footnote* or **2** for *Endnote*

   Or pull down the Layout menu and select *Footnote* or *Endnote*
3. Make one of the selections described in Table 25

TABLE 25   Footnote and Endnote Menu Choices

1   *Create* displays the footnote or endnote screen. Type the note (up to 16,000 lines). Press **F7** to return to the document screen.

2   *Edit* displays the prompt *Footnote number?* or *Endnote number?* followed by the number of the next note. Press **Enter** to edit the suggested number (or letter if you have changed the numbering method), or enter the number (or letter) of another note, and then press **Enter**. The note is displayed on the screen. Edit it, and then press **F7** to return to the document screen.

3   *New Number* displays the prompt *Footnote number?* or *Endnote number?* Enter a new number, and then press **Enter**. This overrides automatic numbering, for example, when different parts of the same document are kept in separate files. Move the cursor down through the text to reform the paragraph, and all following numbers change to reflect the change in the renumbered reference.

4   *Options* displays the Footnote Options (Figure 98) or Endnote Options (Figure 99) menu. Use any of the choices described in Table 26. (Only some of the options are offered for endnotes.) When you are finished changing options, press **F7** to return to the document screen.

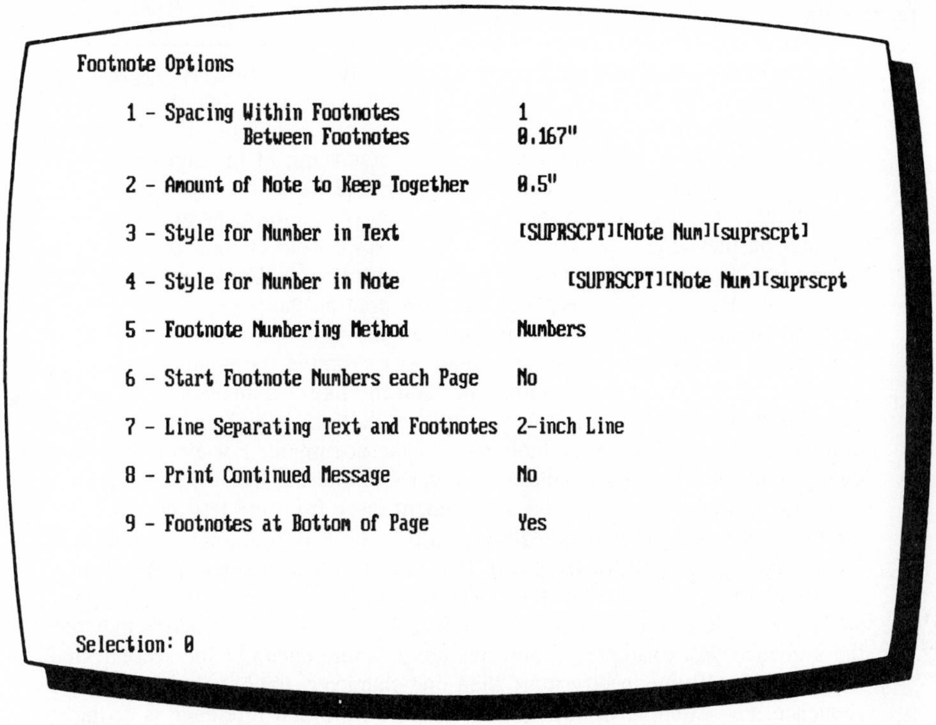

```
Footnote Options

    1 - Spacing Within Footnotes        1
              Between Footnotes         0.167"

    2 - Amount of Note to Keep Together  0.5"

    3 - Style for Number in Text         [SUPRSCPT][Note Num][suprscpt]

    4 - Style for Number in Note               [SUPRSCPT][Note Num][suprscpt

    5 - Footnote Numbering Method        Numbers

    6 - Start Footnote Numbers each Page No

    7 - Line Separating Text and Footnotes  2-inch Line

    8 - Print Continued Message          No

    9 - Footnotes at Bottom of Page      Yes



    Selection: 0
```

FIGURE 98   The Footnote Options Menu.   The Footnote Options menu allows you to specify where and how footnotes are printed.

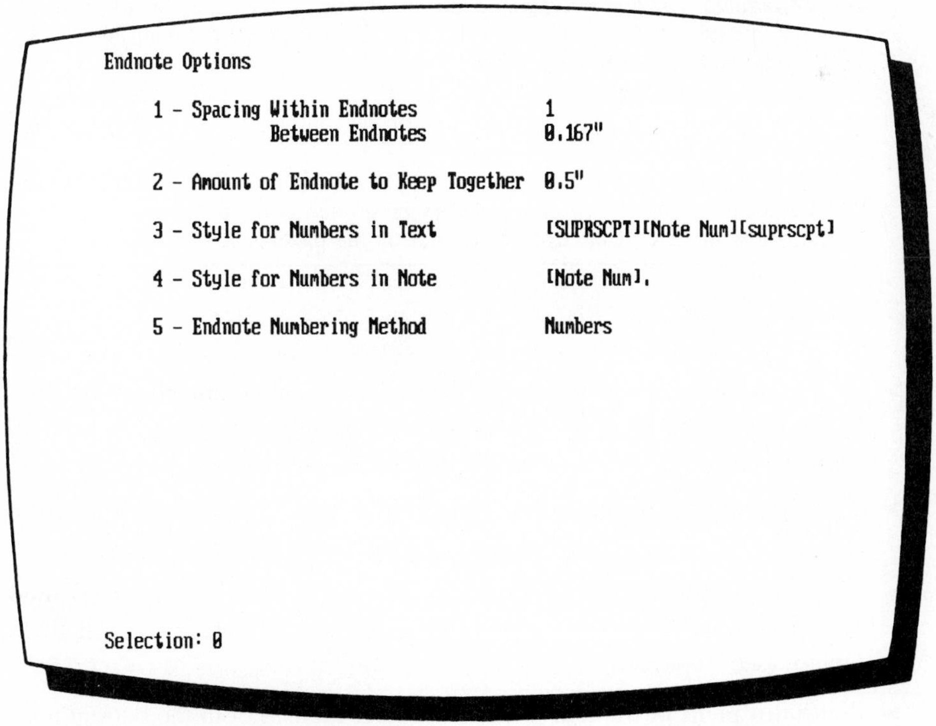

```
Endnote Options

    1 - Spacing Within Endnotes          1
              Between Endnotes           0.167"

    2 - Amount of Endnote to Keep Together  0.5"

    3 - Style for Numbers in Text        [SUPRSCPT][Note Num][suprscpt]

    4 - Style for Numbers in Note        [Note Num].

    5 - Endnote Numbering Method         Numbers



    Selection: 0
```

FIGURE 99   The Endnotes Options Menu.   The Endnote Options menu allows you to specify where and how endnotes are printed.

TABLE 26   Footnote and Endnote Options

1   *Spacing Within/Between Footnotes/Endnotes* controls the line spacing within and between the notes. For the spacing within notes, type **1** for single spacing, **1.5** for one-and-one-half spacing, **2** for double spacing, and so on. For the spacing between notes, enter a setting based on the default unit of measurement. For example, when the default is set to inches, type **.2** for a spacing of 2/10 inch.

2   *Amount of Note/Endnote to Keep Together* controls the number of lines kept together on the same page when the footnote spills onto another page. Enter a setting based on the default unit of measurement. For example, when the default is set to inches, type **1** to keep 1 inch of the note on the page.

3   *Style for Number in Text* controls the style of the footnote or endnote reference numbers in the text area of the document. For example, you can change character attributes (boldface, underline, and the like) or superscript or subscript.

4   *Style for Number in Note* controls the style of the footnote or endnote reference numbers in the footnote or endnote area of the document. For example, you can change character attributes (boldface, underline, and the like) or superscript or subscript, and you can enter spaces to indent them from the left margin.

5   *Footnote/Endnote Numbering Method* controls the way footnotes are numbered. Type **1** for numbers, **2** for letters, or **3** to specify other characters. You can specify as many as five characters. (The default is a single asterisk.) If you specify a single character, like the asterisk, the number of characters indicates the sequence. For example, * indicates the first reference, ** the second, and *** the third. If you specify more than one character, they cycle to indicate the sequence. For example, if you specify * and #, the first reference is *, the second #, the third **, the fourth ##, and so on.

6   *Start Footnote Numbers Each Page* specifies whether footnote numbers run consecutively throughout the document or start over on each page of the document.

7   *Line Separating Text and Footnotes* controls whether a line separates footnotes from the last line of the document. Type **1** for no line, **2** for a 2-inch line, or **3** for a line across the entire page.

8   *Print Continued Message* prints *(Continued...)* on the last line of the first page and *(...Continued)* on the first footnote line of the following page if the footnote continues to the next page.

9   *Footnotes at Bottom of Page* specifies where footnotes are to be printed on pages that are not full. You can specify that they be printed at the bottom of the page or just below the end of the last line of text on the page.

▼**TIPS**

➤ **To see an entire footnote**, use the View Document command on the Print menu, or print the page on which its reference number appears. To print all endnotes, print the last page of the document.

➤ **To delete an endnote or footnote**, delete the code that you entered to create it.

➤ **To search and replace in footnotes and endnotes, use the Extended Search command**. To do so, press **Home** and then **F2** to search or **Alt-F2** to replace (see Topic 20).

➤ **Footnotes print in the text area of the document**, not in the bottom margin. If the footnote is too long to print on a page, ½ inch of it prints on the same page as the reference number, and the rest of the footnote prints on the next page. If there is not enough room to print the first ½ inch of the footnote, both the footnote and the text line that contains the reference number move to the next page.

➤ **Endnotes print below the last hard carriage return on the last page of the document**. To print endnotes on a separate page, put a hard page break (**Ctrl-Enter**) after the last line of text in the document. To add a heading, type it on the last page, and then press **Enter** two or three times so that the first endnote prints that number of lines below the heading.

➤ **If you do not want endnotes to print at the end of the document**, you can enter a code wherever you do want them to print. This is useful when you want endnotes to print together at the end of sections rather than at the end of the document. To enter an endnote code, press **Ctrl-F7** to display the Foot-note menu, and then press **3** for *Endnote Placement*. The prompt reads *Restart endnote numbering? Yes (No)*. Press **Y** to have endnotes start num-bering over below the code, or **N** to have endnotes continue in numerical order. This command inserts a comment into the document followed by a hard page break code so that any following text is printed on a separate page. To calculate the space to be occupied by the endnotes, press **Alt-F5** to display the Mark Text menu. Press **6** for *Generate*, and then press **5** for *Generate Tables, Indexes, Automatic References, etc.* Press **Y** to generate the space. A new comment is inserted that shows the amount of space occu-pied by the endnotes.

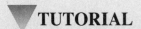

TUTORIAL

TUTORIAL 24A   Entering and Printing Footnotes

In this tutorial, you enter footnotes. To begin this tutorial, you must first load the program. You should insert your data disk into one of the disk drives and make that drive the default. If necessary, clear any existing document from the screen.

Step 1   **Create a Document.** Begin by entering the paragraph shown in Figure 100.

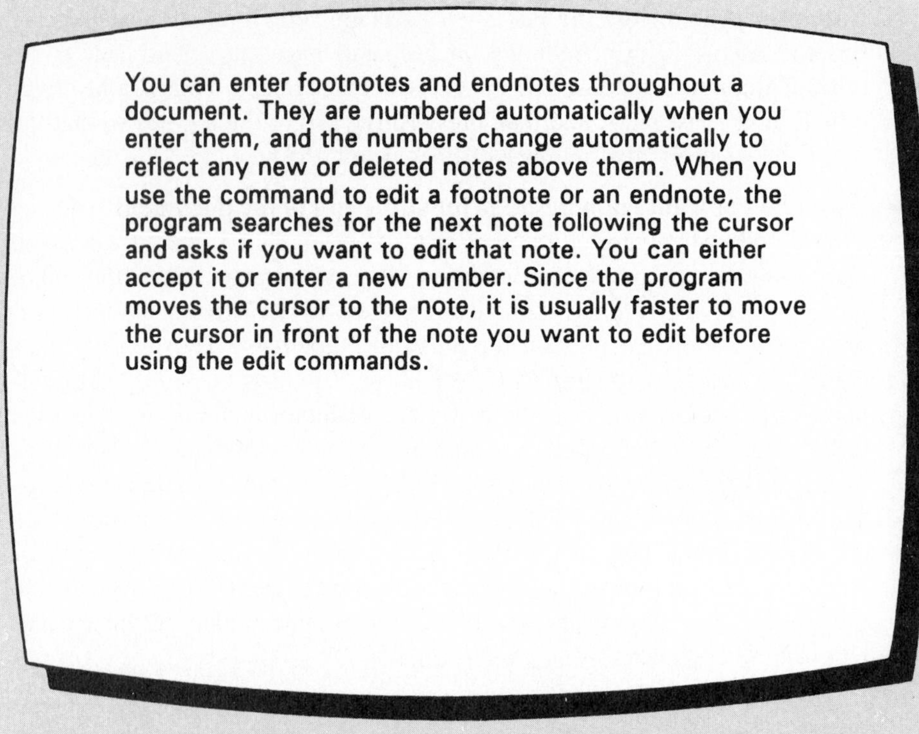

You can enter footnotes and endnotes throughout a document. They are numbered automatically when you enter them, and the numbers change automatically to reflect any new or deleted notes above them. When you use the command to edit a footnote or an endnote, the program searches for the next note following the cursor and asks if you want to edit that note. You can either accept it or enter a new number. Since the program moves the cursor to the note, it is usually faster to move the cursor in front of the note you want to edit before using the edit commands.

FIGURE 100   The FOOTNOTE Document.   You enter this document in this tutorial.

Step 2   **Enter a Footnote**. You can enter footnotes anywhere in the document.

To enter a footnote

Move   the cursor to the space following the period in the sentence *You can either accept it or enter a new number.*

Press   **Ctrl-F7** to display the Footnote menu

Press   **1** for *Footnote*

Press   **1** for *Create*, and the screen goes blank except for the number *1*

Type   **If you enter a new number, the program searches for that footnote and displays the section of the document that contains the specified reference number on the screen after you edit the footnote.**

Press   **F7** to return to the document screen

Result: The number *1* at the cursor's position is the footnote number.

Step 3   **Reveal Codes.** To see the footnote code, press **Alt-F3**. Highlight the code *[Footnote:1;[Note Num]* to display the first 50 characters of the footnote. It ends with *...]*, indicating that there is more to the footnote that is not displayed. Press **Alt-F3** to return to the document screen.

Step 4   **Enter Another Footnote.** Enter another footnote above the first one to see how the program numbers them automatically.

To enter a footnote

Move   the cursor to the space following the period in the first sentence

Press   **Ctrl-F7** to display the Footnote menu

Press   **1** for *Footnote*

Press   **1** for *Create*, and the screen goes blank except for the number *1*

Type   **This is a new footnote.**

Press   **F7** to return to the document screen

Result: The new footnote is now numbered *1*. Move the cursor down through the text to reform the paragraph, and the number of the original footnote changes from *1* to *2*.

Step 5   **Edit a Footnote.** After entering footnotes, you can easily recall them for editing.

To edit a footnote

Press   **Home** twice and then press ↑ to move the cursor to the beginning of the document

Press   **Ctrl-F7** to display the Footnote menu

Press   **1** for *Footnote*

Press   **2** for *Edit* and the prompt reads *Footnote number? 1*

Type   **2** and then press **Enter**

Result: The second footnote is displayed on the screen. Revise it to read *If you enter a new number, the program searches for that footnote and displays it on the screen*. When you are finished, press **F7** to return to the document screen.

Step 6   **Save the Document.** Now that you have finished the document, save it under the filename FOOTNOTE.WP5 so that you can retrieve it later.

Step 7   **Print the Document.** Be sure that the printer is on and has paper in it and that the paper is aligned. Then make a printout of the document. The footnote you entered is printed at the bottom of the page.

Step 8   **Continue or Exit.** You have now completed this tutorial. You may either continue with your own work or exit WordPerfect and return to the operating system. If you are quitting for the day, remove your program and data disks, and then turn off the computer.

▼ EXERCISES

EXERCISE 24A   Enter Footnotes for the RIGHTS Document

Retrieve the RIGHTS.WP5 document that you created in Exercise 6B.

1. Following the heading, enter a footnote that states *All amendments passed unanimously.*
2. Save and then print the document.

EXERCISE 24B   Add a Footnote to the ABUSE Document

Retrieve the ABUSE.WP5 document that you created in Exercise 13A.

1. Add the footnote shown in Figure 101 immediately following the word *TECHNIQUES* in the heading.
2. Save and then print the document.
3. Edit the footnote to italicize the title *Computer-related Fraud and Abuse in Government Agencies.*
4. Save and then print the document.

> [1]The techniques are often used in combination and are identified in Computer-related Fraud and Abuse in Government Agencies, Department of Health and Human Services, Office of the Inspector General, 1983.

FIGURE 101   The ABUSE Footnote.

EXERCISE 24C   Enter a Document That Describes Footnote Formats

If you refer to work by another author in a paper or report, you have to credit the work in footnotes or in a bibliography. In this exercise, you enter footnotes that do not refer to specific works but provide the form and identify the elements that you should use in your citations.

1. Enter the document shown in Figure 102, which lists some typical references you might need.
2. At the end of each reference in the list, add the corresponding footnote shown in Figure 103.
3. Save the document as FOOTFORM.WP5, and then print the document.

---

1. Book with one author

2. Book with two or three authors

3. Book with a corporate author

4. Work in several volumes or parts

5. Works in an anthology or a collection

6. Article in a reference work

7. Article from a weekly, biweekly, or monthly magazine or newspaper

8. Article from a daily newspaper

9. Film

10. Interview

FIGURE 102   The FOOTFORM Document.

[1]First Last, <u>Title</u> (City, State: Publisher, copyright date), pages.

[2]Fist Last, First Last, and First Last, <u>Title</u> (City, State: Publisher, copyright date), pages.

[3]Name of Corporation, <u>Title</u> (City, State: Publisher, copyright date), pages.

[4]First Last, <u>Title</u>, Volume or Part (City, State: Publisher, copyright date), pages.

[5]First Last, "Title of Article," in <u>Title of Publication</u>, ed. (City, State: Publisher, copyright date), pages.

[6]"Title of section," <u>Title of Book</u>, copyright or edition date.

[7]First Last, "<u>Title of Article</u>," Name of Periodical, date, section, page, column.

[8]First Last, "<u>Title of Article</u>," Name of Newspaper, date of issue, page.

[9]First Last, dir., <u>Film Title</u>, with Major Actor, Studio, date or release.

[10]Personal interview with Title, First Last, date.

FIGURE 103   Footnotes to Add to the FOOTFORM Document.

▼QUESTIONS

1. What is the difference between a footnote and an endnote?
2. What happens to a footnote reference number if you insert a new reference number above it?
3. List the steps you would follow to edit a footnote.
4. List the steps you would follow to change the spacing between footnotes.

TOPIC 25
Merge Printing

Instead of individually entering and editing the same letter over and over to different people, merge printing lets you create one form document that then has personalized data entered into each copy as it is being printed. This procedure can greatly increase your speed in preparing form letters and similar documents that are essentially the same except for minor changes from copy to copy.

The data that personalizes each form letter, like the name and address, can be entered from the keyboard or kept in a separate file from which it is automatically inserted into the form letter during the merge process (Figure 104). When stored in a separate file, the information can easily be kept up-to-date and used repeatedly to print letters, envelopes, and mailing labels automatically.

When printing form letters, you begin by creating and coding a primary file. This primary file can contain text, formats, and merge codes. The text and formats appear in each copy that is printed, and the merge codes control the merge-printing process and specify what data are to be inserted where. To merge data automatically, you also create a secondary file that stores the data to be merged in an organized fashion. You edit, save, and retrieve these two types of documents just like any other documents.

To: {FIELD}1˜
Department: {FIELD}2˜

Your new extension is now {FIELD}3˜

A secondary file contains the data that are to be inserted into the primary file.

John{END FIELD}
Finance{END FIELD}
1003{END FIELD}
{END RECORD}
= =
= = = = = =
Mary{END FIELD}
Production{END FIELD}
1004{END FIELD}
{END RECORD}
= =
= = = = = =
Frank{END FIELD}
Sales{END FIELD}
1005{END FIELD}
{END RECORD}
= =
= = = = = =

FIGURE 104   Merge Printing.   A primary file contains text and merge codes like {*FIELD*}*1*˜ that specify where data are to be inserted.

FIGURE 104,   **continued**

```
To: John
Department: Finance

Your new extension is now 1003
```

```
To: Mary
Department: Production

Your new extension is now 1004
```

```
To: Frank
Department: Sales

Your new extension is now 1005
```

When you merge-print the two files, data from the secondary file are automatically printed in place of the merge codes in the primary file, and multiple customized copies are printed.

THE PRIMARY FILE

The primary file contains the unchanging parts of the document (sometimes called the boilerplate or form letter). You also insert codes (called merge codes) into this document to indicate where data are to be merged from the secondary file during merge printing (Figure 104). These merge codes refer to information in the secondary file (see the section "The Secondary File"). For example, one code might specify that the person's name is to be inserted from the secondary file, and another code might specify that the person's street address is to be inserted. The codes are entered into the primary file where this data are to be inserted. When the document is merge-printed, the codes are replaced with data from the secondary file.

 Formatting Primary Files

When you enter codes to format a primary file, keep in mind that WordPerfect merge-prints your documents to the screen (unless you use the {PRINT} code discussed in Topic 26). When it does so, any codes in the primary file are carried to each of the printed copies on the screen. This slows down merge printing and requires more memory. To avoid these problems, enter as many codes as possible as initial codes by pressing **Shift-F8** to display the Format menu, then pressing **2** for *Initial Codes*. Any codes you enter on the Initial Codes screen act just as if they had been entered at the top of the primary file but appear only once in the merged file on the screen. After entering codes, press **F7** twice to return to the document screen.

If you want to hide the merge codes in a primary file so you can see its layout better, you can turn them on and off. To do so, press **Shift-F1** to display the Setup menu, then press **2** for *Display* and **6** for *Edit-Screen Options*. Press **5** for *Merge Codes Display*, then **Y** or **N**. Press **F7** to return to the document screen.

KEY/Strokes

INSERTING MERGE CODES INTO A PRIMARY FILE

---

1. Move the cursor to where you want to enter a merge code
2. Press **Shift-F9** to display the Merge Codes menu (Figure 105)
3. Enter one of the codes listed on the menu and described in Table 27
4. Repeat Steps 1 through 3 for each merge code in the document
5. Save the primary file

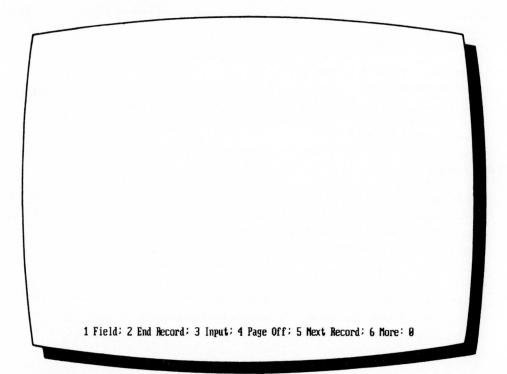

1 Field; 2 End Record; 3 Input; 4 Page Off; 5 Next Record; 6 More: 0

FIGURE 105　The Merge Codes Menu.　When you press **Shift-F9**, the Merge Codes menu lists all the codes that you can insert into a primary file.

You enter fields and records on lines from the top of the document to the bottom. Although you do not actually number them, fields are numbered from top to bottom. The first field in each record is field 1, the second field in each record is field 2, and so on. When entering fields and records, keep the following points in mind:

- The status line indicates the number of the field the cursor is in as soon as you press **F9** to indicate the end of the first field.
- Each record must have the same number of fields.
- You can have as many fields in each record as you like and then specify only those you need during a merge. For example, you may want to maintain phone numbers in a name and address file. When printing letters or envelopes, you do not print the number.
- Fields can contain any number of lines and both soft and hard carriage returns.
- Each field must contain the same category of information. For example, you cannot have a name in field 1 of the first record and an address in field 1 of the second record.
- The fields in each record are separated from each other with an {END FIELD} code that you enter by pressing **F9**. If a field in a record is to be left empty, the {END FIELD} code that ends the field must be entered anyway so that the program knows the field is empty.
- Never separate fields with more than one hard carriage return or insert spaces between the last word in a field and the {END FIELD} code.
- Records are separated from each other with an {END RECORD} code and a hard page break, which you enter by pressing **2** for *End Record* on the Merge Codes menu.

Planning Your Secondary File

When you first create a secondary file, you should plan it carefully so that the data in it are effectively organized.

- If you want to be able to sort a mailing list by ZIP codes, they must be entered into a separate field.
- If you want to use the last name in the salutation, it must be in a separate field. If you have only one field for the entire name, your letter might read ''Dear Mr. John Smith'' instead of ''Dear Mr. Smith.''
- The number of lines used in addresses varies. One address might require only three lines, and another might require five. Set up your fields for the most number of lines. If a particular address is shorter, you can leave those fields blank.
- If in doubt, break information into smaller fields.

In this secondary file, the entire address has been entered as a single field. Each line ends with a hard carriage return *[HRt]*.

```
NAME[HRt]
STREET ADDRESS[HRt]
CITY, STATE, ZIP[HRt]
{END RECORD}
```

```
NAME{END FIELD}
STREET ADDRESS{END FIELD}
CITY, STATE, ZIP{END FIELD}
{END RECORD}
```

In this secondary file, the information has been broken up into individual fields to make it more flexible. Each line ends with an {END FIELD} code.

KEY/Strokes
CREATING A SECONDARY FILE

1. Open a new document file
2. Either type the field's contents. (You can press **Enter** if the data in the field are longer than one line—for example, an inside address—or let word wrap wrap it to the next line.)

    Or leave the field blank
3. Press **F9** to end the field with an {END FIELD} code and move the cursor down to the next line
4. Repeat Steps 2 and 3 for each field in the record
5. When the record is complete, press **Shift-F9** to display the Merge Codes menu and press **2** for *End Record* to end the record with an {END RECORD} code followed by a hard page break
6. Repeat Steps 2 through 5 for each record. Be sure to enter each record's information in the same field sequence
7. When you are finished, save the secondary file

MERGE PRINTING

After creating the necessary files, you merge-print. Merge printing is the process of printing multiple copies of the primary file. Each copy contains a different set of information inserted in place of merge codes in the primary file (Figure 104). When you merge-print a primary and secondary file, the program goes to the first record in the secondary file, inserts data from the specified fields, and then continues printing. After all the requested fields from the first record have been inserted, the first copy advances from the printer, and the process is repeated for the second copy. But this time the program inserts data from the second record. This continues until all the records in the secondary file have been used.

KEY/Strokes

MERGE PRINTING

1. Either press **Ctrl-F9** and then **1** for *Merge*

   Or   pull down the Tools menu and select *Merge*

   The prompt reads *Primary file:*

2. Either type the name of the primary file, and then press **Enter**. (If necessary, you can enter a path in front of the filename if the file is not in the default drive or directory.)

   Or   press **F5** to display the List Files screen, highlight the file you want to merge-print, and then press **1** for *Retrieve*

   The prompt reads *Secondary file:*

3. Either type the name of the secondary file, and then press **Enter**. (If necessary, you can enter a path in front of the filename if the file is not in the default drive or directory.)

   Or   press **F5** to display the List Files screen, highlight the file you want to merge-print, and then press **1** for *Retrieve*

USING MERGE CODES

WordPerfect has a number of merge codes that are very useful (see Table 28). For example, you can enter merge codes that allow you to type text into a document while it is being printed. Moreover, you can specify prompts that appear on the screen when the document is being merge-printed to remind you what information to enter. After you type the data, and then press **F9** to continue, the program inserts the data you typed into the body of the letter in place of the merge code and continues.

There are three ways to display more merge codes

- Press **Shift-F9** twice.
- Press **Shift-F9**, and then select **6** for *More* (Figure 107).
- Pull down the Tools menu, select *Merge Codes*, and then select *More* (Figure 107).

TABLE 28   Merge Codes

- {*COMMENT*}*comment˜* enters a comment in a primary file that is displayed on the screen when you merge-print the document.
- {*DATE*} inserts the current date or time based on the computer's clock.
- {*DOCUMENT*}*filename˜* inserts a file with the specified name into the document when the primary file is merge-printed.
- {*END FIELD*} ends a field in a secondary file.
- {*END RECORD*} ends a record in a secondary file.
- {*FIELD NAMES*}*name1˜...nameN˜˜* assigns names to the fields in a secondary file.
- {*FIELD*}*field˜* specifies the number or name of the field in the secondary file that data are to be inserted from.

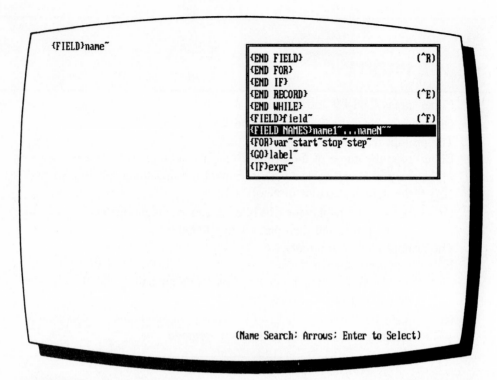

FIGURE 107 Merge Codes Menu.   When you display the Merge Codes menu and then select *More*, a list of additional merge codes is displayed. You can highlight one of them with ↑ or ↓ or by beginning to type its name (without the opening brace (})).

TABLE 28   Merge Codes continued

- *{INPUT}message ˜* stops the merge process and displays a message so that you can type in data from the keyboard. After typing data, press **F9** to continue. If you use this code in a file and only want to enter data from the keyboard, merge-print only the primary file. When prompted to enter a secondary file, just press **Enter**.
- *{KEYBOARD}* is the same as *{INPUT}* but no prompt is displayed when merge pauses.
- *{PAGE OFF}* eliminates the hard page break at the end of a document when all fields have been inserted so that the next record does not begin at the top of a new page.
- *{PAGE ON}* inserts a hard page break at the end of a document when all fields have been inserted so each record prints starting on a new page.
- *{PRINT}* sends text that has already been merged to the printer. You use this when you have too many records to merge-print the files to the screen first.
- *{PROMPT}message ˜* displays a message on the status line during a merge.
- *{QUIT}* stops a merge when it is encountered in a primary or a secondary file.
  - If you want to merge-print only part of a secondary file, for example, names from *A* through *N*, you can enter a *{QUIT}* code at the point in the secondary file where you want the merge to end.
  - When merge-printing letters, envelopes, or labels using a secondary file with a lot of records, you may want to enter this code after the first few records and run a test to be sure that your formats and paper alignment are correct. After testing, remove the code and merge-print the entire secondary file.

TIP

> ➤ **To stop a merge in progress**, press **Shift-F9**.

TUTORIAL

TUTORIAL 25A   Merge-printing a Form Letter

In this tutorial, you merge-print form letters. To begin this tutorial, you must first load the program. You should insert your data disk into one of the disk drives and make that drive the default. If necessary, clear any existing document from the screen.

Step 1   **Create Secondary File.** The secondary file contains three records, each of which has five fields. The fields have to be the same in each record. You will use the following fields:

Field 1 — Name
Field 2 — Company Name
Field 3 — Street Address
Field 4 — City, State, and ZIP Code
Field 5 — Salutation

If one field in a record is empty (for example, the person does not have a company affiliation), that field is left blank. Enter the three records shown in Figure 108. Notice as you do so that pressing **F9** enters an *{END FIELD}* code and moves the cursor down one line.

To enter the first record

Type	**Mr. Robert Smith** and then press **F9**
Type	**Alf Industries** and then press **F9**
Type	**100 Elm Street** and then press **F9**
Type	**Boston, MA 00120** and then press **F9**
Type	**Mr. Smith** and then press **F9**
Press	**Shift-F9** to display the Merge Codes menu
Press	**2** for *End Record* to end the first record

To enter the second record

Type	**Ms. Wendy Lewis** and then press **F9**
Press	**F9** to enter an *{END FIELD}* code for an empty field
Type	**400 Main Street** and then press **F9**
Type	**Los Angeles, CA 90020** and then press **F9**
Type	**Wendy** and then press **F9**
Press	**Shift-F9** to display the Merge Codes menu
Press	**2** for *End Record* to end the second record

To enter the third record

Type	**Mrs. Mary Lockhart** and then press **F9**
Type	**Curtis & Mathers** and then press **F9**
Type	**1000 Oak Road** and then press **F9**
Type	**Chicago, IL 30010** and then press **F9**
Type	**Mrs. Lockhart** and then press **F9**
Press	**Shift-F9** to display the Merge Codes menu
Press	**2** for *End Record* to end the third record

```
        Mr. Robert Smith{END FIELD}
        Alf Industries{END FIELD}
        100 Elm Street{END FIELD}
        Boston, MA 00120{END FIELD}
        Mr. Smith{END FIELD}
        {END RECORD}
        ==========================================
        Ms. Wendy Lewis{END FIELD}
        {END FIELD}
        400 Main Street{END FIELD}
        Los Angeles, CA 90020{END FIELD}
        Wendy{END FIELD}
        {END RECORD}
        ==========================================
        Mrs. Mary Lockhart{END FIELD}
        Curtis & Mathers{END FIELD}
        1000 Oak Road{END FIELD}
        Chicago, IL 30010{END FIELD}
        Mrs. Lockhart{END FIELD}
        {END RECORD}
        ==========================================
```

FIGURE 108   The SECOND Document.   You enter this document in this tutorial.

Step 2   **Print Out a Copy of the Secondary File.** Be sure that the printer is on and has paper in it and that the paper is aligned. Then make a printout of the document. Since it would take three pages if you printed it normally, print the screen display instead. To do so, hold down **Shift** and press **PrtSc** (on an enhanced keyboard, just press the key labeled **Print Screen**). Compare the printout with Figure 108 to be sure they match.

Step 3   **Save the Secondary File.** Now that you have finished the secondary file, save it under the filename SECOND.WP5 so that you can retrieve it later. Before saving the file, change the default drive to the one that contains the disk that you save your files on. This way you will not have to specify the drive in the following steps.

Step 4   **Clear the Screen.** Clear the current document from the screen but remain in the program. When prompted *Save document? Yes (No)*, press **N** (for *No*), since you have previously saved this document.

Step 5   **Create and Code the Primary File.** Now create and code the primary file shown in Figure 109. Since the second field in the second record is blank, enter the question mark code following the field number so that a blank line isn't printed where the blank field occurs.

To code the address

Press	**Shift-F9** to display the Merge Codes menu
Press	**1** for *Field*, and the prompt reads *Enter Field:*
Type	**1** and then press **Enter** twice
Press	**Shift-F9** to display the Merge Codes menu
Press	**1** for *Field* and the prompt reads *Enter Field:*
Type	**2?**and then press **Enter** twice
Press	**Shift-F9** to display the Merge Codes menu
Press	**1** for *Field*, and the prompt reads *Enter Field:*
Type	**3** and then press **Enter** twice

```
Your Name
Your Street
Your City, State ZIP

[Company]
[Street]
[City], [State] [ZIP]

ATTENTION: CATALOG DEPARTMENT

I am a major in (subject) at (school). Would you please
send me a catalog of your titles in the field on (area).

Sincerely yours,


Your name
```

FIGURE 111   The PUBLTR Document.

Company	Street	City	State	ZIP
Allyn & Bacon, Inc.	7 Wells Avenue	Newton	MA	02159
AMACOM Book Division	135 W. 50th Street	New York	NY	10020
Curtin & London, Inc.	P.O. Box 363	Marblehead	MA	01945
Houghton Mifflin Company	One Beacon Street	Boston	MA	02108
Kent Publishing Company	20 Providence Street	Boston	MA	02116
McGraw-Hill Inc.	1221 Avenue of the Americas	New York	NY	10020
Prentice Hall	Sylvan Avenue	Englewood Cliffs	NJ	07632
South-Western Pub. Co.	5101 Madison Road	Cincinnati	OH	45227
Wadsworth, Inc.	10 Davis Drive	Belmont	CA	94002
John Wiley & Sons, Inc.	605 Third Avenue	New York	NY	10158

FIGURE 112   The PUBLIST Document.

3. Merge-print the two files to the screen, and then make a printout. Don't save the merged copies since you can merge them again should you need them.

EXERCISE 25B   Merge-print a Memo

Enter the memo shown in Figure 113.

1. Use the More menu to enter the {DATE}, {INPUT}, and {PRINT} codes shown in italics.

2. Save the memo as MEMO.WP5.

3. Merge-print the memo (press **Enter** when prompted to enter a secondary file name) and enter the names and subjects shown in Figure 114. The document prints one document and then stops.

4. To print one memo after another, enter the merge-code {NEST PRI-MARY}MEMO.WP5˜ on the last line after the {PRINT} code. This new code will call the primary file up again after the first memo is printed. Save the revised file and merge-print it. Fill out two or more memos. To quit at any point, press **Shift-F9**, then press **3** for Stop.

```
{DATE}

To: {INPUT}Type name and press F9~
Fr: {INPUT}Type name and press F9~
Re: {INPUT}Type subject and press F9~

Please call me as soon as you can regarding {INPUT}Type
purpose of memo and press F9~.
{PRINT}
```

FIGURE 113   The MEMO Document.

```
To: John Smith
Fr: (your name)
Re: Meeting
purpose: our plans for Friday's meeting

To: Mary Smith
Fr: (your name)
Re: Inventory
purpose: our current inventory levels

To: Jose Rodriguez
Fr: (your name)
Re: Five-year plan
purpose: your current forecast for sales and profits
```

FIGURE 114   The MEMO Document's Data.

▼QUESTIONS

1. What are the two files you need for automatic merge printing?
2. Describe a primary file and its function.
3. List and describe two codes that you can enter in a primary file.
4. Describe a secondary file and its function.
5. Describe fields and records.
6. List and briefly describe three merge codes that were discussed in this topic.

Since many of the tasks you perform during word processing are repetitive, you often find yourself pressing the same sequence of keys to save, retrieve, or print files; indent paragraphs; boldface or underline words; and so on. WordPerfect allows you to create macros that automate these repetitive tasks.

DEFINING MACROS

You can define (record) and then automatically execute (play back) any sequence of keystrokes, including text and commands. Defining and executing macros is easy and can save you a lot of time if you use the same series of keystrokes over and over again; for example:

- You can record sections of text, like addresses or letter closings, and then insert them into documents where needed.
- You can record and then execute a series of commands. If you have to press five or six keys to execute a command, you can store those keystrokes in a macro and execute it by pressing as few as two keys.
- You can enter a pause in a macro when you define it. When you execute the macro, it executes all keystrokes up to the pause and then waits for you to enter text or other keystrokes from the keyboard. When you do so, and then press **Enter**, the macro continues. This is useful when all but a few of the keystrokes are the same. For example, you can record all the keystrokes needed to retrieve a file from the disk but enter a pause so that you can type in the desired file's name.

There are four steps to defining keystrokes:

1. Press **Ctrl-F10** to tell the program to begin recording keystrokes.
2. Give the macro a name or assign them to an **Alt**-letter key combination.
   - If you assign it a name, you have to enter that name to play it back.
   - If you assign a macro to an **Alt**-letter key combination, you can execute it by holding down **Alt** and pressing the letter you assigned it to.
   - You can press **Enter** to create a temporary macro that is automatically deleted when you exit WordPerfect.
   If you name a macro with a name of an already existing macro, a message informs you that the macro already exists. You can use the displayed menu choices to replace the existing macro, edit it, or view its description.
3. After entering the description of a macro and then pressing **Enter**, the status line flashes *Macro Def*. Any time this message is flashing, you are recording keystrokes. Also when the *Macro Def* message is displayed:
   - You can press **Ctrl-PgUp** to display the Macro Options menu (see Table 29).
   - You can use a mouse to execute commands (but not to move the cursor).
4. Press **Ctrl-F10** to end the macro's definition.

KEY/Strokes

DEFINING A MACRO

1. Either press **Ctrl-F10**

   Or   pull down the Tools menu, select *Macro*, and then select *Define*
   The prompt reads *Define macro:*

2. Either type the name of the macro (up to eight characters), and then press **Enter**

   Or   hold down **Alt** and press a letter (**A** through **Z**) you want to assign the macro to

   Or   press **Enter** to create a temporary macro that is automatically deleted when you exit WordPerfect. (You cannot edit temporary macros.)
   The prompt reads *Description:*. (If you pressed **Enter**, go on to Step 4.) If a macro by the same name already exists, you are prompted to replace or edit it. Press **1** for *Replace*

3. Type a description of the macro (up to 39 characters), and then press **Enter**. The status line flashes *Macro Def*

4. Enter the keys to be recorded in the macro. (To enter options at any point, press **Ctrl-PgUp**—see Table 29.)

5. Press **Ctrl-F10** to end the macro, and the status line no longer flashes *Macro Def*

TABLE 29 Macro Options Menu

1   *Pause* pauses the macro during its execution where **Ctrl-PgUp** is pressed so that you can enter information from the keyboard, for example, to enter a person's name in a salutation or a filename in a save or retrieve macro. When you then enter text and press **Enter**, the macro resumes.

2   *Display* allows you to see the macro perform or turn off the screen update until the macro is finished.

3   *Assign* assigns values to variables. Refer to the WordPerfect manual's section on advanced macros.

4   *Comment* enters comments into the macro definition to help you understand it later when editing it. Comments that you enter are ignored when the macro is played back.

EXECUTING MACROS

When you want to replay the keystrokes that you recorded, you execute the macro. The way you do so depends on how you named it.

- If you assigned it to an **Alt**-letter key combination, you hold down **Alt** while pressing the letter key you assigned it to.

- If you assigned it a name, you press **Alt-F10**, type the name of the macro, and then press **Enter**.

- If is a temporary macro that is automatically deleted when you exit Word-Perfect, press **Alt-F10** and then **Enter**.

KEY/Strokes
EXECUTING A MACRO

1. Move the cursor to where you want the macro played back.
2. Either press **Alt-F10** to display the prompt *Macro:*, type the name of the macro, and then press **Enter**

   Or   hold down **Alt** and press the letter you assigned the keystrokes to

   Or   press **Alt-F10** and then press **Enter** to execute a temporary macro created just for the current session

   Or   pull down the Tools menu, select *Macro*, and then select *Execute*. When the prompt reads *Macro:*, type the name of the macro, and then press **Enter**

EDITING MACROS

WordPerfect also allows you to edit macros so that you can correct any mistakes you may have made or add additional procedures without having to redefine the keystrokes. (You cannot edit temporary macros.)

KEY/Strokes
EDITING A MACRO

1. Either press **Ctrl-F10**

   Or   pull down the Tools menu, select *Macro*, then select *Define*
   The prompt reads *Define macro:*
2. Either type the name of the macro you want to edit, and then press **Enter**

   Or   hold down **Alt** and press the letter you assigned a macro to

   Or   pull down the Tools menu, select *Macro*, then select *Define*. When the prompt reads *Macro:* type the name of the macro, and then press **Enter**

   A message tells you the macro has already been defined and displays menu commands to replace or edit it.
3. Press **2** for *Edit* to display the Macro Edit screen and menu (Figure 115)
4. Edit the description, and then press **Enter** or edit the keystrokes, and then press **F7**
5. Press **F7** to return to the document screen

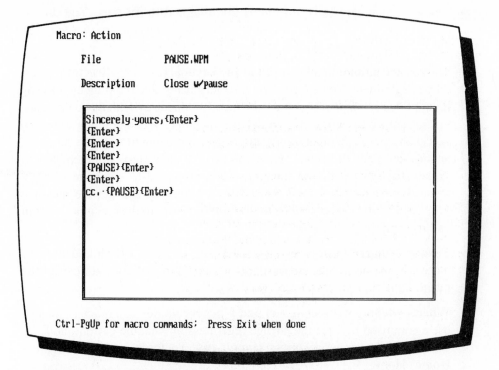

```
Macro: Action

    File            PAUSE.WPM

    Description     Close w/pause

  ┌──────────────────────────────────────────┐
  │Sincerely·yours,{Enter}                    │
  │{Enter}                                    │
  │{Enter}                                    │
  │{Enter}                                    │
  │{PAUSE}{Enter}                             │
  │{Enter}                                    │
  │cc.·{PAUSE}{Enter}                         │
  │                                           │
  │                                           │
  │                                           │
  │                                           │
  └──────────────────────────────────────────┘

  Ctrl-PgUp for macro commands;  Press Exit when done
```

FIGURE 115   The Macro Edit Screen.   The Macro Edit screen displays a menu and the macro. By choosing commands from the menu, you can change the macro's description or keystrokes.

NESTING AND CHAINING MACROS

You can have one macro refer to another so that the second is executed automatically. There are two ways to do so, by nesting or by chaining.

A nested macro is executed before the macro in which it is executed is completed. To nest an existing macro while defining another, just hold down **Alt** and press the macro's letter key at the point where you want it executed in the new macro. When you run the new macro, the nested macro is run at that point; then the new macro resumes executing.

When you chain macros, one begins when the other ends. One way to chain macros is to define the second macro first. You then define the first macro. After recording the first macro's keystrokes, perform either of these procedures:

- Press **Alt-F10** and then press the second macro's **Alt**-letter key command.
- Press **Ctrl-F10** and enter the second macro's name (you could also define a new macro at this point). This records the inserted macro's keystrokes but does not actually execute them until you execute the new macro.

TIPS

➤ **To delete a macro**, delete the file with the same name and the extension .WPM. For example, a macro that you assigned to **Alt-C** is named ALTC.WPM. Macros are stored in the directory specified in the Setup menu's Location of Files command.

➤ **You can see the description you enter when defining a macro** with the Look command on the List Files menu.

➤ **The extension .WPM is automatically assigned to macros**. You do not have to type this extension when defining or executing a macro, but you will see it in the List Files screen.

➤ **Macros are automatically stored in the keyboard/macro directory when they are defined**. You specify this directory using the Setup menu's Location of Files command. If you do not specify a directory with this command, macros are saved on the current default directory. When defining a macro, you can also specify a path in front of the macro name to store the macro in another drive and directory. When you execute the macro, you then have to specify the same path and filename when prompted to enter the macro's name. If you have assigned a macro to a letter key and get the message *ERROR: File not found*, change the default directory to the one it is stored in and try again.

➤ **To stop a macro in progress**, press **F1**. (If you press **F1** while defining a macro, it just inserts the cancel code in the macro and does not cancel the macro definition process.)

➤ **When switching between insert and typeover modes in a macro**, you can use a command to force the change regardless of what the current mode is. To force typeover mode, press **Home**, **Ins**. To force insert mode, press **Home**, **Home**, **Ins**.

▼**TUTORIAL**

TUTORIAL 26A Creating and Using Macros

In this tutorial, you use WordPerfect's macro features. To begin this tutorial, you must first load the program. You should insert your data disk into one of the disk drives and make that drive the default. If necessary, clear any existing document from the screen.

Step 1   **Change the Keyboard/Macros Directory.** When you create macros, they are automatically stored in the directory specified in the Setup menu. Let's use this menu to specify that the macros you create are to be stored on your floppy disk.

To specify the macros directory
Press   **Shift-F1** to display the Setup menu
Press   **6** for *Location of Files*
Press   **2** for *Keyboard/Macro Files*
Type   **A:** (on a hard disk system) or **B:** (on a floppy disk system) and then press **Enter**
Press   **F7** to return to the document screen

Result: No change is seen on the screen, but now any macro that you create will automatically be saved onto your floppy disk.

Step 2   **Record Keystrokes.** Let's record the keystrokes you would use to close a typical business letter.

To record keystrokes
Press   **Ctrl-F10** and the prompt reads *Define macro:*
Type   **CLOSE** and then press **Enter**. The prompt reads *Description:*

Type	**Close for letter** and then press **Enter**. The status line flashes *Macro Def*
Type	**Sincerely yours,** and then press **Enter** four times
Type	**your name** and then press **Enter**
Press	**Ctrl-F10** and the status line no longer flashes *Macro Def*

Result: When you define a macro, it is stored in a file on the current default drive (unless you specify another path when naming it). To see the macro you just defined, press **F5** and then press **Enter**. The file it is stored in is the name you assigned, CLOSE, followed by the extension .WPM. Press **F7** to return to the document.

Step 3 **Play Back Keystrokes.** Once you have recorded keystrokes, you can play them back at any time.

To play back the recorded keystrokes

Press	**Home** twice and then ↓ to move the cursor to the end of the document
Press	**Enter** twice to enter blank lines
Press	**Alt-F10** and the prompt reads *Macro:*
Type	**CLOSE** and then press **Enter**

Result: The macro is played back, and the close is entered at the cursor's position. You can insert this information anywhere in your document by moving the cursor to the desired spot and playing back the recorded keystrokes.

Step 4 **Record Keystrokes with a Pause.** Frequently, you want to be able to enter text from the keyboard when you execute a macro, for example, to enter the name of a person or a file. You can do so by entering a pause when you record the macro. Let's record keystrokes that pause so that you can type your name and any carbon copy initials.

To record keystrokes with pauses

Press	**Ctrl-F10** and the prompt reads *Define macro:*
Type	**PAUSE** and then press **Enter**. The prompt reads *Description:*
Type	**Close w/pause** and then press **Enter**. The status line flashes *Macro Def*
Type	**Sincerely yours,** and then press **Enter** four times
Press	**Ctrl-PgUp** to display the Macro Options menu
Press	**1** for *Pause*
Type	your name and then press **Enter** to end the pause
Press	**Enter** twice to move the cursor down two lines
Type	**cc.** and then press **Spacebar**
Press	**Ctrl-PgUp** to display the Macro Options menu
Press	**1** for *Pause*
Type	your initials and then press **Enter** to end the pause
Press	**Enter** to move the cursor down a line
Press	**Ctrl-F10** and the status line no longer flashes *Macro Def*

Result: The macro is now stored under the name PAUSE.WPM.

Step 5 **Play Back the Macro.** You play back the keystrokes the same way you did the original series.

To play back a macro

Press	**Alt-F10** and the prompt reads *Macro:*
Type	**PAUSE** and then press **Enter**

Result: The macro is played until the first four carriage returns are entered. It then pauses. Type your name, and then press **Enter**. The macro continues until it types *cc.* and enters a space. Type your initials, and then press **Enter**.

Step 6   **Chain Macros.** You can chain macros to each other so that when one is finished, it plays another. Let's create a new macro that moves the cursor to the end of the document, enters two blank lines, and then executes the macro with the pause in it. Here, instead of assigning it a name, you assign it to the **Alt-C** key combination so that you can execute it just by pressing **Alt-C**.

To record keystrokes

Press	**Ctrl-F10** and the prompt reads *Define macro:*
Press	**Alt-C** and the prompt reads *Description:*
Type	**End and then Close** and then press **Enter**. The status line flashes *Macro Def*
Press	**Home** twice and then ↓ to move the cursor to the end of the document
Press	**Enter** twice
Press	**Alt-F10** and the prompt reads *Macro:*
Type	**PAUSE** and then press **Enter** to execute that macro from within the new one
Press	**Ctrl-F10** and the status line no longer flashes *Macro Def*

To play back the recorded keystrokes

Press	**Home** twice and then ↑ to move the cursor to the beginning of the document
Press	**Alt-C** to execute the macro

Result: The cursor moves to the end of the document, and then the PAUSE macro is executed automatically. Type your name and initials, pressing **Enter** after each.

Step 7   **Repeat Macros.** You can use the Repeat command to repeat a macro a specified number of times. Let's use it to enter your name.

To record keystrokes

Press	**Home** twice and then ↓ to move the cursor to the end of the document
Press	**Enter** twice
Press	**Ctrl-F10** and the prompt reads *Define macro:*
Type	**NAME** and then press **Enter**. The prompt reads *Description:*
Type	**Enters name** and then press **Enter**. The status line flashes *Macro Def*
Type	**your name** and then press **Enter**
Press	**Ctrl-F10** and the status line no longer flashes *Macro Def*

To play back the recorded keystrokes

Press	**Esc** and the prompt reads *Repeat Value = 8*
Type	**20** and the prompt reads *Repeat Value = 20*
Press	**Alt-F10** and the prompt reads *Macro:*
Type	**NAME** and then press **Enter**

Result: In a moment, the macro repeats 20 times.

Step 8   **Edit a Macro.** You can edit macros to add or delete keystrokes. Let's edit the PAUSE macro to enter prompts that are displayed when it pauses.

To edit a macro

Press   **Ctrl-F10** and the prompt reads *Define macro:*

Type   **PAUSE** and then press **Enter**. The prompt reads *PAUSE.WPM Already Exists*

Press   **2** for *Edit* to display the Macro Edit screen and menu

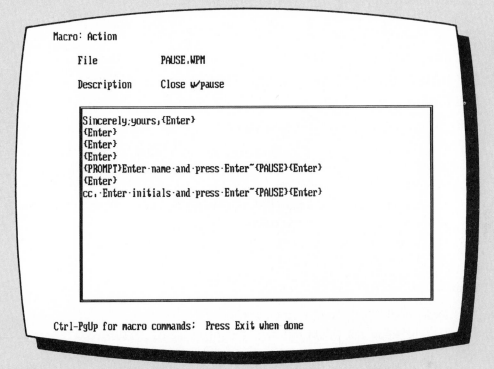

```
Macro: Action

    File            PAUSE.WPM

    Description     Close w/pause

 ┌──────────────────────────────────────────────────┐
 │Sincerely,yours,{Enter}                            │
 │{Enter}                                            │
 │{Enter}                                            │
 │{Enter}                                            │
 │{PROMPT}Enter·name·and·press·Enter~{PAUSE}{Enter}  │
 │{Enter}                                            │
 │cc,·Enter·initials·and·press·Enter~{PAUSE}{Enter}  │
 │                                                   │
 └──────────────────────────────────────────────────┘

    Ctrl-PgUp for macro commands; Press Exit when done
```

FIGURE 116   **The Edited Macro.**   After revising your macro, it should look like this.

Result: The Macro Edit screen and menu is displayed on the screen (Figure 115).

- Position the cursor under the { character in the first {*PAUSE*} code.
- Press **Ctrl-PgUp** to display a menu of macro commands.
- Press ↓ to move the highlight over the command that reads {*PROMPT*}*message~* and then press **Enter**. The {*PROMPT*} code appears in the window with the cursor to its right.
- Type **Enter name and press Enter~**. (The last character, ~, is called a *tilde*. It is usually the leftmost character on the row of number keys. To enter it, you hold down **Shift**.)
- Move the cursor under the { character in the second {*PAUSE*} code, and then repeat the same commands to enter the prompt *Enter initials and press Enter~*.

When you are finished, your screen should look like Figure 116. Press **F7** to return to the document screen. Play back the macro the same way you did in Step 5, and notice how the prompts guide you.

Step 9   **Continue or Exit.** You have now completed this tutorial. You may either continue with your own work or exit WordPerfect and return to the operating system. There is no need to save the document, because the macros themselves have been saved onto the disk. To see them, display the List Files screen. They all have the extension .WPM. If you are quitting for the day, remove your program and data disks, and then turn off the computer.

▼EXERCISE

EXERCISE 26A   Define a Macro That Prints and Saves a Document

Retrieve any document that you have created.

1. Create a macro that saves the document and then prints it. Name the macro SAVEPRT. (On a hard disk system, precede the macro name with a path to the disk from which you retrieved the file, for example, A:SAVEPRT.)

2. Execute the macro. (On a hard disk system, be sure to specify the path to the disk on which you saved the macro.)

3. Clear the screen without saving the document.

▼QUESTIONS

1. Describe the purpose of keyboard macros.

2. List the steps you would follow to record a macro.

3. How do you play back a recorded macro?

TOPIC 27
File Management

You can execute several DOS commands from WordPerfect's List Files menu. You can also access DOS without leaving WordPerfect and, when you are finished, return to exactly where you were.

USING THE LIST FILES MENU

You can execute many DOS commands from the List Files menu (**F5**, **Enter**). These commands are useful when you want to make backup copies of your files or rename or delete them.

Copying Files

You can copy files to other disks or directories or to the same disk or directory if you change its name. The name of a copied and renamed file does not appear on the list of files unless you highlight *<Current>* *<Dir>* at the top of the list of files on the left side of the screen and then press **Enter** twice to update the file list.

 KEY/Strokes
COPYING A FILE

---

1. Display the directory containing the file to be copied
2. Use the arrow keys to highlight the name of the file
3. Press **8** for *Copy* and the prompt reads **Copy this file to:**. (If copying to another floppy disk on a computer with only one floppy disk drive, remove the program disk from drive A, and then insert the disk you are copying to.)
4. Type the path of the drive and directory you are copying the file to, and then press **Enter**. (When copying is completed, insert the program disk into drive A if you removed it.)
5. Press **F7** to return to the document screen

Moving and Renaming Files

You can rename or move files. Renaming them changes their name but leaves them on the same disk or in the same directory. Moving them copies them to another disk or directory and then deletes them from the current one.

KEY/Strokes

RENAMING A FILE

1. Display the directory containing the file to be renamed
2. Use the arrow keys to highlight the name of the file
3. Press **3** for *Move/Rename* and the prompt reads *New name:* followed by the name of the file to be renamed
4. Type the new name of the file (precede it with a path if moving it to another disk or directory), and then press **Enter**
5. Press **F7** to return to the document screen

Deleting Files and Directories

You can delete files that you no longer need or delete empty directories.

KEY/Strokes

DELETING A FILE OR AN EMPTY SUBDIRECTORY

1. Display the directory containing the file or empty subdirectory to be deleted
2. Use the arrow keys to highlight the name of the file or empty directory
3. Press **2** for *Delete*, and the prompt reads *Delete* followed by the name of the file to be deleted
4. Press **Y** to delete
5. Press **F7** to return to the document screen

Using Directories

To move quickly through directories, highlight the directory (including *<Parent>* *<Dir>*, which is the directory one level up), and then press **Enter** twice to display the files it contains. When you locate the directory containing the file you want, highlight the file's name, and then press **1** for *Retrieve*. You can also press **7** for *Other Directory* and then press **Enter** twice to make the highlighted directory the current directory.

To display only selected filenames, highlight *<Current>* *<Dir>* and then press **Enter**. The message reads *Dir PATH*.* To display only selected files, use wildcards. For example, type **B:*.WP5** to list all the files on drive B that end with the extension .WP5.

To change the default directory or create a new one, press **7** for *Other Directory*. Type the new directory (for example, **C:\LETTERS**), and then press **Enter**. If the directory you specify does not exist, the prompt reads *Create:* followed by the name of the directory and the prompt *(Y/N) No*. Press **Y** to create a new directory.

KEY/Strokes

CREATING A NEW DIRECTORY

1. Press **F5** and the prompt reads *Dir* followed by the current default drive and directory and the prompt *(Type = to change default Dir)*
2. Either press **=** (the equal sign)

    Or   press **Enter** to display the files in the directory, and then press **7** for *Other Directory*

    The prompt reads *New directory =*
3. Type the new directory (for example, **C:\LETTERS**), and then press **Enter**. The prompt reads *Create:*, followed by the name of the directory and *(Y/N) No*
4. Press **Y** to create the directory
5. Press **F7** to return to the document screen

ACCESSING DOS

You can access DOS without leaving WordPerfect. When you are finished, you return to exactly where you were. To do so (if using a floppy disk system, insert a disk with the COMMAND.COM file into drive A), press **Ctrl-F1**, and the menu lists two commands you can use to access DOS:

- *1 Go to DOS:* displays the command prompt so that you can execute as many commands as you want. When finished with DOS, type **EXIT** and then press **Enter**. When you are finished, always return to WordPerfect, and then quit the program correctly.
- *2 DOS Command* executes a command you type, and when it is completed, WordPerfect automatically reappears.

When you access DOS from WordPerfect, do not use the CHKDSK/F or DELETE commands on the WordPerfect program disk.

KEY/Strokes

ACCESSING DOS FROM WITHIN THE PROGRAM

1. If using a floppy disk system, insert a disk with the COMMAND.COM file into drive A
2. Either press **Ctrl-F1**

    Or   pull down the File menu and select *Go to DOS*
3. Either press **1** for *Go to DOS* to display the command prompt, and execute DOS commands. When finished, type **EXIT** and then press **Enter**

    Or   press **2** for *DOS Command*, type a command, and then press **Enter**. When the command is completed, you automatically return to Word-Perfect

▼ **TIP**

➤ **If you want to copy or delete a group of files, you can mark them**.
  ▪ To mark or unmark individual files, move the highlight over the desired files, and then press **Shift-*** (or just the asterisk on the numeric keypad).
  ▪ To mark or unmark all files, press **Alt-F5**.

▼ **TUTORIAL**

TUTORIAL 27A   Using List Files to Manage Files

In this tutorial, you practice using the List Files screen and menu. To begin this tutorial, you must first load the program. You should insert your data disk into one of the disk drives. If necessary, clear any existing document from the screen.

Step 1   **Change the Default Drive and Display the List Files Screen and Menu**. Now change the default drive to B on a floppy disk system or drive A on a hard disk system.

To change the default drive

Press	**F5** and the message reads *Dir* followed by the current directory
Press	= (the equal sign), and the prompt reads *New directory* = followed by the current directory
Type	**B:** (on a floppy disk system) or **A:** (on a hard disk system), and then press **Enter**. The message reads *Dir* followed by the path of the new default drive and directory
Press	**Enter** again to display the list of files on the new default drive and directory

Result: The default drive is now drive B on a floppy disk system or A on a hard disk system, and a list of the files in that drive is displayed.

Step 2   **Copy a File**. Now copy the ENTER1.WP5 file and rename the duplicate file ERASE.WP5 in the same step.

To copy a file

Highlight	*ENTER1.WP5* on the list of files
Press	**8** for *Copy*, and the prompt reads *Copy this file to:*
Type	**ERASE.WP5** and then press **Enter**
Highlight	*<Current> <Dir>* at the top of the list of files on the left side of the screen, and then press **Enter** twice to update the file list

Result: The new ERASE.WP5 file is now listed on the file list.

Step 3   **Delete a File**. Now let's delete the ERASE.WP5 file.

To delete a file

Highlight	*ERASE.WP5* on the list of files
Press	**2** for *Delete*, and the prompt reads *Delete A:\\ERASE.WP5? (Y/N) No* or *Delete B:\\ERASE.WP5? (Y/N) No*
Press	**Y** to delete the file

Result: The new file is no longer listed on the file list.

Suzanne Franks
2 Jenevein Avenue
San Bruno, California 94066
(415) 555-1212

Corporate Development, Inc.
101 4th. Street
San Francisco, California 94107

ATT: Karen Hernandez

Dear Ms. Hernandez:

I am responding to your advertisement that appeared in the August 1 issue of the <u>San Jose Mercury News</u>. The possibility of becoming involved in all phases of a computerized learning center is very exciting, and I would welcome the opportunity to discuss it with you in more detail. I have extensive experience in all phases of Macintosh and IBM PC computer operations. More important, however, I work very well with all kinds of people, and love to convey to them not only knowledge, but a sense of excitement about computers and their applications. My experience in fund raising is limited to my undergraduate days when I participated in Purdue alumni telethons and fund raising for the Purdue student chapter of a national industrial design association. Although limited in experience, I recognize the importance of this phase of the activity and expect that I would both enjoy it and perform it well, given my ability to convey both enthusiasm and a sense of joining in a shared goal.

I will call you on Monday, August 4, to see if a personal meeting can be arranged at your convenience. I look forward to meeting with you to exchange ideas, to tell you more about myself, and to show you some of the creative computer projects that I have been involved with.

Sincerely yours,

Suzanne Franks

enc. Resume

B.

FIGURE 1   (continued)

STEPS

1. Prepare a cover letter for a position you might be interested in.
2. Save your letter as CVRLTR3.WP5 and then make a printout.
3. Proofread and edit the printout, and then enter the changes into the file. Spell check it again, and then make another printout. Be sure to save your revisions.
4. Revise your letter so that you can send it to a second person. Save your revised letter as CVRLTR4.WP5 and then make a printout.

PROJECT 2
Creating a Resumé

▼ BACKGROUND REQUIRED

To complete this project, you must have completed the following topics:

Topic 10	Tab Stops and Indents
Topic 12	Working with Blocks of Text
Topic 16	Text Alignment
Topic 21	Changing Fonts

▼ PROJECT DESCRIPTION

When searching for a job, you need a resumé that describes your background. In this project, you prepare your own resumé. Figure 2 shows some typical resumés that you can use as guides and sources of ideas when preparing your own resumé. Read the "Concepts" section and each of the sample resumés carefully, and highlight ideas you might want to incorporate into your own resumé. Then prepare a resumé for a job you might be seeking.

▼ CONCEPTS

Resumés give the employer written evidence of your qualifications. When creating a resumé, you need two kinds of information: facts about yourself and facts about the job you want. With this information in hand, you can present the facts about yourself in terms of the job.

Begin by assembling information about yourself. Some items appear on virtually every resumé, including the following:

- Name
- Current address and phone number—if you are rarely at home during business hours, try to give the phone number of a friend or relative who will take messages for you. Alternatively, you can get an answering machine. These are becoming increasingly more acceptable.
- Job sought or career goal
- Experience (paid and volunteer)—date of employment, name and full address of the employer, job title, starting and finishing salary, and a brief description of your responsibilities
- Education—the school's name, location, the years you attended there, the diploma or certificate you earned, and the course of studies you pursued
- Other qualifications—hobbies, organizations you belong to, honors you have received, and leadership positions you have held
- Special talents
- Office machines, tools, and equipment you have used and skills that you possess
- References—often just a statement that references are available on request; however, their names are worth listing

Personal information—height, weight, marital status, and physical condition are not important according to recruiters. In fact, employers are prohibited by law from asking for some of it. If some of this information is directly job related (the height and weight of a bouncer may be important to a disco owner), list it. Otherwise, save space, and add more information about your skills.

Next, gather specific information about the jobs you are applying for. You

Judy L. Antonio
19 Fernwood Drive
Williamsville, New York 14221
(716) 555-1313

EDUCATION

College	State University College at Buffalo
Degree	Bachelor of Science degree in Education
Certification	Elementary Education

TEACHING EXPERIENCE

11/87-12/87   Student Teacher
Central Elementary School
155 Central Road
Williamsville, NY 14221
Planned and implemented lessons for all subjects in the second and third grades.

9/87-10/87   Student Teacher
Country Parkway Elementary School
35 Hollybrook Drive
Williamsville, NY 14221
Planned and implemented lessons for all subjects in the first grade.

EXPERIENCE/WORK HISTORY

3/85-4/87   Teacher Substitute
Campus Child Care Center, Inc.
SUNYAB
Buffalo, NY 14214
Started as teacher aide and in May, 1985, was promoted to teacher substitute.

11/84-6/86   Teacher's Assistant
Central Day Care Center
15 Jewett Parkway
Buffalo, NY 14214
Before and After School Program: planned and implemented various activities for children, ages 5-7.

1979-1986   Counselor and Program Staff
Cradle Beach Camp (summer resident camp)
Old Lake Shore Road
Angola, NY 14006
Responsibilities included: arts and crafts staff, cabin staff, pool staff and cabin counselor with physically handicapped, mentally retarded, and/or deprived boys and girls, ages 9-17. Certified in advanced lifesaving.

REFERENCES

Available upon request from:
State University College at Buffalo
Grover Cleveland Hall, Room 306
1300 Elmwood Avenue
Buffalo, NY 14222

A. A Chronological Résumé

FIGURE 2   Sample Résumés. These illustrations show two typical resumés: one arranged chronologically and the other functionally.

need to know the pay range (so that you can make their top offer your bottom offer), education and experience required, and hours and shifts worked. Most important, you need to know the job duties (so that you can describe your experience in terms of those duties). Study the job description. Some job announcements, especially those issued by a government, even have a checklist that assigns a numerical weight to different qualifications so that you can be certain which is the most important; looking at such announcements will give you an idea of what employers look for. If the announcement or ad is vague, call the employer to learn what is sought.

Once you have the information you need, you can prepare a resumé. You may need to prepare more than one master resumé if you are going to look for different kinds of jobs; otherwise, your resumé will not fit the job you seek.

Allison Springs
15 Hilton House
College de l'Art Libre
Smallville, CO 77717
(888) 736-3550

Job sought: Hotel Management Trainee

Skills, education, and experience

Working with people. All the jobs I have had involve working closely with people on many different levels. As vice president of the junior class, I balanced the concerns of different groups in order to reach a common goal. As a claims interviewer with a state public assistance agency, I dealt with people under very trying circumstances. As a research assistant with a law firm, I worked with both lawyers and clerical workers. And as a lifeguard (five summers), I learned how to manage groups. In addition, my work with the state and the law office has made me familiar with organization procedures.

Effective communication. My campaign for class office, committee projects, and fund raising efforts (which netted $15,000 for the junior class project) relied on effective communication in both oral and written presentations.

Organization and management. My participation in student government has developed my organization and management skills. In addition, my work with the state government and a law office has made me familiar with organization procedures.

Chronology

September 1988 to present	Attended College de l'Art in Smallville, Colorado. Will earn a Bachelor of Arts degree in political science. Elected vice president of the junior class, managed successful fund drive, directed Harvest Celebration Committee, served on many other committees, and earned 13 percent of my college expenses
January 1992 to present	Worked as research assistant for the law office of McCall, McCrow, and McCow, 980 Main Street, Westrow, Colorado 77718. Supervisor: Jan Eagelli (666) 654-3211
September 1991 to December 1991	Served as claims interviewer intern for the Department of Public Assistance of the State of Colorado, 226 Park Street, Smallville, Colorado 77717. Supervisor: James Fish (666) 777-7717
1985-1990	Worked as lifeguard during the summer at the Shilo Pool, 46 Waterway, Shilo, Nebraska 77777

Recommendations available upon request

B. A Functional Résumé

FIGURE 2   (continued)

Reverse chronology is the easiest method to use. It is also the least effective because it makes when you did something seem more important than what you did. It is an especially poor format if you have gaps in your work history, if the job you seek is very different from the job you currently hold, or if you are just entering the job market. About the only time you would want to use such a resumé is when you have progressed up a clearly defined career ladder and want to move up a rung.

Resumés that are not chronological may be called functional, analytical, skill oriented, creative, or some other name. The differences among them are less important than their similarity, which is that all stress what you can do. The advantage to a potential employer—and, therefore, to your job campaign—should be obvious. The employer can see immediately how you will fit the job. This format also has advantages for many job hunters because it camouflages gaps in paid employment and avoids giving prominence to irrelevant jobs.

You begin writing a functional resumé by determining the skills the employer is looking for. Again, study the job description for this information. Next, review your experience and education to see when you demonstrated the ability sought. Then prepare the resumé itself, putting first the information that relates most obviously to the job. The result will be a resumé with headings such as "Engineering," "Computer Languages," "Communication Skills," or "Design Experience." These headings will have much more impact than the dates that you would use on a chronological resumé.

The way you arrange your resumé depends on how well your experience seems to prepare you for the position you want. You can either describe your most recent job first and work backward (reverse chronology) or group similar skills together. Whichever format you use, the following advice generally applies:

- Use specifics. A vague description of your duties will make only a vague impression.
- Identify accomplishments. If you headed a project, improved productivity, reduced costs, increased membership, or achieved some other goal, say so.
- Keep the length down to two pages at the most.
- Remember your mother's advice not to say anything if you cannot say something nice. Leave all embarrassing or negative information off the resumé, but be ready to deal with it in a positive fashion at the interview.
- Proofread the master copy carefully, and then have someone else do the same.

▼ **STEPS**

1. Enter and format your own resumé.
2. Save the resumé as RESUME.WP5 and then make a printout.
3. Proofread and edit the printout, and then enter the changes into the file. Spell check it again, and then make another printout. Be sure to save your revisions.

PROJECT 3
Preparing a Follow-Up Letter

▼ **BACKGROUND REQUIRED**

To complete this project, you must have completed the following topic:

Topic 10   Tab Stops and Indents

▼ **PROJECT DESCRIPTION**

After you have had a job interview, you should immediately send a follow-up letter to the person who interviewed you. In this project, you complete a follow-up letter so that you can mail it after an interview. Figure 3 shows a typical follow-up letter that you can use as a guide and source of ideas when preparing your own

Dear

I would like to thank you for spending time with me last (Friday) to discuss your opening for an entry level (position). I am impressed with the quality of your organization and would like to reiterate my interest in discussing the position further.

As I mentioned to you, I feel that I could contribute to your company's objectives for a number of reasons.

■ I am able to work well with coworkers and am very much a team player.

■ My previous experience at (previous job) has given me enough experience to understand the responsibilities of the position and I hope will give me a head start in becoming a contributing employee.

Since the interview, I have been giving a great deal of thought about our discussion and would also like to make the following points:

■ While working on the school newspaper, I gained interviewing experience that should make me better at completing the surveys you mentioned would be required as part of the position's responsibilities.

■ I have earned over 50 percent of my college expenses and in the process have established a solid employment record over the past four years. I have proved my reliability in this position and hope you will call Mr. Jones at 212-555-1212 to hear his opinions of the contributions that I have made.

Again, thank you for your consideration, and I look forward to hearing from you. If there is any additional information I might be able to supply, please let me know. I am anxious to hear from you.

Sincerely yours,

FIGURE 3   Sample Follow-Up Letter.   This illustration shows a sample follow-up letter that is sent after a job interview.

letter. Read the "Concepts" section and the sample letter carefully, and highlight ideas you might want to incorporate into your own letter. Then prepare a follow-up letter for a job you might be seeking.

▼CONCEPTS

The purpose of a follow-up letter is to remind the person who interviewed you that you are interested in the position you discussed. You might refer to points you made in the interview that you want the interviewer to remember. You are selling yourself in the follow-up letter just as you did in the cover letter, resumé, and interview. Your advantage in the follow-up letter is that you have had time to consider how the interview went, so you can address points you forgot to make or would like to reinforce. Keep the letter short, and if possible, itemize key points so that the interviewer can read it quickly and still get the points you are making.

▼ STEPS

1. Prepare a follow-up letter for a position you might be interviewed for. Save your letter as FOLLOWUP.WP5 and then make a printout.
2. Proofread and edit the printout, and then enter the changes into the file. Spell check it again, and then make another printout. Be sure to save your revisions.

DOS COMMANDS QUICK REFERENCE

Command	Description	Type
Basic Commands		
VER	Displays DOS version number	Internal
DATE	Displays system date	Internal
TIME	Displays system time	Internal
Drive Commands		
A:	Makes drive A the default drive	Internal
B:	Makes drive B the default drive	Internal
Data Disk Formatting Commands		
FORMAT	Formats a data disk	External
FORMAT/V	Formats a data disk with a volume name	External
System Disk Formatting Commands		
FORMAT/S	Formats a system disk	External
FORMAT/S/V	Formats a system disk with a volume name	External
Copying Commands		
COPY	Copies individual files	Internal
COPY A:*.* B	Copies all files from A to B	Internal
COPY B:*.* A	Copies all files from B to A	Internal
Duplicating Disks Command		
DISKCOPY	Duplicates a disk	External
Comparing Disk Command		
DISKCOMP	Compares duplicated disks	External
File Renaming Commands		
RENAME	Renames files	Internal
REN	Renames files	Internal
File Erase Commands		
ERASE	Deletes files from disk	Internal
DEL	Deletes files from disk	Internal
Disk Checking Commands		
CHKDSK *.*	Looks for noncontiguous blocks	External
	Indicates status of memory	
	Indicates disk space	
Directory Commands		
MD	Creates a new directory	Internal
CD	Changes the default directory	Internal
RD	Removes a directory	Internal
CD	Returns to the root directory	Internal
CD ..	Returns to one level up	Internal
TREE	Displays a list of directories	External
TREE/F	Displays a list of directories and files	External

FIGURE 4 Quick Reference Card. This illustration shows a listing of the most frequently used DOS commands.

PROJECT 4
Preparing a Quick Reference Card for DOS

▼BACKGROUND REQUIRED

To complete this project, you must have completed the following topics:

Topic 10	Tab Stops and Indents
Topic 21	Changing Fonts

▼PROJECT DESCRIPTION

When working with any program on a computer, you have to understand the DOS commands that you use to copy, rename, and delete files; format disks; change default drives; and perform other tasks. In this project, you prepare the quick reference card shown in Figure 4 that describes the basic DOS commands you should be familiar with.

▼CONCEPTS

DOS commands fall into two classes: internal and external. Internal commands are always available whenever the operating system's command prompt is displayed on the screen. External commands are stored in their own individual files on the disk and are loaded only when you execute the command. To load an external command, the file in which it is stored must be on a disk in one of the drives when you execute the command. If the file can't be found, the computer displays an error message.

▼STEPS

1. Enter and format the table shown in Figure 4. When you are finished, save the document as DOS.WP5 and then make a printout.
2. Proofread and revise your table. Make a new printout, and then save the finished document.

APPENDIX

Understanding DOS

All applications programs that operate on a microcomputer require an operating system. Because the operating system coordinates activity between any applications program you run and the computer hardware, you must load the operating system into the computer's memory before you load an applications program. Most applications programs that you buy from publishers do not contain the operating system. To use these programs, you must first load the operating system from another disk, or copy the appropriate operating system program files to the applications program disk or your hard disk. This is necessary because the operating system may have been published by one company and the applications program by another. Even if the same company publishes both, they are not sure which version of their operating system you may be using, so they cannot anticipate which version to put on the disk.

When IBM developed the original IBM PC, they contracted the development of its operating system to Microsoft, which developed an operating system called MS-DOS (Microsoft Disk Operating System). The IBM PC version of this program was named PC-DOS. The PC-DOS version usually runs on IBM PC computers, and the MS-DOS version usually runs on compatibles made by manufacturers other than IBM. These two versions of the operating system are essentially identical in the way they work and the commands you use to operate them; usually they are interchangeable. Since the IBM PC set the standard for microcomputers, MS-DOS and PC-DOS are the most widely used operating systems.

As computers have evolved, so have operating systems. When major changes are made in the operating system, it is released as a new version. For example, DOS was initially released as version 1.0, and over the years, versions 2.0, 3.0, and 4.0 have been released. Minor changes also are introduced periodically. These are usually identified with numbers following the decimal point. For example, DOS is available in versions 3.0, 3.1, 3.2, 3.3, 4.0, and 4.01. Normally, programs that run on an early version will also run on a later version. This appendix discusses all versions of releases 3 and 4, so they are referred to as DOS 3 and DOS 4. The major difference between DOS 3 and 4 is the addition of the Shell to DOS 4. This version allows you to execute many of the most commonly used commands from these menus.

Note: All of the instructions in this appendix describe procedures that you follow when DOS's command prompt is displayed. If you are using DOS 3, the command prompt is displayed when you first load the operating system. (If you are working on a computer connected to a network, ask your instructor how you display this prompt.) However, if you are using DOS 4, your system may be set up to display the Shell. To follow the procedures described in this appendix, you must remove this Shell and display the command prompt. To do so, you have two choices:

- Press F3 from Start Programs to remove the Shell from memory. (You first have to press F3 if you are in the File System, or Esc if you are in the DOS Utilities' subgroup, to return to Start Programs.) You can also select *Exit Shell* from the Start Programs' Exit menu on the Action Bar. After using either command, type **DOSSHELL** and then press ENTER to return to the Shell if you want to display it again.
- Press SHIFT-F9 to leave the Shell in memory and load a second copy of the COMMAND.COM file. You can also select *Command Prompt* from the Start Programs' Main Group. These commands make it faster to return to the Shell when you want. To do so, type **EXIT** and then press ENTER. If you use this command, and there is not enough room in memory for the second copy of the COMMAND.COM program, an error message is displayed. Use the first procedure to display the command prompt.

1. UNDERSTANDING DISKS AND DISK DRIVES

When you work on a computer, the programs and files you work on are stored internally in the computer's random-access memory (RAM). This memory is a limited resource, yet it must serve many uses. Not only do you load different applications programs, you also create files for your own work, and there can be a lot of them. The computer's memory is not large enough to store all the programs, documents, and other computer-generated files you work on. Moreover, most memory will lose its data when you turn the computer off.

For these reasons, external storage (also called auxiliary or secondary storage) is provided. You use this storage to store programs and data that you are not using at the moment. Once data is stored externally, you can reload it into the computer's internal memory without having to rekeyboard it.

Computers usually use magnetic disks to store programs and files externally. Magnetic disks, and the devices used to store and retrieve data on them, fall into two major classes: floppy disks and disk drives and hard disk drives.

FLOPPY DISKS AND DISK DRIVES

Floppy disks for microcomputers come in two sizes: $5\frac{1}{4}$ and $3\frac{1}{2}$ inches. Each size works only with drives specifically designed to accept it. Though they vary in size, they have certain features in common (Figure 1):

1. A storage envelope protects $5\frac{1}{4}$-inch disks from scratches, dust, and fingerprints. Some envelopes are treated to eliminate the static buildup that attracts abrasive grit. These envelopes are not used on the better protected $3\frac{1}{2}$-inch disks.
2. A plastic outer covering protects the disk itself while allowing it to spin smoothly inside the jacket. $5\frac{1}{4}$-inch disks are protected by flexible plastic jackets, whereas $3\frac{1}{2}$-inch disks are mounted in a rigid plastic housing. The jacket or housing is permanently sealed and contains lubricants and cleaning agents that prolong the life of the disk.
3. The read/write slot in the jacket is where the disk drive's read/write head contacts the surface of the disk. This read/write head stores data on (writes) and retrieves data from (reads) the surface of the disk as the disk spins inside the drive. On $3\frac{1}{2}$-inch disks, the read/write slot is protected by a sliding metal cover called the shutter. When you insert the disk into the drive, this shutter

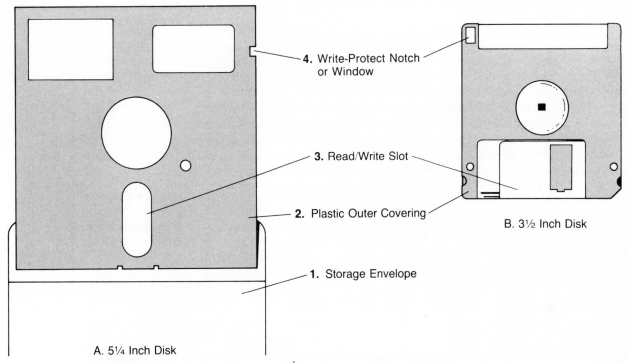

4. Write-Protect Notch or Window

3. Read/Write Slot

2. Plastic Outer Covering

B. 3½ Inch Disk

1. Storage Envelope

A. 5¼ Inch Disk

FIGURE 1   Floppy Disk Characteristics.   5¼-inch and 3½-inch disks have many features in common.

is automatically pushed aside so that the read/write slot is exposed, and the drive can come in contact with the floppy disk within.

4. The write-protect notch or window allows you to write on a disk when it is not write-protected and prevents you from writing on the disk when it is (see the section "Write-Protect Your Disks"). A switch, or photoelectric circuit, inside the disk drive determines if the disk is write-protected. If it finds that it is, the switch disables the drive's ability to write information onto the disk.

If you were to remove the plastic jacket or housing of a floppy disk, you would find a round piece of plastic covered with a metallic oxide similar to the magnetic recording material used on audiotapes and videotapes. The round disk is sandwiched between two sheets of a soft, feltlike material, which is impregnated with a lubricant that protects the disk when it is spinning in the drive.

The floppy disk drive is the device that the floppy disk is inserted into so that you can store data to and retrieve data from it. The floppy disk drive has two parts you should be familiar with: the slot and the light (Figure 2).

2. Light

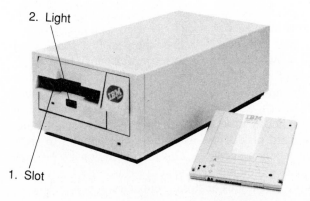

1. Slot

FIGURE 2 A Floppy Disk Drive. The floppy disk drive has two parts that you should be familiar with: the drive's slot and the drive's light. Here they are shown on a standalone drive, but most disk drives are built into the computer. *Courtesy of IBM Corporation*

Types of Floppy Disks

Since there is variation among computers, the disks you buy must be appropriate for the system you want to use them on. On every box of disks, and on most disk labels, are several terms that you should be familiar with. Knowing the number of sides, the density, and the sectors used by your system allows you to select and use the correct disks with your system.

SIDES

Disks are rated as single or double sided. Single-sided disks can store data on only one side of the disk. Double-sided disks can store data on both sides of the disk if your system's disk drive is capable of writing to both sides.

DENSITY

Data are stored on a disk on tracks, narrow concentric bands around the disk somewhat like the grooves on a $33\frac{1}{3}$ record (al-though a record's groove is one continuous spiral and not a series of concentric circles). To store more data, the tracks are placed closer together. The spacing of these tracks is measured as tracks per inch (TPI). The maximum density that can be used to store data on a disk is indicated on the disk label and box.

- Single-density disks can store data on 24 TPI.
- Double-density disks can store data on 48 TPI or up to 360KB (KB stands for kilobytes).
- High-density disks (also called high-capacity or quad-density disks) can store data on 96 TPI.
- $3\frac{1}{2}$-inch floppy disks can store 720KB or 1.44MB (MB stands for megabytes) on a double-sided disk. These smaller disks can store more data than the larger $5\frac{1}{4}$-inch disks because they can store data on 135 TPI.

1. The slot is where you insert a floppy disk into the drive (see the box "Inserting Floppy Disks" in Topic 1).
2. The light on the front of the drive goes on when the drive is operating. When the light is on, you should not open the door or eject a disk. Doing so can damage the disk and cause you to lose data. If you make a mistake and the drive spins when the door is open or without a disk inserted, do not close the door or insert a disk. In a few moments, a message will usually appear telling you the drive's door is open or no disk is in the drive. When the light goes out, close the door or insert a disk, and then follow the instructions displayed on the screen.

HARD DISK DRIVES

Hard disk drives (also called fixed disks or Winchester disk drives after their code name while being developed at IBM) were not commonly used with microcomputers until recently because of their high cost. But over the past few years, their cost has dropped dramatically. Lower cost and superior performance have made hard disk drives the first choice of serious computer users. Moreover, their storage capacity greatly reduces the number of disk "swaps" that have to be made when working with floppy disk drives. Since many operating systems and applications programs come on several floppy disks, this can save a great deal of time.

Instead of a floppy disk, hard disk drives use rigid metal platters to store data. This allows them to store data more densely. This increased density plus the number of platters greatly increases their storage capacity. Hard disk drives generally provide 10, 20, 40, or more megabytes of storage capacity, much more than a floppy disk. In addition, a hard disk drive spins at 3600 rpm, about ten times faster than a floppy disk drive, allowing data to be stored and retrieved faster.

In a floppy disk drive, the read/write heads are in contact with the disk. In a hard disk drive, they fly over its surface on a cushion of air with a space smaller than a piece of dust separating the head from the rapidly spinning disk. To imagine the small tolerances involved, picture an airplane flying at high speed $\frac{1}{2}$ inch above the ground without making contact. With the high speeds and small spaces involved, even a particle can cause the read/write head to come in contact with the disk's surface, creating a head crash. With the disk spinning at almost 60 mph, this can cause a lot of damage to the disk and the data stored on it.

When you use a hard disk drive, the read/write head is positioned on the disk where data is stored. If you are going to move your computer, use the park program (found on a disk that comes with your computer) to park the read/write head. This program moves the read/write head to a section of the disk that has no data, thus preventing the head from damaging data on the disk should it move. Even slightly jarring your computer may damage your files.

PROTECTING AND CARING FOR YOUR FILES AND DISKS

When you enter data into the computer, it is not stored permanently until you save it onto disks. But even then the data is not protected from loss or damage. No one ever heeds this advice until they loose important information and have to spend hours or days recreating it. Don't be like everyone else; follow these recommendations before you lose data.

Floppy Disk Storage

When you first start working on a microcomputer, the number of disks you work with is manageable. But before long, keeping disks filed in an orderly way can present quite a problem. Several disk filing systems have been developed, including plastic sleeves that can be inserted in three-ring binders, plastic cases, and sophisticated filing cabinets for large collections.

Labeling Your Disks

An unwritten rule among computer users is that an unlabeled disk contains no valuable files. People often do not take the time to check what files, if any, an unlabeled disk contains. Thus the first step when you use a disk is to label it. Always write the disk title, your name, the date, and the operating system version that you are using on the labels (Figure 3).

If you are using 5¼-inch floppy disks, be sure also to fill out labels before you affix them to the disks. If you write on a label that is already on a disk, you can damage the disk if you press down too hard. If you must write on a label that is already on a disk, use a felt-tip pen, and write very gently. Do not apply pressure.

Write-Protect Your Disks

When you save files onto a disk, format a disk, or erase files from a disk, you can damage files if you make a mistake. If a disk is write-protected, you can read files on the disk, but you cannot save files on it, format it, or erase files from it. When you have an important disk that you want to protect the files on, write-protect it so that you do not inadvertently damage or delete files (Figure 4).

- When the write-protect notch on a 5¼-inch floppy disk is not covered, you can save, copy, and erase files on a disk. When the write-protect notch is

A. Data Disks

DATA DISK--ORIGINAL Your Name / The Date Formatted with DOS 4	DATA DISK--BACKUP Your Name / The Date Formatted with DOS 4

B. Program Disks

PROGRAM DISK--ORIGINAL Your Name / The Date Formatted with DOS 4	PROGRAM DISK--BACKUP Your Name / The Date Formatted with DOS 4

FIGURE 3   Disk Labels.   Disks labels should indicate the type of disk, whether it is an original or backup copy, your name, the date the disk was formatted, and the format used.

covered by tape, you cannot. You must use a write-protect tape that light cannot shine through since many drives use a light to determine if the notch is covered or not. If you use a transparent tape, the light will shine through the notch just as if it were not covered, and the drive will assume it is not write-protected.

* 3½-inch floppy disks have a sliding tab that you press to open or close the write-protect window. When closed, you can save, copy, and erase files on a disk. When open, you cannot.

Backup Copies

Always make backup copies of your important files and disks, and save them a safe distance from your working area. Make sure the same accident cannot happen to both the original disk and its backup copy. The information on the disk is usually worth much more than the disk itself, so don't take chances. You can back

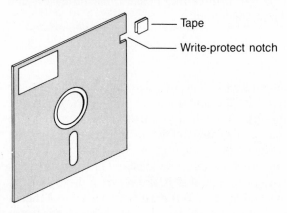

Tape

Write-protect notch

FIGURE   4   Write-Protecting Floppy Disks.
A. Write-protecting a 5¼-inch disk
B. Write-protecting a 3½-inch disk

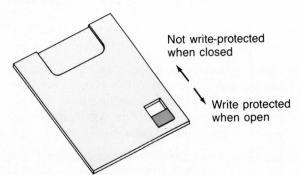

Not write-protected when closed

Write protected when open

up floppy disks using the Copy or Diskcopy commands described in Sec. 6 or 7, and hard disks using the Backup command described in the DOS manual.

Caring for Your Disks

Disks, both hard and floppy, are very reliable storage media. However, the data they contain can be lost or damaged if you do not take a few precautions. Floppy disks are relatively durable under ordinary conditions and have a useful life of about forty hours' spinning time. But that life can be shortened or abruptly ended by improper handling. Proper care ensures that disks will accurately store and play back the data you need.

Care of Hard Disk Drives

DON'T drop or jar them. They are very sensitive.

DO use the park program to move the drive's read/write head to a safe place on the disk before moving the computer.

Care of Floppy Disk Drives

DON'T use commercial cleaning kits too often. Overuse can cause problems with the drive.

DO insert the cardboard protectors that came with 5¼-inch disk drives and close the doors when moving the computer.

Care of Floppy Disks

DO keep disks in their protective storage envelopes. These envelopes reduce static buildup, which can attract dust that might scratch the disk.

DO keep disks dry, away from sneezes, coffee, or anything wet. A wet disk is a ruined disk.

DO prevent disks from getting too hot or too cold. They should be stored at temperatures of 50°–150°F (10°–52°C). Extremes of temperature can destroy a disk's sensitivity, so treat them the same way you treat photographic film; that is, keep them out of direct sunlight, do not leave them in a car exposed to temperature extremes, and so forth.

DO keep disks at least 2 feet away from magnets. The magnets found in copy stands, telephones, radio or stereo speakers, vacuum cleaners, televisions, air conditioners, novelty items, electric motors, or even some cabinet latches can ruin a disk's data.

DON'T touch a disk's recording surface. Handle them only by their protective covers.

DON'T use a hard-tipped pen to write on a disk label that is affixed to the disk. This can crease the disk inside the protective cover and cause you to lose data. Write on the label before affixing it to the disk, or use a felt-tip pen with very light pressure.

DON'T leave a disk in a nonoperating disk drive with the door closed for long periods. Open the drive door to lift the read/write head from the surface of the disk.

DON'T insert or remove a disk from the drive when the disk drive is running (that is, when the drive's light is on).

DON'T bend, fold, or crimp disks.

DON'T use paper clips to attach a floppy disk to a file folder or copy of a printout. Special folders are available that let you keep disks and printed documents together.

DON'T expose disks to static electricity. In dry climates or in heated buildings, static builds up when you walk on carpeted and some other kinds of floors. If you experience shocks when you touch metal objects, you are discharging the static that has built up. If you touch a disk when still charged with this static, you can damage the data. To prevent this, increase the humidity in the air, use static-proof carpets, or touch something like a typewriter to discharge the static before you pick up a disk.

Even with the best of care, floppy disks can last only so long. Close to the end of their useful life, they show their own form of senility by losing information or giving invalid commands. These are signs that it is time to replace the disk, which ideally, you have already made another backup copy of.

2. SPECIFYING DRIVES

CONCEPTS

When you first turn on your computer and load the operating system, drive A spins. If a disk in that drive contains the necessary operating system files, the operating system is loaded. Drive A operates because the computer's designers have placed a program in the computer's ROM telling it that it should address this drive when first turned on. Since it addresses drive A automatically, drive A is the default drive (Figure 5).

Although you cannot change the default drive that the computer addresses when you first turn it on, you can, and often do, copy, rename, delete, and save files from a drive other than the default drive. There are two ways to do this (Figure 6). You can change the default drive, or you can specify the other drive in the command.

Procedures

When working from the command prompt, you can quickly change the default drive by typing the letter of the drive and a colon (and an optional backslash) and then pressing ENTER. For example, if the default drive is set to A, and you want to change it to B, type **B:** or **B:** and then press ENTER. The command prompt indicates the current default drive. For example, *B>* or *B:\>* indicates that drive B is the default drive.

To specify a drive in a command, you enter the letters of the desired drives in the command followed by colons. For example, when you want to copy a file from drive A to drive B, you type the command **COPY A:FILENAME.EXT B:**.

FIGURE 5   The Default Drive.   The default drive is the drive the computer automatically addresses when you execute commands or copy files. It's like a model railroad where you can set a switch to send a train down one track or another.

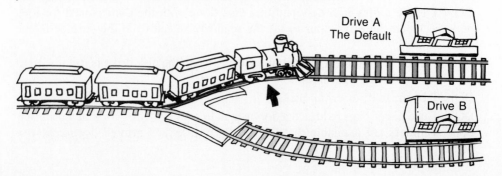

Drive A
The Default

Drive B

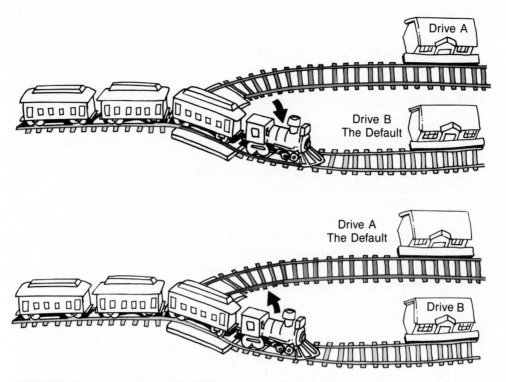

FIGURE 6   Addressing Another Drive.
A. You can change the default drive so that the program automatically addresses another drive rather than the original default drive. It's like changing the position of the switch on a model railroad to send the train down another track.
B. You can leave the default drive unchanged and specify another drive in your commands. This ignores the setting for the default drive and sends the command (or file if copying) to the drive that you specify. It's like sending a model train down a specified track regardless of how the switch is set.

When executing DOS's external commands, you have to specify drives in the commands. If the program is on the disk in the default drive, you have to type only its name to execute the command. Let's say you want to use the CHKDSK command to check a disk in drive B, and the operating system disk is in drive A. If the default drive is A, all you have to type is **CHKDSK B:**. But if the default drive is B, you have to type **A:CHKDSK B:**.

 3. FORMATTING DATA DISKS

CONCEPTS

When you buy new blank disks to store your data or program files, you have to prepare them to run on your computer. This step is necessary because most disks are designed to be used on a wide variety of computers. Many computers and their operating systems use different methods to save files, so the blank disks must be customized for each type of system. This process is called formatting a disk.

The FORMAT command completely erases any data on a disk, so you should be careful. You should never format a previously used disk or a program disk unless you are sure you will not need any of the files on it. You also should never format a hard disk drive unless you are willing to lose every file on the disk. To see what files are on a disk before you format it, display the files on the disk as described in Sec. 4.

271

Procedures

To format a data disk from the command prompt, you use the FORMAT command. The FORMAT.COM file must be on one of the drives since this is an external command.

To Format a Data Disk from the Command Prompt

1. On a floppy disk system, insert the disk with the FORMAT.COM file into drive A and the disk to be formatted into drive B. Make drive A the default drive.

   On a hard disk system, insert the disk to be formatted into drive A. Make drive C the default drive.

2. Type **FORMAT B:** (on a floppy disk system) or **FORMAT A:** (on a hard disk system), and then press ENTER. The prompt reads *Insert new diskette for drive x: and press ENTER when ready.* (The *x* is the specified drive and varies depending on the system you are using.)

3. Since the disks were inserted in Step 1, press ENTER to continue. A message indicates the command's progress. In a few moments, a message reads *Format complete.*

   The status of the disk is displayed, and then a prompt reads *Format another (Y/N)?.*

4. Either press N and then press ENTER to quit formatting and return to the command prompt.

   Or   insert a new disk into the same drive as you did in Step 1, press Y and then press ENTER to display the prompt asking you to insert a new disk. Press the designated key to continue.

▼ 4. ASSIGNING AND LISTING FILENAMES

CONCEPTS

When you save your work in files on a disk, the operating system uses filenames to keep track of individual files. In this topic, we introduce you to filenames and how to list the names of files on your disks.

Assigning Filenames

The files for the programs you use have already been assigned names. When you use these programs to create and save your own work, you must assign names to your files. The number and type of characters that you can use in a file's name are determined by the operating system you are using. For example, with DOS you can create filenames that have only eight characters and an optional period and three-character extension (Figure 7). The characters that are allowed are called legal characters and are listed in Table 1. Using any other character results in a name the computer will not accept.

TABLE 1   Characters That Can Be Used in Filenames

Characters	Examples
Letters	**A** through **Z** (uppercase or lowercase)
Numbers	**0** through **9**
Characters	! @ # $ % ^ & ( ) − _ { } ˜ ′ `

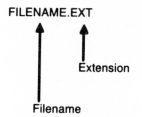

FILENAME.EXT

↑ Extension

↑ Filename

FIGURE 7 Filenames. File-names have two parts: the filename and an extension.

```
A:\>DIR

 Volume in drive A is RESOURCE
 Volume Serial Number is 3025-12EF
 Directory of  A:\

FILE1     TXT       19 01-01-80     4:31a
FILE3     TXT       17 02-20-89     1:47a
FILE5     TXT       17 02-20-89     1:47a
FILE6     TXT       17 01-30-91     1:48a
FILE7     TXT       17 01-30-91     1:49a
FILE8     TXT       17 01-30-91     1:49a
FILE9     TXT       17 01-30-91     1:49a
FILE10    TXT       18 01-30-91     1:49a
FILE11    TXT       18 01-30-91     1:50a
CHPT1     BAK     1024 01-30-91     1:50a
CHPT1     DOC     1024 01-30-91     1:51a
CHPT2     BAK     1024 01-30-91     1:51a
CHPT2     DOC     1024 01-30-91     1:51a
CHPT3     BAK     1024 01-30-91     1:52a
CHPT3     DOC     1024 01-30-91     1:52a
CHPT4     BAK     1024 01-30-91     1:52a
CHPT4     DOC     1024 01-30-91     1:52a
CHPT5     BAK     1024 01-30-91     1:52a
CHPT5     DOC     1024 01-30-91     1:52a
DBASE     BAT        9 01-30-91     1:54a
BUDGET91  WK1     5596 02-15-89     6:57p
WP5       BAT        7 01-30-91     1:54a
123       BAT        7 01-30-91     1:55a
BUDGET92  WK1     5596 02-15-89     6:58p
NAMES     BDF      982 02-15-89     7:00p
TEXTBOOK  DBF     1228 02-15-89     7:01p
README    BAT       10 01-30-91     2:02a
README    TXT       10 01-30-91     2:02a
FILE      TXT       18 01-01-80     1:36a
WHATSUP   DOC     9465 02-19-89    12:44p
GIVEUP    HUH     1051 02-19-89     6:55p
MYFILE    TXT      113 01-01-80     9:02p
EDIT      TXT      212 03-03-89     9:58a
BANKLOAN  WK1    12048 03-03-89    10:26a
BANKLOAN  PRN     3318 03-03-89    10:26a
FILELIST  BAT      117 01-01-80    10:12p
NAMES     DBF      982 02-15-89     7:00p
1-2-3         <DIR>    07-16-89     1:26p
DBASE         <DIR>    07-16-89     1:26p
WORD          <DIR>    07-16-89     1:26p
PLACEST   DBF     4676 08-08-89     9:44a
       44 File(s)     1384448 bytes free

A:\>
```

FIGURE 8 A Directory Displayed from the Command Prompt. Besides listing the filenames and their extensions, the DIR command also displays:
• The volume name
• The size of each file in bytes
• The date and time the file was last saved (useful only if you set the date and time each time you turn on the computer)
• The number of files on the disk
• How much free space is left on the disk

You can type filenames in uppercase letters, lowercase letters, or a combination of uppercase and lowercase. If you enter lowercase letters, the computer automatically converts them to uppercase on the disk.

Each filename you use must be unique if the file is not stored on a separate disk or in a separate directory on a hard disk drive (see Sec. 10). If you assign a file with the same name and extension as a file that is already on the disk, the new file will overwrite the previous file and erase it. However, you can use the same filename with different extensions, for example, LETTER.DOC and LETTER-.BAK. You can also use the same extension with different filenames.

Listing Files

Since a disk can hold many files, it is often necessary to find out what files are on a particular disk. The names of the files on a disk are held in a directory. To display this directory, you use the DIR command from the command prompt or display the DOS 4's File System.

PROCEDURES

With the operating command prompt on the screen, you can display filenames with the DIR command (Figure 8). If you do not specify a drive, the command lists the files on the default drive. To display the files in another drive, specify that drive in the command, for example:

- To list the files on the disk in drive A, type **DIR A:** and then press ENTER.
- To list the files on the disk in drive B, type **DIR B:** and then press ENTER.

If a list of files is too long to be displayed on the screen, some of the filenames will quickly scroll up and off the screen. Two commands prevent this: DIR/W or DIR B:/W and DIR/P or DIR B:/P. The /W and /P following the commands are parameters that modify the basic command.

- The /W parameter (for Wide) displays the filenames horizontally instead of vertically. This command drops the file size, date, and time information to make room for a horizontal listing of filenames. Because only the filenames are displayed and they are arranged horizontally on the screen, many filenames can be displayed on the screen at one time.
- The /P parameter (for Page) displays filenames until the screen is full. To display additional files, simply press any key. Since many screens can display only twenty-three filenames, this command is useful when more than twenty-three files are on a disk.

▼ 5. SPECIFYING FILES

CONCEPTS

In many operating system commands, you specify the name of a single file. Frequently, however, you want to work with groups of files. For example, when making a backup disk, you might want to copy all the files from one disk to another. Instead of working with one file at a time, you can work with several files at once.

To copy one or more files, you must specify the source and target drives in the COPY command only if they are not the default drives, for example:

- If the default drive is set to A, and you want to copy a file named LETTER on drive A to drive B, you would type **COPY LETTER B:**. This command reads "copy the file named LETTER in the default drive to drive B." You do not need to specify drive A because that is the default drive. If you did, you would type **COPY A:LETTER B:**.
- If the default drive is set to B, and you want to copy a file named LETTER on drive A to drive B, you would type **COPY A:LETTER**. The command reads "copy the file named LETTER in drive A to the default drive." You do not need to specify drive B because that is the default drive.
- Regardless of which drive is the default, you can specify both the source and target drives as a precaution. For example, to copy the file named LETTER from drive A to drive B regardless of which drive is the default drive, type **COPY A:LETTER B:**. This command reads "copy the file named LETTER in drive A to drive B."

To Copy Files from Drive A to Drive B from the Command Prompt

1. Insert the source disk into drive A and the target disk into drive B.
2. Type **A:** and then press ENTER to change the default drive to drive A.
3. Either type **COPY *.* B:** and then press ENTER to copy all files.

   Or type the file's name, and then press ENTER to copy a single file.
4. Repeat Steps 1 through 3 for each disk that you want to copy. (Remember, you can press F3 and then ENTER to repeat the COPY command.)

7. DUPLICATING DISKS

CONCEPTS

As you have seen, you can use the COPY command with wildcards to copy all the files from one disk to another to make a backup copy. The DISKCOPY command (an external command) also lets you make a backup copy of a floppy disk. So why are there two commands to do the same thing?

- The DISKCOPY command does not require you to format the disk you are copying the files to. The DISKCOPY command automatically formats the disk before it begins to copy the files. You cannot use this command to copy files to a disk that already contains files unless you want to erase the existing files.
- The COPY command does not make an exact duplicate of a disk. It copies the files but not their exact location on the disk. When you want to make an exact duplicate of a disk, use the DISKCOPY command. If a disk is full and files are stored in noncontiguous sectors, it takes the drive longer to save and retrieve them. The COPY *.* command will copy them so that they are all on contiguous sectors, but the DISKCOPY command will not. If you are making backup copies, it is better to use the COPY *.* command.

PROCEDURES

To duplicate a disk from the command prompt, insert the operating system disk that contains the DISKCOPY.COM file into drive A, type **DISKCOPY A: B:** and then press ENTER. A prompt asks you to insert the source and target disks. Insert the source disk (the one you are copying from) into drive A. (Write-protect it so that you do not inadvertently erase it.) Insert the target disk (the one you are copying to) into drive B, and then press any key to continue. When the first disk is duplicated, a prompt asks if you want to duplicate more. Press the specified keys to quit or continue.

To Duplicate a Disk in Drive A to Drive B from the Command Prompt

1. On a floppy disk system, insert the DOS disk that contains the DISKCOPY-.COM file into drive A, and then make that the default drive. On a hard disk system, make drive C the default drive.
2. Type **DISKCOPY A: B:** and then press ENTER. You are prompted to insert the source and target disks. (On a hard disk system with a single floppy disk drive, you are only prompted to insert the source disk.)
3. On a floppy disk system, insert the source disk (the one being duplicated) into drive A, and insert the target disk (the duplicate) into drive B.

   On a hard disk system, insert the source disk into drive A. Remove it, and then replace it with the target disk when prompted to do so.

   When ready, press any key to continue. A message indicates the sectors and tracks being copied. In a few moments, the prompt reads *Copy another diskette (Y/N)?*.
4. Either insert the new disk(s) into the same drive(s) as you did in Step 3, press Y and then press any key to duplicate additional disks.

   Or press N to stop and return to the command prompt.

▼ 8. RENAMING FILES

CONCEPTS

There are times when you want to change the name of a file on a disk. To do this, you use the RENAME or REN commands (internal commands).

PROCEDURES

To rename files from the command prompt, you use the RENAME command (an internal command). You can also use REN, a shorter version of the command, to do the same thing. When using this command from the command prompt, you must specify the old name and the new name. You can add specify a path for the source but not for the target name. For example, when the *A>* command prompt is on the screen, and a disk in drive B has a file named OLDNAME.EXT that you want to change to NEWNAME.EXT, you type **RENAME B:OLDNAME.EXT NEWNAME.EXT** and then press ENTER.

▼ 9. DELETING FILES

CONCEPTS

Monitoring the amount of free space on a disk is important because many applications programs misbehave when you ask them to save files on a full disk, or they may create temporary files that take up a lot of space. Most people tend to keep files long after they are useful. It is good practice to occasionally use the File System or DIR command to list the files on a disk and then delete any files no longer needed.

PROCEDURES

When you want to delete one or more files, you use the ERASE or DEL command. These two commands are interchangeable and work exactly alike. For example, with the *A>* command prompt on the screen, and a disk in drive B that you want to delete a file named FILENAME.EXT from, you type **ERASE B: FILENAME.EXT** or **DEL B:FILENAME.EXT** and then press ENTER.

You can use wildcards with the ERASE and DEL commands, but it is dangerous to do so. Miscalculating even slightly the effects that wildcards have can cause the wrong files to be deleted. However, there are precautions you can take:

- One way to use wildcards safely is to preview which files will be affected by specifying the planned wildcards with the DIR command. If only the files you want to delete are listed, the same wildcards are safe to use with the ERASE or DEL command. For example, if you want to delete all files with the extension .BAK, type **DIR *.BAK.** If the list of files can all be deleted, type **DEL *.BAK.**
- To be prompted for each file when using DOS 4, use the /P parameter. For example, to delete all files with the extension .BAK, type **DEL *.BAK/P.** Before each file is deleted, a prompt reads *Delete (Y/N)?.* Press Y to delete the file, or press N to leave the file on the disk.
- If you use the *.* wildcards, a prompt reads *Are you sure (Y/N)?.* Press Y to continue and delete all the files, or press N to cancel the command.

To Delete Files from a Disk from the Command Prompt

1. Select the name of the file(s) you want to delete. (If you plan on using wildcards, preview the results of the ERASE or DEL command by typing **DIR** followed by a filename. Use the ? wildcard to stand for a specific character or the * wildcard to stand for any group of characters.)
2. Type **ERASE** or **DEL** followed by the name of the file to be deleted. (If using wildcards, use the ones you entered to preview the results.)
3. Press ENTER to delete the files.

▼10. USING DIRECTORIES

CONCEPTS

When using DOS, you can divide a hard (or floppy) disk into directories, which help you organize files on these disks. Imagine if you used a file drawer to store all of your memos, letters, and reports. Before long, the drawer would become so crowded that you could not find anything. But with a little organization and planning, the documents could be organized into folders, making it easier to locate the needed document (Figure 12).

A hard disk is like an empty drawer in a new filing cabinet: It provides a lot of storage space but no organization (Figure 13). To make it easier to find items in the drawer, you can divide it into categories with hanging folders. You can file

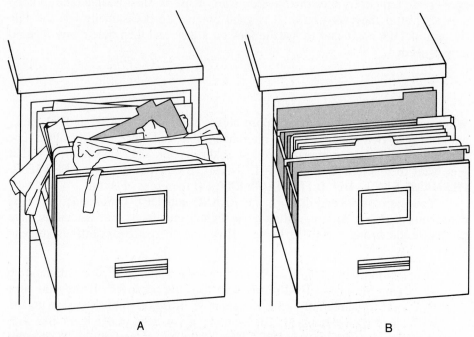

FIGURE 12   File Drawers.   Unorganized file drawers make it difficult to find files when you need them (a). Organized file drawers make it easy to find the files you want (b).

documents directly into the hanging folders, or you can divide them into finer categories with manila folders. A directory is like a hanging folder, and a subdirectory is like a manila folder within a hanging folder. A file in a directory or subdirectory is like a letter, report, or other document within either a hanging folder or a manila folder.

Directories on a hard disk drive are organized in a hierarchy (Figure 14). The main directory, the one not below any other directory, is the root directory. Below it, directories can be created on one or more levels. These directories can hold files or subdirectories.

PROCEDURES

Any disk may be divided into directories and subdirectories. You will often find floppy disks with directories, and almost every hard disk has them. To work with these disks, you have to know how to move around through the directories and display the names of files that you want to work with.

Changing Directories

To change directories from the command prompt, you use the CHDIR or CD command. To change the default directory, type **CD** then type the name of the drive and directory, and then press ENTER. If you are changing more than one level, list the directories in order, separated by a backslash. For example, to change to a directory named OLD that is a subdirectory of a directory named LETTERS, type **CD\LETTERS\OLD.** There are several versions of these commands; for example, in Figure 15:

A. To make the subdirectory OLD the default directory, you type **CD\LETTERS\OLD** and then press ENTER.

B. To move up one directory, for example, from OLD to LETTERS, you type **CD..** and then press ENTER.

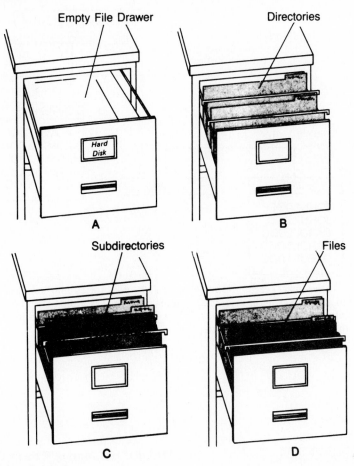

FIGURE 13   Hard Disks.
A. A new hard disk is like an empty file drawer. It has lots of room for files but no organization.
B. You can divide the hard disk into directories, which is like dividing the file drawer with hanging folders.
C. You can then subdivide the directories into smaller subdirectories, which is like dividing the hanging folders with manila folders.
D. You can then save files in any of these subdirectories the same way you would file a document in one of the manila folders.

C. To move down to a subdirectory within the current directory, type **CD** press SPACEBAR then type the name of the directory, and then press ENTER. For example, to change from LETTERS to NEW, you type **CD NEW**.
D. To return to the root directory from any other directory, you type **CD** and then press ENTER.

To display the default directory on the current drive, type **CD** and then press ENTER. To display the current default directory on another drive, type **CD** followed by the drive identifier, and then press ENTER. For example, to display the current directory on drive C, type **CD C:** and then press ENTER.

Displaying Files

When you want a list of your hard disk's organization, you use the TREE command (an external command) (Figure 16). When you want a list of the directories, and the files they contain, you use the /F parameter, for example, TREE/F (Figure 17). This command, unlike the DIR command, lists files in all directories.

Root Directory ————▶

Directories ————▶

Subdirectories ————▶

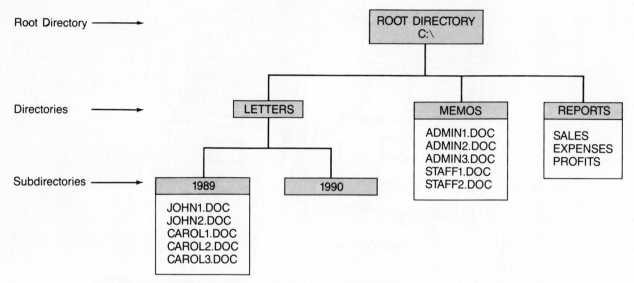

FIGURE 14   Directory Trees.   On the hard disk, directories and subdirectories are organized into a treelike hierarchy. The topmost directory is called the root directory. Directories below it are called directories. When directories are subdivided into additional directories, they are called subdirectories.

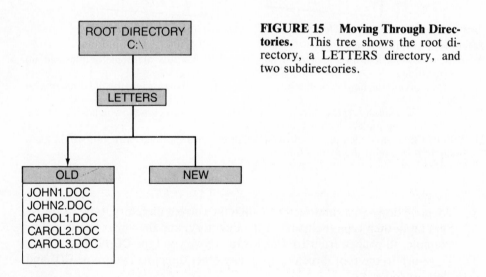

FIGURE 15   Moving Through Directories.   This tree shows the root directory, a LETTERS directory, and two subdirectories.

Directory PATH listing for Volume RESOURCE
Volume Serial Number is 09F8-0958

FIGURE 16 The TREE Command.   The TREE command lists just the directories on the disk.

Directory PATH listing for Volume RESOURCE
Volume Serial Number is 09F8-0958

FIGURE 17 The TREE/F Command. The TREE/F command lists directories and files on the disk.

```
B:.
    │   FILE1.TXT
    │   FILE2.TXT
    │   FILE3.TXT
    │   FILE4.TXT
    │   FILE5.TXT
    │   FILE6.TXT
    │   FILE7.TXT
    │   FILE8.TXT
    │   FILE9.TXT
    │   FILE10.TXT
    │   FILE11.TXT
    │   CHPT1.BAK
    │   CHPT1.DOC
    │   CHPT2.BAK
    │   CHPT2.DOC
    │   CHPT3.BAK
    │   CHPT3.DOC
    │   CHPT4.BAK
    │   CHPT4.DOC
    │   CHPT5.BAK
    │   CHPT5.DOC
    │   BUDGET91.WK1
    │   BUDGET92.WK1
    │   NAMELIST.DBF
    │   PUBLISH.DBF
    │   README.BAT
    │   README.TXT
    │   FILE.TXT
    │
    ├───1-2-3
    │       README.TXT
    │       └───OLD
    │               README.TXT
    │
    ├───DBASE
    │       README.TXT
    │
    └───WORD
            README.TXT
```

To List Directories and Files from the Command Prompt

- To display a list of directories, type **TREE** and then press ENTER.
- To display a list of directories and the files they contain, type **TREE/F** and then press ENTER.

▼11. MAKING AND REMOVING DIRECTORIES

CONCEPTS

When you want to organize your work on a hard disk drive, you create directories. When the directories are no longer needed, you remove them (after deleting all the files they contain).

When creating directories, you should have some kind of a plan. It makes sense to follow these rules:

- Keep only essential files, like AUTOEXEC.BAT and CONFIG.SYS, in the root directory.

285

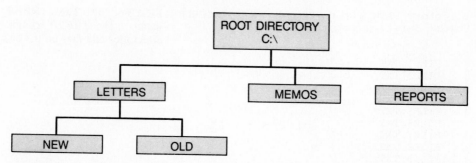

FIGURE 18 Making Directories. This tree shows the root directory, a LETTERS directory, and two subdirectories.

- Store all program files related to a program in their own directory. For example, you might want a directory for DOS, 1-2-3, WordPerfect, and dBASE.
- Do not store the data files that you create in the same directory as the program files. Keep all related data files in their own directories. For example, you might have separate directories for letters, reports, financial documents, and name and address lists. You might also create separate directories for the files you create with different programs. For example, you might have separate directories for WordPerfect documents, 1-2-3 worksheets, or dBASE database files.
- Do not create too many levels since it takes time to move around them. Most disks can be well organized with no more than three levels, including the root directory.

When creating and deleting directories, here are some rules to keep in mind:

- When you create directories, you assign them names. These names follow the same conventions that you use for filenames. However, you should not use a period and extension, or you might confuse directories with filenames at some later date. Files and subdirectories in one directory can have the same names as files and subdirectories in other directories.
- Before you can remove a directory, you must delete all the files it contains. If the directory contains subdirectories, you must first also delete the files they contain, and then delete the subdirectories.
- You cannot delete the current directory or the root directory.
- You can create as many directories and subdirectories as you want, but the path (see Sec. 12) cannot exceed sixty-three characters.

PROCEDURES

To make a directory from the command prompt, you type **MKDIR** (or **MD**) followed by the name of the directory you are creating. The form of the command depends on whether you are working in the directory off of which you want to create a directory or subdirectory. For example, if you wanted to create the directories shown in Figure 18, you type:

- **MD\LETTERS** and then press Enter
- **MD\MEMOS** and then press Enter
- **MD\REPORTS** and then press Enter

To make the two subdirectories off the LETTERS directory, you type:

- **MD\LETTERS\NEW** and then press Enter
- **MD\LETTERS\OLD** and then press Enter

If you first changed directories so that LETTERS was the default directory, you could create the two subdirectories by typing:

- **MD NEW** and then pressing ENTER
- **MD OLD** and then pressing ENTER

To Create Directories from the Command Prompt

- To create a directory off the root directory regardless of the directory you are in, type **MD** followed by the name of the directory.
- To create a directory off the root directory of another drive, type **MD** followed by the drive identifier, a slash, and the directory name.
- To create a subdirectory in the current directory, type **MD** followed by the directory name.

Removing Directories

To remove a directory from the command prompt, you must first delete all the files that it contains. Next, you have to move to the directory above the one to be removed. To do so, type **CD..** and then press ENTER. Now, type **RMDIR** (or **RD**) followed by the name of the directory you are removing. If you want to remove a directory that contains subdirectories, you must first remove the subdirectories. You cannot delete the current default directory from the command prompt.

12. SPECIFYING PATHS

CONCEPTS

In previous topics, you frequently specified drives when executing commands that copied, moved, or deleted files on disks. When a disk is divided into directories, you not only must specify a drive, you also must specify a directory in many commands. Specifying the drive and directories is called specifying a path.

Paths are instructions to the program that tell it what subdirectory a file is located in or where it should be placed. It is like telling someone that "the letter to ACME Hardware is in the manila folder labeled ACME in the hanging folder labeled Hardware in the third file cabinet from the right." These precise instructions make it easy to locate the file.

Paths are simply a listing of the directories and subdirectories between where a file is and where you are or want the file to be copied to. To specify a path, you must indicate:

1. The drive
2. The name of the directory (or directories)
3. The filename

PROCEDURES

To specify a path from the command prompt, you must indicate the drive, then the name of all subdirectories, and then the filename. All elements must be separated from one another by backslashes (\), for example, C:\LETTER\NEW\FILE-1.DOC. When copying or moving files from the DOS 4 Shell's File System, you have to specify only a path to the target directory in the *To:* field of the Copy or Move pop-up.

When specifying paths from the command prompt, you have to consider both the source and target directories:

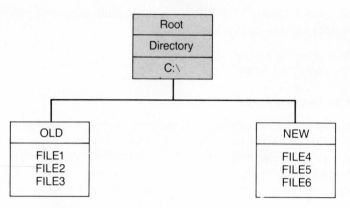

FIGURE 19 Default Directories and Paths When Copying or Moving Files. This figure shows the root directory and two subdirectories.

- If the source directory is the default, you have to specify only the path to the target.
- If the target directory is the default, you have to specify only the path to the source.
- If neither the target nor the source directory is the default, you have to specify the path for both.

For example, let's assume your disk has the directories and files shown in Figure 19.

- When copying or moving files from the command prompt, you have to specify a path only when the source or target directory is not the default.
  - When OLD is the default, the path you specify to copy FILE1 to the NEW directory is specified only for the target. For example, from the command prompt, you type **COPY FILE1 C:\NEW.**
  - When NEW is the default, the path you specify to copy FILE1 to the NEW directory is specified only for the source. For example, from the command prompt, you type **COPY C:\OLD\FILE1.**
  - When the root directory is the default, the paths you specify to copy FILE1 to the NEW directory are for both the source and the target. For example, from the command prompt, you type **COPY C:\OLD\FILE1 C:\OLD.**
- When you want to display a list of the filenames in a directory, the same principles work.
  - When the root directory is the default, you can display its directory by just typing **DIR** and then pressing ENTER.
  - To display the files in the OLD directory, you type **DIR C:\OLD** and then press ENTER.
  - To display the files in the NEW directory, you type **DIR C:\NEW** and then press ENTER.
- When you want to delete a file, the same principles work. For example, when OLD is the default directory:
  - To delete FILE1, you type **DEL FILE1** and then press ENTER.
  - To delete FILE4, you type **DEL C:\NEW\FILE4** and then press ENTER.

Index

A

Absolute tabs, 126
Action Bar (Shell), 22
Align commands, 168
Aligning text, 167–74. *See also* Tab
    stops
  alignment characters, 124–25, 131
  centering, 168–70
    on columns, 169, 173
      horizontal, 169, 172
      vertical, 170, 172–73
    flush right, 168, 171, 172
    headers and footers, 205, 208
    justification, 167–68
    with margins, 171–73
Alt-keys, 37–38, 238
Appending blocks, 145, 146–47
Application programs, 11, 21
Arabic page numbers, 118, 120
Arrow keys, 5, 63, 66, 75
Assign macro option, 239
* (wildcard), 59, 76, 275
AUTOEXEC.BAT file, 15
Auto line height setting, 161, 180, 182
Auxiliary storage, 264. *See also* Floppy
    disks; Hard disks

B

Backspace key, 5, 42, 63, 65–66, 80
  typing mode and action of, 79
Backups, floppy disk, 268–69
Basic program, 16
Binding Offset command, 89, 93–94
Block Command (**Alt-F4** or **F12**), 113,
  146
Blocks, 142–54
  appending, 145, 146–47
  boldfacing and underlining in,
    151–53
  column, 142–43, 146, 149–50
  copying, 145–51
    between windows, 157
  deleting, 145, 146–47, 148, 150–51

format preservation in, 148, 161
line, 142, 146, ·150
moving, 145, 146–47, 148, 149
predefined, 147–48, 151
printing, 146
rectangular, 143–44, 146
saving, 145–46
selected, 145–47, 190–91
selecting, 144–45, 148
unselecting, 148
Body of letter, 254
Boilerplate, 221
Boldface command (**F6**), 63, 67
Boldfacing, 67, 69–71, 160, 164, 166
  in blocks, 151–53
Booting the computer, 11, 16
Buffer, 80
  printer, 95

C

Cancel command (**F1**), 26, 42
Cancel Job(s) command, 93
Caps Lock key, 25, 31–32, 63
Carriage returns, 64–65
  hard, 64–65
    dormant, 114
    joining lines of text separated by,
      106
  soft, 64
CD (DOS command), 282–83
Center command (**Shift-F6**), 124, 168,
  205
Centering text, 168–70
  on columns, 169, 173
    horizontal, 169, 172
    vertical, 170, 172–73
Characters, deleting, 63
CHKDSK (DOS command), 271
Chronological resumé, 257, 258
Clearing the screen, 53
Clicking mouse, 44
Clock, system, 11, 13
Closing paragraph, 254

Codes
  editing, 99–110
    deleting and editing, 106–9
    list of, 100–103
    open, 103–4, 108
    paired, 103, 104–5
    revealing, 99–100, 108
  font change, 94
  hard tab, 129
  merge, 221–23, 227–28
  replace, 191–92
  tab, 129
Cold boot, 16
Column blocks, 142–43, 146, 149–50
Columns, centering text on, 169, 173
COMMAND.COM, 264
Command prompt, 13–14. *See also*
    DOS (Disk Operating System)
  loading files at, 56
  loading WordPerfect from, 21, 24,
    28–29
  from Shell, 15, 18
Commands, executing, 35–48
  getting help for, 35–37, 45–46
  with mouse, 43–45
  prompts and, 42–43
  with pull-down menus, 38–40
  selecting menu options, 40–42
  using function keys, 37–38
{*COMMENT*} comment ~ code, 228
Comment macro option, 239
Compose (**Ctrl-V**), 191
Conditional End of Page command,
  114
Conditional page breaks, 112, 113,
  114
Context-sensitive help, 36
Continuous-form paper, loading, 85
Control Printer Menu, 88, 92–93
COPY (DOS command), 277–79
Copying blocks, 145–51
  between windows, 157
Copying files, 247, 250, 251, 277–79
Cover letters, 253–55
Ctrl-Alt-Del (warm boot), 16

Notes

Notes

Notes

Notes

Notes

Notes

Notes

Notes

Notes

Notes

Proofreaders' Marks

⊙	Insert period	*rom.*	Roman type
⋀	Insert comma	*caps.*	Caps—used in margin
:	Insert colon	≡	Caps—used in text
;	Insert semicolon	*c+sc*	Caps & small caps—used in margin
?	Insert question mark	≡	Caps & small caps—used in text
!	Insert exclamation mark	*l.c.*	Lowercase—used in margin
=/	Insert hyphen	/	Used in text to show deletion or substitution
⋁	Insert apostrophe		
⋁⋁	Insert quotation marks	૬	Delete
⊥	Insert 1-en dash	૬	Delete and close up
⊥	Insert 1-em dash	*w.f.*	Wrong font
#	Insert space	⌣	Close up
ld>	Insert ( ) points of space	⊐	Move right
shill	Insert shilling	⊏	Move left
⋁	Superior	⊓	Move up
⋀	Inferior	⊔	Move down
(/)	Parentheses	‖	Align vertically
[/]	Brackets	=	Align horizontally
☐	Indent 1 em	⊐⊏	Center horizontally
☐☐	Indent 2 ems	⊔⊓	Center vertically
⁋	Paragraph	*eq.#*	Equalize space—used in margin
no ⁋	No paragraph	⋁⋁⋁	Equalize space—used in text
tr	Transpose [1]—used in margin	....	Let it stand—used in text
∼	Transpose [2]—used in text	*stet.*	Let it stand—used in margin
sp	Spell out	⊗	Letter(s) not clear
ital	Italic—used in margin	*run over*	Carry over to next line
___	Italic—used in text	*run back*	Carry back to preceding line
b.f.	Boldface—used in margin	*out, see copy*	Something omitted—see copy
∿∿∿	Boldface—used in text	૬/?	Question to author to delete [3]
s.c.	Small caps—used in margin	⋀	Caret—General indicator used to mark position of error.
▬▬▬	Small caps—used in text		

---

[1] In lieu of the traditional mark "tr" used to indicate letter or number transpositions, the striking out of the incorrect letters or numbers and the placement of the correct matter in the margin of the proof is the preferred method of indicating transposition corrections.

[2] Corrections involving more than two characters should be marked by striking out the entire word or number and placing the correct form in the margin. This mark should be reserved to show transposition of words.

[3] The form of any query carried should be such that an answer may be given simply by crossing out the complete query if a negative decision is made or the right-hand (question mark) portion to indicate an affirmative answer.